Better Homes and Gardens®

Creative Crafts and Stitchery

Contents

BETTER HOMES AND GARDENS BOOKS

Editorial Director: Don Dooley
Managing Editor: Malcolm E. Robinson   Art Director: John Berg
Production and Copy Chief: Lawrence D. Clayton   Asst. Art Director: Randall Yontz
Associate Editors: Marie B. Schulz, Susan Rosenthal, Jo Moore Stewart
Designers: Faith Berven, Harijs Priekulis, Sheri Veenschoten
Contributing Editor: Joan Cravens

Welcome to the Craft Jamboree

Creative Crafts and Stitchery encompasses a melange of handcraft techniques — weaving, rug making, sewing, crocheting, knitting, embroidery, needlepoint, basketry, furniture making and caning, cornhusk toy construction, decoupage, rosemaling, preserving flowers and more. Most of these date back hundreds of years and, at one time, were done of sheer necessity.

But as the Industrial Age emerged, early machines mass-produced duplicates of these same items at a breathtaking pace and with a surprising degree of accuracy, thus taking away the incentive for home crafts. Also, it became fashionable to purchase these ready-mades rather than to make your own.

Luckily, as the Industrial Revolution gained momentum, other machines appeared that reduced housework chores to a minimum and also lessened the workday hours in industries. This trend allowed people more leisure time to pursue the activities that gave them the greatest personal gratification.

Today, people of all ages in cities large and small and in the country take great pride in creating handmade articles — not because they have to but because they want to produce something that is truly their own handwork.

Another contributing factor to the craft boom is the availability of materials. Designers and manufacturers alike are keeping pace with the needs of craftsmen by introducing materials and tools solely for the hobbyist. Wherever you live, you're bound to find a well-stocked hobby shop and needlework shop nearby. Besides these sources, you may also find craft materials at variety and discount stores, hardware stores, building supply dealers, thrift shops, and garage sales.

In this 288-page volume you discover 146 designer projects representing 50 different craft and stitchery techniques. Each project is pictured, has diagrams and drawings wherever they will be helpful to the reader, a list of materials, and complete easy-to-follow step-by-step directions. You will also find a glossary of terms for each technique and drawings of stitches or procedures for handy reference.

Projects include fashion accessories and wearing apparel for every member of the family, decorative and functional items for every room in the home, and endearing toys for the playroom set.

So, whether you're the all thumbs- or nimble fingers- type, you'll find a multitude of designs in this book tailored to your tastes and talents. First, decide which area you wish to explore and assemble materials and tools in a convenient work area, and then follow the directions one step at a time.

Here is a hobbyist's dream come true — a stitchery and craft work studio built into a cozy storage corner where everything can disappear when workshop time is over. Incorporate some of these ideas into your work area — a wine rack chest that acts as a novel stashaway for bulky balls of yarn, Indian baskets that hold neatly rolled-up drawings, and a flip-top table that snaps closed to conceal half-finished needlework. Add room-darkening window shades for light control, easy-care floor covering, and decorate with plants, pillows, and wall hangings.

Embroidery

Stitchery is back in style! And what better way to show off your stitchery skill than with home accessories or wearing apparel embroidered in colors and patterns suited to your own taste. To inspire you and increase your skills, this chapter includes projects using techniques ranging from traditional hand embroidery to the more recent machine embroidery.

Embroidered Bedroom Rug

A fabric, an accessory, or a wallpaper can inspire the decor of an entire room, but the finishing touch that says the room is you is in the handwork. Here, an embroidered rug punctuates a crisp and airy room inspired by the wallpaper border.

Materials
- White wool rug, 42x68 inches
- 1 4-oz. skein light green knitting yarn
- 1 4-oz. skein dark green knitting yarn
- Tissue paper
- Large-eyed needle

Directions
Begin by sketching the corners of the rug border. Mark a right angle on a piece of tissue. Draw a second corner two inches inside the first one. Next, trace the rug motif directly from the wallpaper into the corner on the

paper. The leaf design on this rug was arranged on one side of the angle and then reversed for the opposite side. Make four copies of the pattern.

With regular thread, baste a guide for the border six inches from the edge around the rug. Baste again two inches inside the first border. Pin the patterns in the corners.

Embroider the corner motif directly over the tissue. Work the large leaves in light green satin stitch angled upward from the center of each leaf, and outline them in stem stitch (directions are on page 29). Outline the leaves at the top of the stem and in the corners in dark green stem stitch. Fill them with light green French knots. Work the small dark green leaves in a detached chain stitch filled with a single straight stitch.

Following the basted guidelines, work the border in dark green stem stitch. Add French knots, 1½ inches apart, down the center. Remove the tissue and the basting stitches when the embroidery is finished.

For the fringe, cut two 8-inch strands of each color yarn. Fold the strands in half. Fasten them to the short end of the rug by slipping the fold between the wool threads and inserting the ends into the loop made by the fold. Repeat at both ends of the rug.

Embroidered Dinner Napkins

Let nifty napery take its cue from a china pattern. Stitch up a casual look in lots of color, as on these large napkins. For elegance, try white-on-white embroidery or white thread against a dark background.

Materials
- 1½ yards of 54-inch white homespun or linen for 4 24x24-inch napkins
- 2 skeins red embroidery floss
- 2 skeins pink embroidery floss
- 4 skeins yellow embroidery floss
  4 skeins gold embroidery floss
- 5 skeins light green embroidery floss
- 7 skeins dark green embroidery floss
- Needle
- Tracing paper
- Dressmaker's carbon paper

Directions
Cut four 24x24-inch napkins on the straight grain of the fabric. Machine-baste close to the edges and again 1½ inches inside the edges. Mark the bias with basting stitches.

Transfer the pattern below to the napkin corner with dressmaker's carbon. Center the pattern on the bias. Remove the bias basting.

Using six strands of floss, work the leaves and large petals in dark green, red, and gold satin stitch. Outline them in lighter shades of the same colors worked in chain stitch. Work the stems, small flower, and circle in chain stitch, filling with the dark shades and outlining with the light ones. Stitch directions are on pages 28-29.

Next, remove the outer row of basting stitches, and fringe the edges. Machine-stitch along the top of the fringe. Finally, remove the remaining basting stitches.

If you use your own pattern, trace the design from a plate of your choosing. Some designs will be just the right size for the corner of a napkin, but many will need to be adapted. Either an entire design or part of one may be enlarged (see page 31 for directions). If you have embossed china, copy and enlarge the pattern and work it in a corner or in a border around the edge of the napkin.

1 Square = ½ Inch

Stylized Floral Embroideries

Not all your embroideries need be inspired by designs in the house. Here are some dramatic stitcheries from the garden. These stylized flowers, with their earthy browns and greens and warm plums and magentas would be a lively accent in a cool, modern room. We show these embroideries as wall hangings, but they can easily be made up as pillows.

Materials
- ½ yard beige linen or homespun
- 3 small skeins burnt orange Persian yarn
- 3 small skeins magenta Persian yarn
- 3 small skeins light brick Persian yarn
- 2 small skeins brick Persian yarn
- 1 small skein plum Persian yarn
- 1 small skein brown Persian yarn
- 2 small skeins olive Persian yarn
- 1 small skein navy Persian yarn
- 1 small skein bronze Persian yarn
- Crewel needle
- Tissue paper
- Dressmaker's carbon paper
- 2 sets 15-inch artist's stretchers

Directions:
Enlarge the patterns on tissue paper according to the directions on page 31. The full size pattern should be 15x15 inches. Cut the fabric into two pieces, each 18x18 inches. Center the patterns on each piece of fabric; tape them in place, and transfer the designs with dressmaker's carbon paper.

Staple or tack each piece of fabric to a set of 15x15-inch artist's stretchers. Make sure the design is centered and the grain of the fabric is straight.

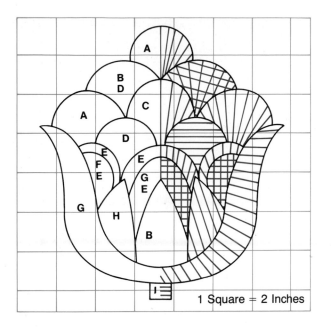

1 Square = 2 Inches

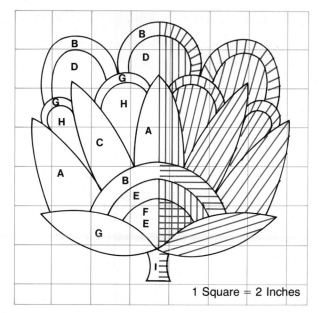

1 Square = 2 Inches

Color Key
A. Burnt orange
B. Magenta
C. Light brick
D. Brick
E. Plum
F. Brown
G. Olive
H. Navy
I. Bronze

Embroider each design with three strands of yarn. The lines in the pattern indicate the type and direction of the stitches. Work long-line areas in satin stitch (see the glossary on pages 28-29 for directions).

Work the crisscross areas in a weaving stitch. Lay down long, straight stitches along the length of the shape. These should be approximately ¼ to ⅜ inches apart. Next, starting on one edge of the shape, bring the needle to the surface and weave under and over the straight stitches to the other side. Insert the needle in the fabric and bring it up again ¼ to ⅜ inches away. Weave across the straight stitches again, this time passing the needle *over* the threads you went under on the first trip across, and *under* those you went over. Continue until the shape is filled.

When the embroidery is finished, frame each piece as shown, hang without a frame, or make each one into a pillow cover.

Basic Embroidery Tips

• Store fabric and yarns in a plastic bag to keep them clean.
• Choose one of three simple ways of transferring a design to fabric: 1) trace over dressmaker's carbon paper 2) iron over a transfer made with a hot transfer pencil or 3) baste over a design on tissue paper.
• Don't be afraid of using brightly colored yarns and flosses. The colors will not be as bright on the fabric as they are in the skeins.
• Use an embroidery needle with an eye large enough for the thread to pass through easily without breaking. If crewel needles are too small, use chenille needles, which have larger eyes and sharper points.
• For surface embroidery or counted-thread work, keep on hand a supply of blunt-end tapestry needles.
• Use a thimble. Embroidery should be a pleasant pastime, not a painful one.
• Work in a comfortable chair and good light. A lamp that does not cast shadows between you and the work is best.

Spanish Blackwork Embroidery

The wall hanging and pillow opposite only *look* modern. They are, in fact, examples of Spanish blackwork, a very old form of counted thread embroidery that is currently enjoying a much-deserved revival.

Blackwork became popular in sixteenth-century England when the Spanish ladies of Catherine of Aragon began adapting English designs for use in their embroideries. Traditionally worked in black thread on white fabric, it was widely used for clothing decoration. Neck ruffs, bodices, sleeves, cuffs, caps, and even the gloves of lords and ladies were often lavishly covered with intricate and delicate stitches in highly stylized motifs. Today, blackwork adorns many things other than clothing. Its designs are crisp, contemporary, and limited only by your creativity.

After embroidering our blackwork patterns, you may want to design your own. First, find or sketch a pattern with some large shapes for fillings. Fill the shapes with light, medium, and dark pencil tones, until the contrast is pleasing. Then, select light, medium, or heavily stitched patterns to fill the areas. Remember you can use threads ranging from the finest to the heaviest for widely differing effects. You can also fill the spaces with either "square" stitches that cross over a few threads in any direction or straight stitches worked in closely spaced rows like pattern darning.

Materials
- Tapestry and crewel needles — size to be determined by fabric density
- Embroidery hoop

Wall hanging
- 18x18 inches white or off-white fabric (see general instructions)
- 20 yards No. 5 black pearl cotton

Even-weave Fabric

- 20 yards No. 8 black pearl cotton
- 11x14 inch picture frame
- 11x14 inch cardboard
- 13x15 inches thin foam or quilt batting

Pillow
- 20x20 inches white fabric for the front (see general instructions)
- 20x20 inches black velvet for the back
- 1¾ yards cording
- 30 yards No. 5 black pearl cotton
- 30 yards No. 8 black pearl cotton
- Polyester stuffing

Directions
General instructions: Select a fabric that is woven evenly, with an equal number of threads to the inch in either direction (see the diagram above). The threads must be free of irregularities, easy to see, and easy to count. They may be fine or coarse. Linen, homespun, and wool are good choices.

Trace the design on a piece of paper, then transfer it to the fabric. Tape the pattern and the fabric to a window, being sure to match the grain of the fabric with the straight lines of the design. Trace the design onto the fabric with a pencil or *waterproof* pen. If you use a pen, touch the fabric very lightly and work quickly to keep the ink from staining the fabric.

Stretch the fabric taut in a hoop so the thread counting is easier.

(continued)

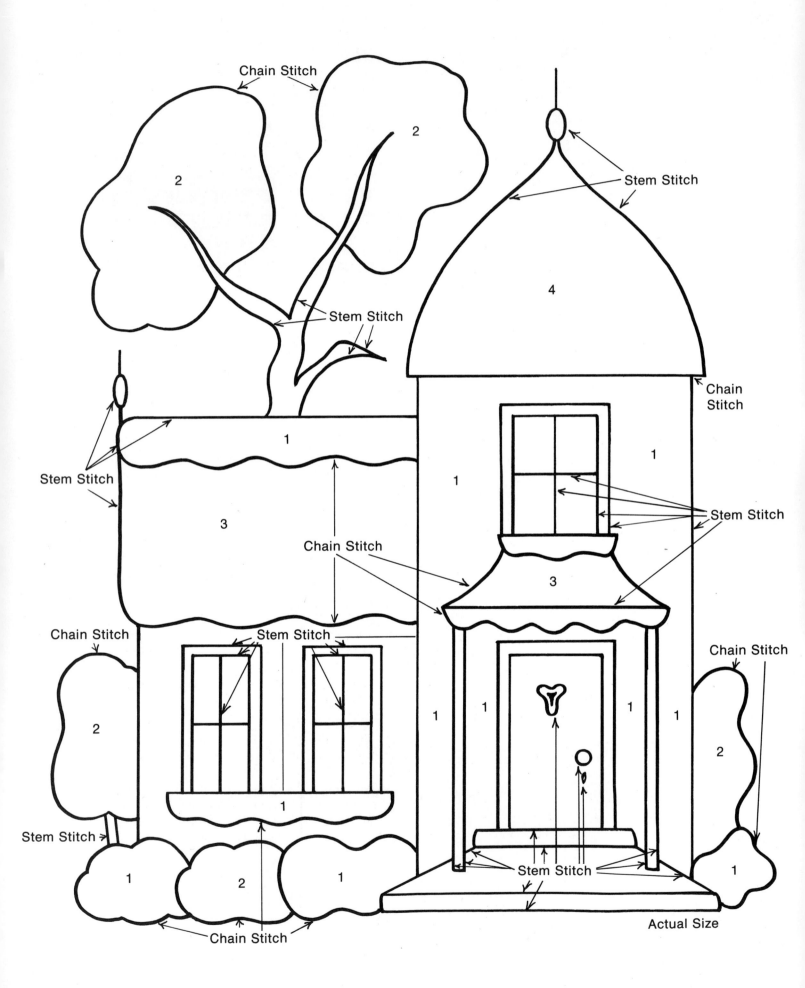

Chain Stitch

2

2

Stem Stitch

Stem Stitch

Stem Stitch

4

Chain Stitch

1

Stem Stitch

1

1

1

Chain Stitch

3

3

Stem Stitch

Chain Stitch

Chain Stitch

Stem Stitch

2

1

1

1

1

2

Stem Stitch

1

1

2

1

Stem Stitch

Chain Stitch

Actual Size

First, work the fillings in No. 8 black pearl cotton with the tapestry needle. Pass the needle through the spaces between the threads (shown in black on the diagram on page 13) to avoid splitting the threads.

Black thread carried from stitch to stitch on the back of white fabric may cast a shadow on the front of the work. To eliminate shadows, use the double-running, or Holbein, stitch wherever possible. Instructions for this stitch are in the glossary at the end of the chapter.

It is a good idea to practice the double-running stitch, as it is used in each of these designs, on a scrap of fabric until you understand the direction the needle must take. Once you are comfortable with the rhythm of each design, your stitches will be more uniform and more attractive.

After filling, outline each part of the design with the No. 5 black pearl cotton in the crewel needle.

Do not use knots on the back of the fabric to secure the thread ends. Instead, knot the end of the thread and insert it from the *front* to the back in the center of the area to be filled. Next, bring the thread to the front along the edge of the design and take two tiny stitches. These will be covered later by the outline stitches. Finally, lift the knot away from the fabric and cut it, allowing the thread end to pull to the back of the fabric.

Weave the tail end of the first thread into the back of the embroidery. Also, weave the front ends and tail ends of all the succeeding threads into the back of the work.

Begin the filling near the outline at the widest point of the design. Complete as many whole stitches as possible inside the shape. Then, fill the spaces near the edges of the shape with partial stitches.

Upon completion, block the embroidery by dampening the back; stretching it so the grain lines are straight; and tacking it to a towel-covered board to dry. If necessary, press lightly on the wrong side.

(continued)

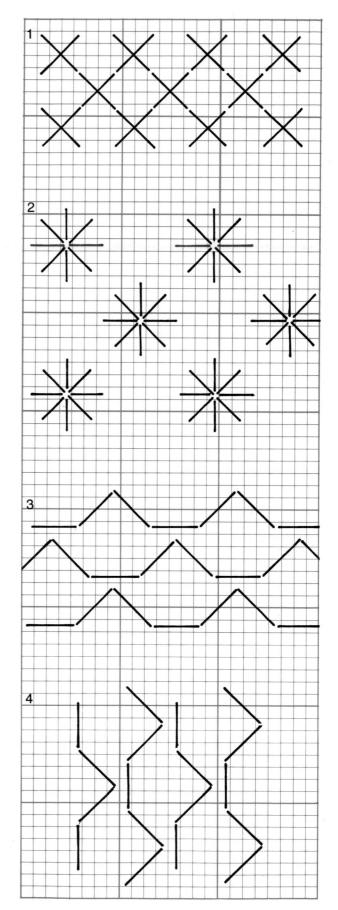

15

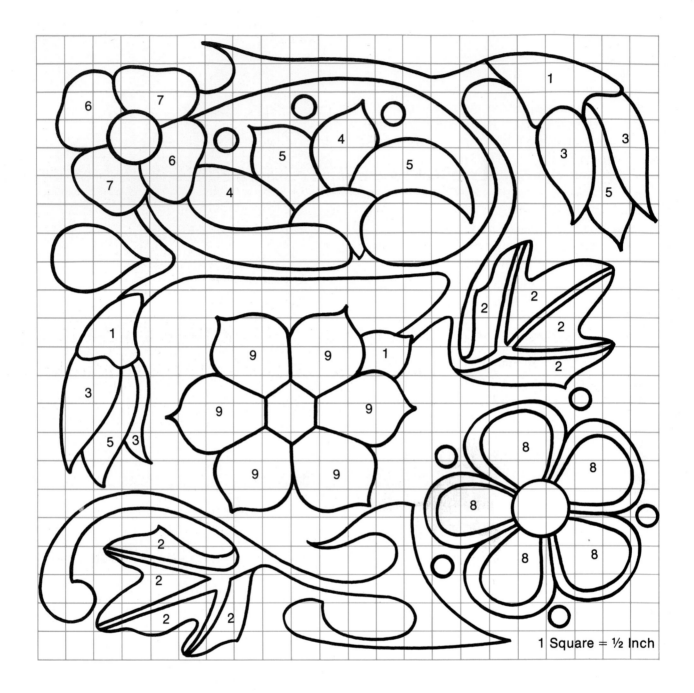

1 Square = ½ Inch

Wall hanging: Cut a piece of fabric 14x17 inches and staystitch the edges. Use the remaining fabric for practice stitches.

Transfer the pattern to the fabric. Fill in the shapes of the house, trees, and shrubs with the stitches in the diagram on page 15. Each square in the grid represents a space between the threads. Lines meeting in the same square represent threads that enter the same space in the fabric.

After working the filling stitches, outline each part of the design with chain or stem stitches (see the glossary on page 28 for directions for each of the stitches).

To frame your embroidery, first mount it on padded cardboard. If necessary, trim the cardboard a bit to allow for the thickness of the fabric and the padding. Cut the padding 1 inch larger than the cardboard.

Lay the fabric face down and center the padding with the cardboard on top.

(continued)

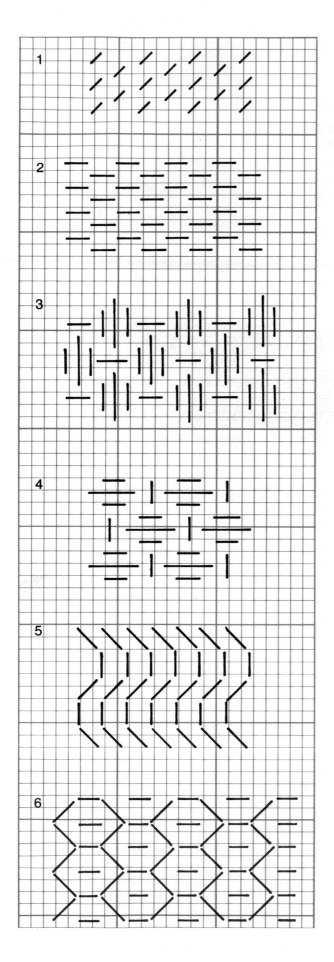

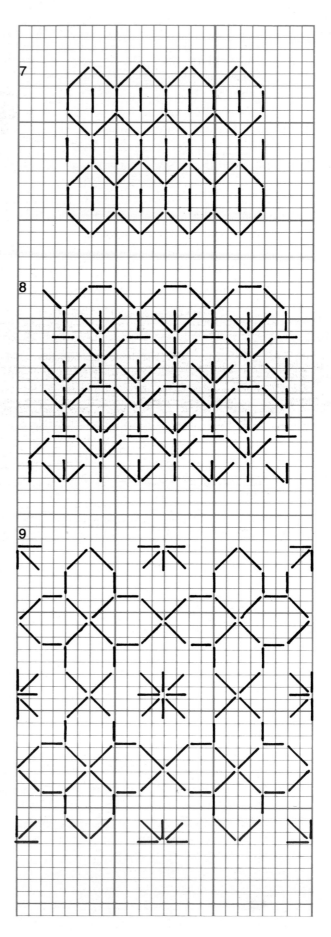

17

Fold the fabric to the back, and secure it with tape on the center of each side. Miter the corners and trim the excess fabric. Hand stitch the folded corners together with heavy thread. Finally, remove the tape, and lace together the top and bottom and then the sides with long stitches.

Add a coat of soil-resistant finish to protect the fabric before inserting it in the frame. Then mount and secure the embroidery in the frame, following the manufacturer's instructions. Glue a piece of brown paper to the back of the frame to keep out dust.

Pillow: Cut a piece of white fabric 16x16 inches for the pillow front, and staystitch around the edges. Use the remaining white fabric for practice stitches.

Enlarge the pattern according to the directions on page 31, and transfer it to the fabric. Fill in the flowers and leaves with the patterns shown in the diagram.

Pattern number 1 is a short diagonal stitch that can be worked vertically as a simple running stitch. Number 2 is a darning stitch (see pages 28-29 for directions). Numbers 3 and 4 are darning stitches worked horizontally and vertically.

Pattern number 5 is a double-running stitch. In numbers 6 and 7, the diagonal stitches can be worked as double-running stitches, with the rest of the pattern worked in darning stitches.

Pattern numbers 8 and 9 can be embroidered a number of ways. On the extra fabric, practice working vertical and horizontal double-running stitches, adding the adjacent forked or star stitches, and decide which are easier for you. Then, fill the large flower petals with the appropriate stitches.

After the fillings are completed, work the stems and outlines in stem stitch.

Block the finished embroidery. Then, cut a piece of velvet 16x16 inches for the back. Cut and piece the remaining velvet to cover 58 inches of cording. Stitch the covered cord 1 inch from the edge around the pillow front. With the right sides together, stitch the front to the back, leaving one side open. Grade the seam allowances and clip the corners. Then, turn and stuff the pillow, and slipstitch the opening closed.

Child's Shawl

Wrap up some big smiles for yourself when you present this Swedish embroidered warmer to a child. Worked in bright colors kids love, it is designed for three- to eight-year olds. Older children can get in on the fun of making the warmer, for it is embroidered in variations of two simple stitches.

See the photograph on page 124 for a back view of the shawl.

18

Materials

- ⅔ yard brown wool fabric
- ⅔ yard lining fabric
- 2 small (8.8 yard) skeins red 3-ply Persian wool
- 2 small skeins purple 3-ply Persian wool
- 2 small skeins gold 3-ply Persian wool
- 1 small skein aqua 3-ply Persian wool
- 3⅔ yards ½-inch-wide crocheted red edging
- Crewel needle
- Tailor's chalk

Directions

If you intend to wash the shawl, pre-shrink the fabric and the yarn before beginning.

Enlarge the pattern according to the instructions on page 31, adding ½ inch to the curved edges for the seam allowance. Transfer the pattern to tissue or brown paper. Fold the fabric along the grain and pin the pattern along the fold. Cut out the scarf, and cut a piece of lining fabric to match.

Using the tailor's chalk, lightly sketch each line of the embroidery on the right side of the fabric. You need not sketch each stitch, just mark the lines each series of stitches is to follow. To provide general stitching guides for the red flowers, mark circles approximately 1¼ inches in diameter and space them about 1¼ inches apart.

Work all the embroidery with two strands of yarn. Directions for each stitch are on pages 28-29 at the end of the chapter.

The red flowers are each made up of eight detached chain stitches. Work the checkered-chain stitch borders in gold and purple. Work the single line of chain stitches in aqua. Work the line of spaced buttonhole stitches in purple.

When the embroidery is finished, steam press the scarf on the reverse side. Baste the crocheted trim along the seam line. With right sides together, stitch the scarf to the lining in a ½-inch seam, leaving a six-inch opening at one end of the scarf to turn it. Turn the scarf right side out, clip the corners, and grade the seams. Press the scarf and slipstitch the opening closed.

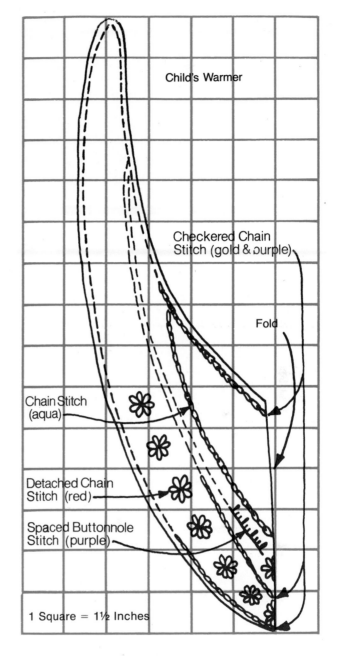

Child's Warmer

Checkered Chain Stitch (gold & purple)

Fold

Chain Stitch (aqua)

Detached Chain Stitch (red)

Spaced Buttonhole Stitch (purple)

1 Square = 1½ Inches

Make two yarn ties. Cut two 45-inch strands of each color yarn for each tie. Twist the strands together tightly in one direction, then fold the twisted strand in half, and twist it in the opposite direction. Tie a knot about ½ inch from the loose ends, and trim the ends evenly to form a tassel. Tack a tie to the center of each end of the scarf.

Embroidered Sweaters

Turn your knits into knockouts with a sweep of embroidered flowers or a striking monogram. Sweaters are a perfect starting point for creative stitchery. Next, you can try decorating scarves, mittens, and caps.

Materials
- Embroidery hoop
- Petit point needle

Floral trimmed sweater:
- V-neck sweater
- 2 small skeins (8.8 yards) cranberry 3-ply Persian wool
- 1 small skein pink 3-ply Persian wool
- 1 small skein dark green 3-ply Persian wool

Monogrammed sweater:
- Crew-neck sweater
- 1 large skein (40 yards) light blue 3-ply Persian wool
- 1 large skein dark blue 3-ply Persian wool
- Tissue paper

Directions
General Instructions: If the sweater will be washed, shrink the yarn or embroidery thread before you begin. Soak the yarn or thread in cold water and dry thoroughly.

While it helps to have a design sketched before you begin, it is not necessary to transfer the pattern to the sweater unless it is an exact design, like the monogram shown. Instead, embroider the design freehand (as was done on the green sweater). First, stitch the central motif and one side of the design, and then reverse the design for the opposite side of the neckline. You can also work the design freehand within a basted square, triangle, or other outline.

For the monogram, or any design requiring precise lines, transfer the pattern to tissue paper. Use a waterproof pen, for a pencil may leave a smudge on light-colored fabric. Pin or tape the paper in the exact position desired. To center the design, baste along the vertical center of the sweater and mark the vertical center of the pattern. Then match the lines. Clamp the tissue and the sweater into an embroidery hoop and hand- or machine-baste around the outline.

When machine-basting the design, back the fabric with another layer of tissue paper to protect the sweater from the pulling action of the feed dogs on the sewing machine. Put the wider embroidery hoop beneath the sweater so it will lie flat against the base of the machine as you stitch. Run the machine slowly and smoothly over the tissue. Remove the paper carefully, and begin embroidering.

Use an embroidery hoop while working so the tension on the knit is even in all directions. Also, be careful not to pull the stitches too tightly, causing unsightly holes in the knitted fabric. Avoid knots on the back of the sweater (which would surely be uncomfortable) by weaving thread ends into the back of the design. Where knots are unavoidable, triple knot the yarn and do not cut the excess too close to the knot, because wool is springy and the knot may come undone.

Floral trimmed sweater: For the embroidery around the neck of this sweater, pick up the colors in the companion shirt. Embroider daisy-like cranberry flowers in satin stitch with a pink French knot in the center. Work the leaves on these flowers in satin stitch. Do the stems in stem stitch. Work the other flowers by embroidering a stem first, and then adding a cluster of pink French knots at the top and along the sides. Directions for all the stitches are in the glossary on pages 28-29.

This embroidery was worked without a pattern by first stitching the center motif, then one side, and, finally, the other side of the neckline. If you prefer to work with guidelines, mark the position and diameter of the large flowers with a square basted with regular sewing thread. Then baste the stem line in place. The basting stitches will give you an indication of how well-balanced your design will be before you actually begin the embroidery.

Monogrammed sweater: Design your monogram from typefaces in newspapers and books, patterns in art and stitchery books, or by doodling. Let a child design his or her own monogram. Children often put faces or favorite motifs in the enclosed letters that are charming when worked up in stitches. Once you have settled on a design, transfer it to tissue paper and baste the outline onto the sweater.

While the sweater shown is primarily beige, it also has some blue in it which is nicely accented by the blue monogram. Fill the letters with rows of light blue split stitch, and work the shadows in dark blue satin stitch. Work the outline around the letters and shadows in stem stitch.

Tips for Embroidery

• Cut yarn for embroidery no more than 18 inches long. Longer pieces tend to flatten, twist, and look a bit worn.

• Use small-bladed scissors to cut out mistakes. You will be less apt to accidentally snip the fabric.

• Practice new stitches on spare pieces of fabric. Save the practice pieces to work up into patchwork samplers so you have a record of the stitches themselves and of the way they look done up in different weights of thread.

• If you are not used to working with a hoop or frame, do try it. You can clamp the fabric into a large hoop, lace it to a needlepoint frame, or tack it to artists' stretchers. If your frame does not stand, rest one side against a table and the other in your lap. Work with one hand on top of the fabric and one below. Your work will go faster and the tension on your thread will be more uniform, resulting in a nicer finished work.

Butterfly Embroidered with Inlays

Embroidery floss and glossy metal inlays are the secret to this spectacular and sparkling butterfly. And while this shimmering creation looks intricate, with exquisite stitches, it is really quite simple to recreate.

If you are ready for something new in embroidery, this project is for you. Working with metal inlays is fun, and after mastering the technique, you may want to go on to work with mirrors, glass, or gems.

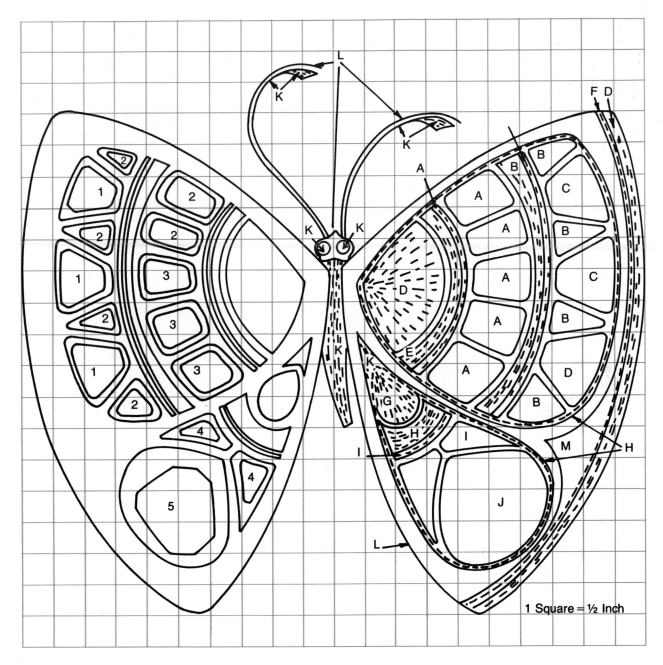

1 Square = ½ Inch

Color Key — Left Wing — Metal Segments
1. Emerald green
2. Blue
3. Turquoise
4. Lime green
5. Green-gold

Color Key — Body and Right Wing — Embroidery
A. Medium turquoise
B. Dark turquoise
C. Cobalt blue

Color Key — Body and Right Wing — Cont.
D. Medium blue
E. Blue-violet
F. Purple
G. Dark green
H. Medium green
I. Light green
J. Lime green
K. Brown
L. Black
M. Painted black, unembroidered

(continued)

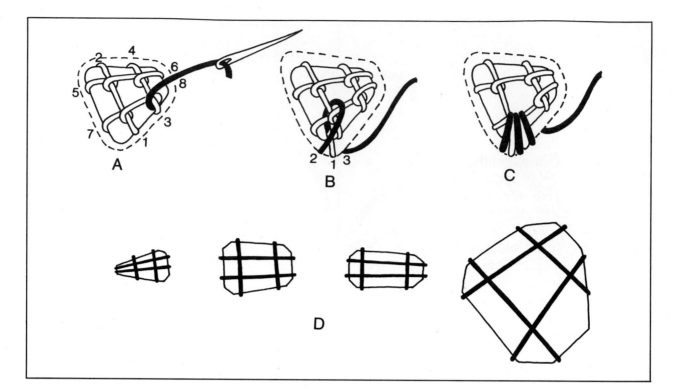

Materials

- ½ yard off-white sailcloth or other firmly woven fabric
- ½ yard white flannel
- 1 skein cobalt blue embroidery floss
- 1 skein blue-violet embroidery floss
- 1 skein purple embroidery floss
- 1 skein dark green embroidery floss
- 1 skein light green embroidery floss
- 1 skein brown embroidery floss
- 2 skeins medium turquoise embroidery floss
- 2 skeins dark turquoise embroidery floss
- 2 skeins medium blue embroidery floss
- 2 skeins medium green embroidery floss
- 2 skeins lime green embroidery floss
- 4 skeins black embroidery floss
- Waterproof, fine-point, black felt pen
- Large embroidery hoop
- Tracing paper
- Dressmaker's carbon paper
- Heavy cardboard or macrame board
- Aluminum soft-drink cans in green, blue, turquoise, lime green, and green-gold
- Tin snips or heavy shears
- White glue
- 13x13-inch square of ⅜-inch plywood
- Spray adhesive
- Staple gun, or small tacks and hammer
- 13x13-inch picture frame

Directions

Enlarge the butterfly body and the left wing on tracing paper (see page 31 for directions on enlarging). Omit the dotted lines and numbers. Reverse the wing pattern and trace it on the right side of the butterfly body.

Stretch the fabric and pin it to a piece of cardboard. Center the pattern on the fabric and trace it, using dressmaker's carbon paper. Fill the black areas shown in the left wing pattern with the felt-tip pen. The ink will bleed a bit. Do not use the pen on the feelers, and do not paint completely to the edges of the outlines.

Prepare metal inlays by first removing the tops and bottoms of the soft-drink cans. Next, use the tin snips to cut the cans along the seams and to remove the seams and rims. Flatten the cans by rolling them gently in the direction opposite the curl. Be careful not to scratch the metal.

Following the color key for the metal inlays, cut shapes from the unprinted areas on the cans. The dotted lines on the pattern indicate the sizes to cut the pieces. Pieces must be at least ⅛ inch smaller than the areas to be embroidered. Square-type shapes from ½-1½ inches in size are easiest to work. Remove sharp points.

Stretch the fabric tightly in a large embroidery hoop. Glue the inlays in place with a dot of white glue. Dry them thoroughly.

Using three strands of floss, anchor each inlay in a thread frame (see diagram A). Bring up the thread close to the metal at 1; go over the inlay and insert the needle at 2. Pull the thread taut. Bring the thread up again at 3, and down at 4, pulling it taut. Take a tiny back stitch on the back to anchor the thread, and bring it up again at 5. Wrap the thread around the first crosswise thread and pull it taut. Then wrap it around the next thread, and insert it at 6. Cross the first two threads again (see diagram A); this will secure the metal and make a frame for the stitches that will surround the inlay. Next, anchor the thread securely on the back and clip the excess.

The thread frames can secure pieces of different shapes as long as they are set well inside the corners and edges (see diagram D). Otherwise, the edges of the metal may be exposed by the drawing action of the embroidery. The little "windows" created by the thread will vary in size, but they will all be square-like ovals in shape.

Following the color key for the right wing, and using six strands of floss, work the inlaid areas (see diagrams B and C). Bring the needle out on a corner of the outline at 1 (Diagram B). Go *under* and then over the threads of the frame, and reinsert the needle at 2. Pull the loop tightly enough to draw the frame slightly without distorting the fabric. Come out at 3; go under and over the thread frame again, and reinsert the needle next to the first stitch. Work the needle carefully under the frame to avoid scratching the metal.

Continue this backward-forward sequence of stitches until the metal is completely encircled (Diagram C). Unwind the thread periodically as you work to keep it flat and smooth.

Next, outline the remaining areas with long and short back stitches (directions are on pages 28-29). Starting with the body, fill the inside colored areas with long-and-short stitches (directions are on pages 28-29). Reposition the pattern over the wings before completing the black outlines and blue edges. If the stitches have been drawn too tightly, causing distortion of the wings, re-draw the lines. Finish the embroidery.

Block the embroidery by stretching and pinning it to the cardboard, face down. Dampen the back, and allow it to dry. Press the back with a warm iron if necessary.

Coat the face of the plywood with adhesive and smooth the flannel over it, fuzzy side up. Trim the edges flush with the wood. Center the embroidery over the flannel. Starting in the middle of each side, pull the fabric to the back and staple it. Miter the corners. Trim away the excess fabric.

Following the manufacturer's directions, assemble the picture frame and insert the embroidery and secure it in place.

Tips for Creative Stitchery

• Use good-quality fabric and thread for finished embroidery. Also, sign and date your original designs. That may be your piece of work in a museum 300 years from now!

• Free your imagination for creative stitchery with new and unusual colors and textures, materials, and techniques. Try thick and thin threads in cotton, linen, silk, wool, or metal. Try ribbons and twine and fabric strips. Add beads and buttons and feathers and seeds. Add layers of applique, or cut away some areas for reverse applique or drawn-thread work. Mix a joyful feast for the eye and the spirit.

Embroidery on the Machine

Have you ever been tempted to help yourself to a fancy hotel towel? Help yourself instead to your sewing machine, some plain towels, and the patterns for these stylish hotel logos. If you have not tried machine embroidery yet, this is a good project to start with. Large letters filled in a solid color work up quickly once you've mastered the do's and don'ts of machine stitchery.

Don't be discouraged if you have a straight stitch machine. Fill the letters with closely spaced rows of running stitches. Or swing your hoop forwards and backwards for the look of long and short stitches.

Do be sure your machine is in good order before you begin to embroider.

Do visit your fabric shop for a look at the new machine embroidery threads. They come in a host of colors and shades and have the sheen of traditional embroidery floss.

Most of all, do have a grand time with machine embroidery. It is fun and fast, and the finished work looks spectacular.

Materials
- Purchased white terry cloth towels
- 8-inch embroidery hoop

- Organdy or lightweight, nonwoven pattern-tracing fabric
- Blue machine embroidery thread
- Gold machine embroidery thread

Directions

Enlarge one of the patterns below for the embroidery, or design your own pattern. (See page 31 for instructions for enlarging a design.) Trace the full-size design onto organdy or pattern-tracing fabric.

Center the fabric pattern on the towel. Add another layer of tracing fabric to the back of the towel to prevent the terry loops from snagging as you stitch. Clamp all three layers into an embroidery hoop, with the larger hoop on the underside of the fabric.

Prepare your machine for embroidery before you begin. Remove the presser foot. Lower or cover the feed dogs so you can move the fabric freely as you stitch. Lessen the top tension on the machine. Test the adjustments to the machine and practice stitching on an extra piece of terry cloth before actually tackling a design on a towel.

Begin to embroider with the stitch regulator set for a narrow zigzag. Slide the hoops under the needle and lower the presser bar. Insert the needle into the fabric and bring the bobbin thread to the surface. Holding both thread ends out of the way, take a few stitches to anchor the threads. Then, snip off excess thread. Begin stitching, running the machine at an even speed (slowly for beginners), and move the embroidery hoop back and forth slowly and evenly for uniform stitches. Perfection of your design depends on moving the hoops in a steady, relaxed manner. Practice helps!

If the thread loops on the fabric, the tension on the machine is too loose. If it breaks, the tension either on the spool or on the bobbin, is too tight.

Outline all the letters with the machine set for a narrow zigzag stitch. Then fill the letters with wide zigzag stitching. The finished stitching will look something like long and short stitches in hand embroidery.

When the embroidery is finished, trim away excess organdy or tracing fabric from the front and back of the design. Tie off and clip all the loose thread ends.

Hotels   1 Square = 1½ Inches

Tips for Machine Embroidery

- Always use an embroidery hoop.
- Before stitching, clamp organdy over sheer, high-pile, or looped fabrics.
- Check color books for simple designs.
- As you become more adept, try subtle shading with machine embroidery threads on traditional crewel designs.

Basic Embroidery Stitches

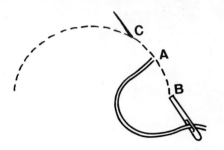

Back Stitch: Bring the needle up at A, a short distance from the end of the line, and down again at B. Bring it up again at C, to the left of A. For even back stitching, make all stitches the same length. For long-and-short back stitching, vary the length of the stitches as you go along.

Checkered Chain Stitch: Thread the needle with two colors of thread. As you work, hold only one color under your thumb for the loop. Keep the other thread out of the way. After taking one stitch, hold the other thread down for a loop. If the thread you are not working with doesn't disappear completely, pull it gently from the underside of the fabric. Repeat this process, alternating the colors.

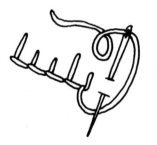

Buttonhole Stitch: Bring the needle up at A. Holding the thread down with your thumb, go down at B, above and to the right of A. Come up again at C. The needle should go *over* the thread held by the thumb.

Detached Chain Stitch: Tie down each stitch by inserting the needle outside the loop after each chain stitch is formed.

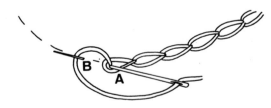

Chain Stitch: Bring the needle out at A. Hold the thread with your left thumb to form a loop, and reinsert the needle at A. Bring it up again at B, a short distance ahead and inside the loop held by the thumb.

Darning Stitch: This is a running stitch commonly worked in patterns. Bring the working thread up and over three or four threads of the fabric. Pick up only one or two threads between the long stitches. Rows should be close together.

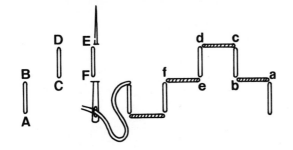

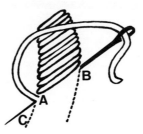

Double-running Stitch: Work a running stitch in one direction (A-B, C-D, E-F), and when you reach the end of the line turn around and work back to cover the empty spaces (a-b, c-d, e-f) by going into the same holes.

Satin Stitch: Bring the needle up at A, down at B, and up again at C right next to A. Continue, making straight stitches that lie close together side by side.

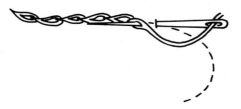

French Knot: Bring the needle up and wrap the thread over it one or more times, depending on how large a knot you want. Then reinsert the needle in the same place, and pull the thread through to the back.

Split Stitch: This stitch is like the stem stitch except that as you work, let the tip of the needle come up through the strands of previous stitch, splitting them.

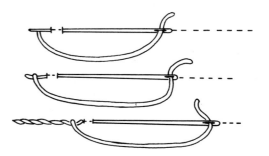

Long-and-short Stitch: Begin stitching at the outer edge of the area to be filled. Where rounded shapes taper to a point, mark a few radiating lines from the tip to the edge to help you distribute the stitches evenly. Work a row of alternately long and short satin stitches around the edge. Then fill the following rows with stitches that are all the same length and lie evenly.

Stem Stitch: Work from left to right. Bring the needle up and take a short back stitch. Keeping the thread below the needle, take another back stitch, and bring the needle out where the previous stitch went in.

Needlepoint

Needlepoint, one of the oldest and most elegant of the many needle arts, actually is a form of embroidery worked on canvas. Once you master a few basic stitches, put your nimble fingers to work. You'll take great pride in your artistic creations as you explore this fascinating hobby. This chapter contains a representative sampling of needlepoint.

Bride and Groom Dolls

People of all ages will be intrigued by the whimsy and charm of this demure bride and formally attired bridegroom. Each figure stands about 24 inches high and is about 8 inches wide at the broadest point.

Materials
- 1 yard No. 14 mono canvas for each doll
- Off white (No. 1) needlepoint wool
- Dark pink (No. 2) needlepoint wool
- Light pink (No. 3) needlepoint wool
- Flesh (No. 4) needlepoint wool
- Medium blue (No. 5) needlepoint wool
- Lichen—gray/green (No. 6) needlepoint wool
- Lettuce green (No. 7) needlepoint wool
- Chartreuse (No. 8) needlepoint wool
- Pale peach (No. 9) needlepoint wool
- Medium peach (No. 10) needlepoint wool
- Apricot (No. 11) needlepoint wool
- Deep yellow (No. 12) needlepoint wool
- Pale yellow (No. 13) needlepoint wool
- Medium yellow (No. 14) needlepoint wool
- Gold (No. 15) needlepoint wool

- Medium brown (No. 16) needlepoint wool
- Lighter brown (No. 17) needlepoint wool
- Light gray (No. 18) needlepoint wool
- Medium gray (No. 19) needlepoint wool
- Dark gray (No. 20) needlepoint wool
- Black (No. 21) needlepoint wool
- ¾ yard backing fabric, such as velvet, velveteen, or no-wale corduroy.
- Polyester/dacron fiberfill for stuffing
- Tapestry needle
- Masking tape
- Waterproof marking pen

Directions
General Instructions: The amount of yarn you use depends on how tightly you stitch. If you are not able to judge your own yarn gauge, enlarge and trace pattern on canvas and do several sample rows. Take sample with you to your needlepoint shop and get help in estimating amounts of yarn. Make sure you buy sufficient yarn in the right dye lot to complete the project.

To enlarge your pattern, select paper large enough to accommodate finished design (brown wrapping paper works well). Then, draw horizontal and vertical lines one inch apart, and transfer your drawing onto it.

(continued)

Color Key
1 off white
2 dark pink
3 light pink
4 flesh
5 medium blue
6 lichen (grey/green)
7 lettuce green
8 chartreuse
9 pale peach
10 medium peach
11 apricot
12 deep yellow
13 pale yellow
14 medium yellow
15 gold
16 medium brown
17 lighter brown
18 light grey
19 medium grey
20 dark grey
21 black

Cross-hatching on bride's dress

band of hat
19

Stripes in pants
19
Stripes in pants
21

Figure out how lines pass from square to square, and whether you move in a straight, curved, or diagonal line. As you practice, it becomes easier to reenact the path of the line as it moves from one square to the next one.

Needlepoint yarn usually comes in 3-ply strands. To save working time, cut yarn into 18-inch pieces, separating yarn into 2-ply strands as you work. To prevent confusion among similar shades, first divide and label all yarn according to corresponding numbers on color key.

Press canvas with a dry iron, and bind all edges with masking tape to keep canvas from fraying and yarns from catching in rough edge of canvas as you work.

Bride doll: Lay canvas over enlarged doll pattern and pin in place. (See general instructions on page 31.) Using a light-colored waterproof marking pen, carefully trace outline of doll pattern onto canvas. *Be sure to use a waterproof marker,* so the tracing does not bleed through onto the yarn when you block the finished piece.

It is not necessary to color the canvas before you begin stitching. For correct placement of colors, simply refer to numbered sections of pattern and to accompanying color key as you work. It is important to cover canvas evenly. Before beginning, experiment on a corner of the canvas to make sure you are not pulling the yarn too tight.

Outline all areas of canvas first in a single row of continental stitch in the appropriate color. Work all solid areas of pattern in basketweave stitch. Although basketweave takes a little more skill and about a third more yarn to work than the continental stitch, you will find it is less likely to pull canvas out of shape.

Both continental and basketweave stitches are illustrated on pages 40-41.

After outlining each section of canvas in continental stitch, work the small, detail areas. Then, proceed to basketweave stitch larger areas such as the bride's gown and veil. Finally, add extra rows of stitching around outer outline of doll. (This extra margin will be taken up when you sew needlepoint piece to backing fabric.)

If your finished piece is out of shape, dampen back of canvas, gently pull back into shape, and tack down on all sides. When canvas is dry, dampen again and press with a warm iron and press cloth on wrong side.

Lay finished piece of needlepoint on backing fabric with right sides together. Baste needlepoint piece to backing piece to prevent shifting. Next, machine stitch needlepoint piece to backing piece, running machine stitches inside the two extra rows of needlepoint stitches. Stitch again, ⅛-inch outside the first row of machine stitching. Leave the bottom of the bride doll open for turning and stuffing. Trim away the excess canvas. Turn doll to right side and press lightly. Stuff with polyester filling. Slipstitch edges closed.

Groom doll: Enlarge and trace pattern of groom doll just as you did for bride doll. After outlining each section of canvas in continental stitch, work the small, detail areas of the canvas, and then proceed to basketweave stitch larger areas such as the groom's coat. Finish the groom doll in same manner as you did bride doll.

No. 14 Mono Canvas

34

Art Nouveau Wall Hanging

This needlepoint picture suggests an alternative to framing. It is mounted unframed on velvet backing so that the soft textural quality of the stitchery adds beauty to the reproduction of the Art Nouveau poster.

This also has the claim of authenticity, since the earliest weavings were hung on walls and doors as protection against cold.

Materials
- 22x30-inch piece of No. 12 mono canvas
- 2 ounces avocado needlepoint wool
- 2 ounces medium blue needlepoint wool
- 2 ounces orange-red needlepoint wool (for hair)
- 1 ounce flesh color needlepoint wool
- 1 ounce light pink needlepoint wool
- 1 ounce medium pink needlepoint wool
- 1 ounce yellow needlepoint wool
- 1 ounce dark blue needlepoint wool
- 1 ounce olive green needlepoint wool
- 1 ounce brown needlepoint wool
- 1 ounce black needlepoint wool
- 1 yard velvet for backing and loops
- 1 yard lining for backing and loops
- 22-inch piece of ½-inch dowel
- 2 finials (one for each end of dowel)
- Tapestry needle
- Dressmaker's weights

Directions
Note: See general instructions on page 31 before you start this project.

Enlarge the design shown on page 36 so that the size of the pattern measures 18x26 inches. Center the enlarged design face up under the No. 12 mono canvas. Using a waterproof marking pen, trace the design onto the canvas.

Work the entire wall hanging in basket-weave stitch (see pages 40-41), and extend the design one row around all four edges.

Block the piece of needlepoint by dampening it and tacking it to the blocking board. First, anchor the corners with stainless T-pins or rustproof tacks; then, place the tacks an inch apart along the four sides of the canvas. Keep the needlepoint canvas on the blocking board until you mount it. This keeps the canvas from losing its shape. Then, sew a row of machine stitching on the excess canvas about ½ inch from the needlepoint (see Fig. 1 below).

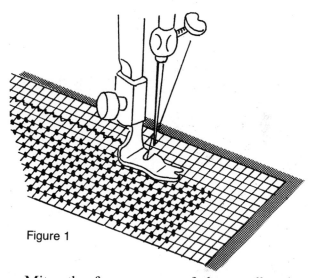

Figure 1

Miter the four corners of the needlepoint and tack excess canvas to back of stitching, making sure that the rows of stitching are perfectly straight and that no unstitched canvas shows along the edges (see Fig. 2).

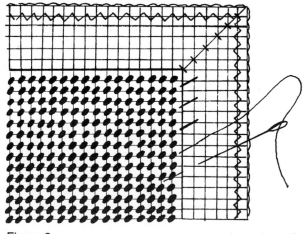

Figure 2

(continued)

1 Square = 1 Inch

To make each of the three velvet loops, follow this procedure: Lay one of the 3x12-inch velvet strips face down on its lining and sew the long side seams of both together, ½ inch in from the edges (see Fig. 3). Turn the strip right side out and steam flat. Fold the fabric strip in half and stitch the open ends together ½ inch in from the ends of the strip (see Fig. 4).

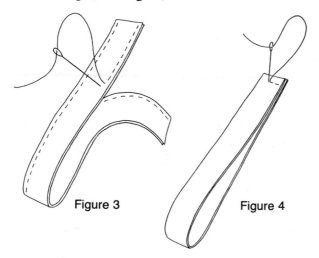

Figure 3   Figure 4

Lay the lining for the hanging face up. Place the loops on top of the lining with their raw ends extending 1½ inches beyond the edge of the lining. Place one loop at each end and one loop in the center (see Fig. 5). Baste each loop securely in place.

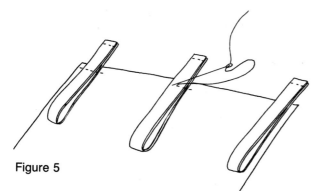

Figure 5

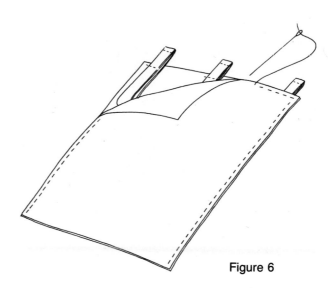

Figure 6

Lay the large piece of velvet face down over the loops and lining. Baste and then sew the top and both sides together, leaving a ½-inch seam allowance all around (see Fig. 6). Cut away the excess material at the corners and slip the wooden dowel through the pockets in the loops. Sew dressmaker's weights to the bottom of the lining about 1 inch from the edge.

Turn right side out and steam the seams flat. Turn the lining and the velvet under ½ inch at the bottom and blindstitch the two pieces (see Fig. 7).

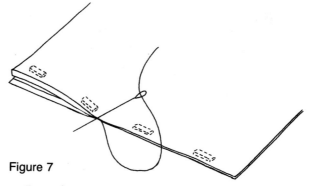

Figure 7

Lay the needlepoint on the velvet backing, centering from side to side, but leaving a slightly wider border at the bottom than at the top. Blindstitch the needlepoint to the velvet backing (see Fig. 8).

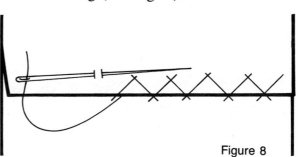

Figure 8

Remove masking tape and trim around completed needlepoint, leaving margin of three unstitched rows of canvas. Fold edges under and press flat. Cut backing ½ inch larger than canvas. Fold backing edges under ¼ inch and slipstitch them to needlepoint on three sides.

Bend wire into rectangle slightly smaller than needlepoint strip, twist ends together, and insert between needlepoint and backing. Slipstitch fourth side closed.

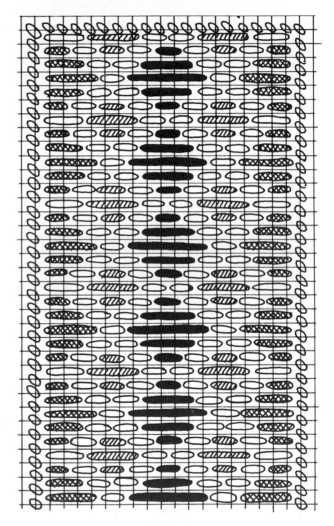

½ of napkin ring pattern
12 Squares = 1 Inch

☐ gold/yellow pearl cotton

■ dark green Persian wool

▨ light green Persian yarn

▩ magenta Persian yarn

Bargello Napkin Rings

Add interest to your table setting with hand-made needlepoint napkin rings. Materials listed are sufficient for six rings. Basic needlepoint stitches are shown on pages 40-41.

Materials
- ½ yard No. 12 mono needlepoint canvas
- ½ skein magenta needlepoint wool
- ½ skein dark green needlepoint wool
- ½ skein light green needlepoint wool
- 3 small skeins yellow-gold pearl cotton
- ½ yard fabric for lining
- Tapestry needle
- Lightweight wire
- Masking tape

Directions
Cut a 2½x8-inch strip of canvas for each ring. Bind with masking tape. Work canvas in Bargello weave stitch as shown in drawing. Fill in with diamond stitch, following color guide in drawing. Outline outside edges with row of continental stitches.

Mini Pillows

These small-size needlepoint pillows are an excellent project for beginners. They require only one basic stitch and the diagonal stripes are created automatically by changing yarn colors at the ends of the rows.

Choose colors that form a pleasing combination and vary the widths of the stripes. Each pillow measures 9x12 inches and is backed with a solid color durable fabric.

Materials
- 9x12-inch piece of No. 12 mono canvas for each pillow top
- 12 cards of needlepoint wool per pillow in the colors of your choice
- No. 18 needlepoint needle
- 9x12-inch backing fabric such as velveteen, corduroy, or hopsacking
- Polyester fiberfill
- Masking tape

Directions
Cut the canvas to measure 9x12 inches. Bind the edges with masking tape to prevent raveling. Use short lengths of needlepoint yarn, between 18 and 24 inches. Study the sketch below carefully before beginning. If you're a novice, practice on a piece of scrap canvas.

Start at top right of canvas, holding it diagonally with stitch 1-2 at the top. Do not knot end of yarn. Holding canvas firmly, push threaded needle through from back, leaving a 1-inch end in back. Hold the end of yarn by pressing it against the canvas with the left forefinger. After a few stitches, it will stay in place.

Follow the sketch and stitch down diagonally from left to right, then back up to the left for the next row and back to the right. Starting with stitch 21-22, then 23-24, and 25-26, notice how you are stitching between the jogs formed by stitches 17-18, 15-16, and 13-14.

Do not tie knots at ends of rows. To change colors or continue a color, finish off by weaving yarn through the finished work on the wrong side. Start a new color as explained above. When you finish needlepointing, remove the masking tape.

If the needlepoint piece is out of shape, dampen it and pin it to a board. Align the corners and straight edges, and let the piece dry. Remove it from the board and stitch the finished design to the pillow backing, right sides together. Leave the fourth side open to turn. Trim the seams and turn right side out. Stuff with polyester fiberfill and slip-stitch the opening closed.

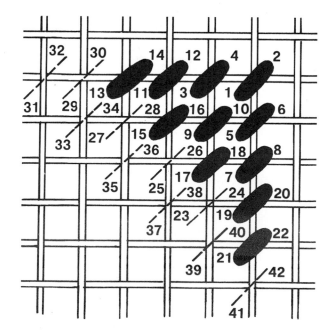

Needlepoint Stitches

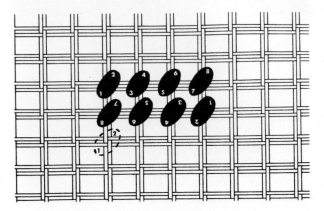

Half Cross Stitch: This is the simplest of all needlepoint stitches; it requires the least amount of yarn, and must be worked on Penelope (double-thread) canvas.

Work half cross stitch from right to left, from left to right, or from bottom to top, working vertically. (Use whichever method is easiest for you.) It forms a straight stitch on the back.

Use the plain half cross stitch for small items which need no padding on the back, or which will not be subject to hard wear. This stitch requires about one yard of yarn for a square inch of canvas.

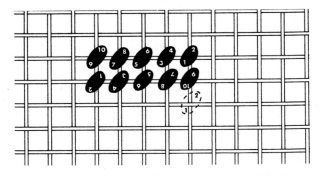

Continental Stitch: This can be worked on mono (single mesh) canvas or Penelope (double-thread) canvas. This stitch works up with more thickness on the back than on the front. Blocking is always necessary because the canvas becomes distorted.

Always start this stitch in the upper right-hand corner. Work from right to left. Bring the needle out a mesh ahead and slanting.

This method produces the half cross stitch on the top and a slanting stitch on the back. The continental stitch uses about 1¼ yards of yarn a square inch.

This stitch is ideal for use on articles that receive heavy wear such as chair seats, foot stools, bench tops, and rugs.

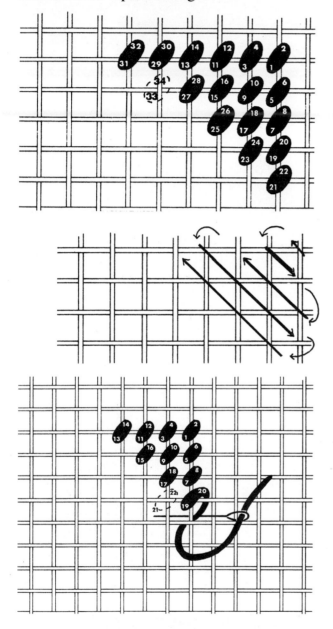

Basketweave Stitch: This stitch is named for the woven pattern it forms on the back of the canvas. It is the most durable stitch and causes the least distortion of the canvas. It can be worked on mono (single mesh) canvas or Penelope (double thread) canvas.

Begin the stitch at the upper right hand corner and increase one stitch each side until you have attained the desired width.

Stitches will be in diagonal rows rather than along horizontal or vertical threads. The sequence of stitching follows the direction indicated by the arrows.

Each individual basketweave stitch is formed in the same way. The thread crosses the intersection of the canvas from the southwest corner to the northeast corner. Until you become experienced enough to tell an "up" row from a "down" row by looking at the backing, put your needlework aside only when you are in the middle of a row. Then, insert your needle in the canvas so it is poised for the next stitch.

Basketweave stitch is perfect for backgrounds and large areas of color. It may be worked without turning the canvas.

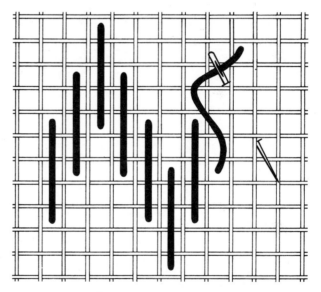

Bargello or Florentine Stitch: This consists of a series of upright stitches passing over three or more meshes of the canvas to form a particular pattern. The most common pattern is called the flame stitch and is worked in varying shades of one or more colors.

It is necessary to use fluffy yarns for Bargello because all the stitches are upright, and cover only the horizontal threads.

41

Appliqué

Along with many other needlecraft techniques, the fine art of appliqué is experiencing a revival in popularity. Layer smaller cutout fabric motifs on a larger background, and create fabric collages that lend themselves to many handcraft projects. Accomplish the following appliqué projects by hand-stitching, by machine-stitching, or by gluing.

Appliquéd Doily Wall Hanging

Ingenuity and economy are the name of the game. Select knitted, crocheted, tatted, or needle lace doilies from a personal collection, antique stores, or garage sales. Remember your baker when you choose. The doilies that accompany his cakes are beautifully designed, but they should be glued, rather than stitched. With doilies in hand, you're ready to arrange a large, attractive 2½x4-foot display. Use your creative eye and decide where your doily design can best blossom into the decor of the room.

Materials
- 5 doilies (knitted, crocheted, tatted, or needle lace) for flowers
- Transparent fabric, such as net or organdy, for stems
- Bits of old lace, nylon, net, and eyelet fabric for leaves
- 1 3x4-foot piece of lightweight upholstery fabric, such as duck or sailcloth
- Thread to match
- Embroidery floss or crochet cotton to match
- 2½x4-foot plywood board (½-inch)
- Frame to fit
- Staple gun and staples
- Picture hangers

Directions
Arrange the five doilies on the upholstery fabric in a bouquet pattern. In case your doilies are small, cut larger circles from organdy or net fabric and center a doily on each. Cut stems for each flower from organdy or net, and cut leaves from small pieces of lace and eyelet fabric. Experiment with different arrangements until you have arrived at the one you like best. Note positions of all pieces.

Pin stems and then leaves in place. Machine sew with a zigzag stitch around the edges. Retrace zigzag stitches with machine satin stitching. Next, pin the doilies in place and sew with a single thread in tiny overcast stitches round the edges.

Embroider French knots, couching, satin stitches, or small single stitches (see pages 28-29) around the doilies, using four to six strands of embroidery floss.

Stretch upholstery fabric over the ½-inch plywood board and staple in place; frame, apply picture hangers, and hang.

Appliquéd Doily Accessories

Appliqué delicate doilies onto such accessories as ordinary pillows, a simple shower curtain, hand towels, and a lid cover.

Watch these everyday items acquire a new personality. They become elegant accessories with an air of nostalgia.

Materials
Bathroom Accessories
- Assortment of doilies
- Clear shower curtain
- White fabric glue
- Assorted bands of lace
- Hand towels
- Toilet lid cover
- Thread to match

Doily Pillows
- Assorted doilies
- Assorted pillows in bright colors
- Thread to match

Directions
Bathroom Accessories: Working on the outside of the shower curtain, arrange doilies and attach with fabric glue. Let glue dry and hang the curtain.

To trim the hand towels, pin the lace trim onto the towels and sew in place with a small whipstitch. (See the diagram on page 77 to learn how to whipstitch.)

To make the doily toilet seat cover, pin doily to lid cover and fasten down with tiny whipstitches. Secure the center of the doily with whipstitches, if necessary.

Doily Pillows: Center and pin doilies in place on each pillow; smooth out any wrinkles. Secure the edges and the center with tiny, hidden whipstitches.

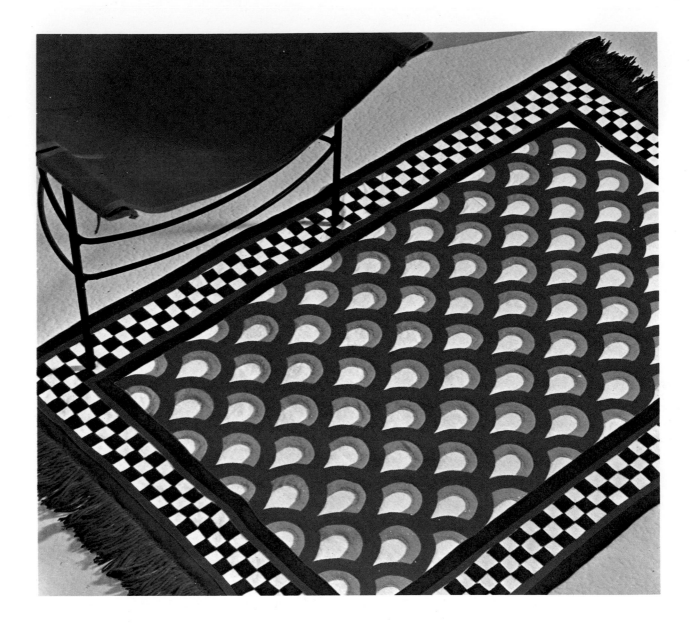

Brightly Colored Appliquéd Rug

The colorful 3x4½-foot felt rug brightens any room. It looks difficult to make, but you simply enlarge the pattern pieces, cut out the felt, and stitch the layers together.

Materials
- 1½ yards blue felt
- 1 yard white felt
- 1⅛ yards orange felt
- ⅞ yard yellow felt
- 2⅛ yards blue yarn fringe
- Dressmaker's carbon paper
- Tracing wheel
- Thread to match
- Cardboard
- Paper
- Compass

Directions
Divide an 8½x11-inch piece of paper into 2½-inch squares. Using a compass, duplicate the semicircular pattern. Diameters of semicircles are 5 inches, 3¼ inches, and 1½ inches, respectively. Draw short vertical lines (see pattern).

Note color designations for each area; O (orange), Y (yellow), and W (white).

Using dressmaker's carbon and tracing wheel, transfer pattern onto two pieces of 8½x11-inch cardboard. Label one piece No. 1

and the other No. 2. On No. 1, cut out all areas designated W (smallest semicircles and V-shaped one below it). On 2, cut out all areas marked W and all areas marked Y (larger semicircle and V-shaped area below it).

Cut Y felt into a 25x42½-inch piece and divide into 2½-inch squares with light pencil marks. Place cardboard No. 1 along 25-inch edge and trace outline of cutout areas. Pick up cardboard, move it to the right, align it, and repeat until 25-inch edge has been covered with pattern.

To repeat pattern lengthwise, place bottom row of cutouts in correct position on felt and repeat procedure until entire piece has been covered. Align edges properly.

Cut a 25x42½-inch piece of O felt and divide into 2½-inch squares. Place cardboard No. 2 over it and repeat tracing.

Cut out traced area from Y and O felt. Cut a 37x53-inch piece of W felt and a 37x54-inch piece of blue felt. Place O felt directly over Y felt; line up properly, and baste together. Center and pin this two-layered piece to W felt. Zigzag stitch around top and two sides. Trim ½ inch off bottom row and stitch to W felt.

Cut 1-inch wide blue felt strips as follows: two 27 inches, two 37 inches, two 44 inches, and two 54 inches. Cut ½-inch wide strips from O felt: two 28 inches, two 35 inches, two 45 inches, and two 52 inches. Cut 237 1-inch blue felt squares.

Hold a 27-inch blue strip perpendicular to a 44-inch blue strip. Miter corner and sew together. Repeat for other 27- and 44-inch blue strips. Join the two pairs, mitering corners. You now have a large rectangular outline that will border the design perfectly. Pin to edge and zigzag stitch.

Make a large O rectangular border in same manner, using two 28-inch strips and two 45-inch strips. Join to blue border strip in same manner with zigzag stitches.

Arrange blue squares on W felt, as shown in diagram, and zigzag stitch around edges. Stitch remaining O strips to W felt around edges. Pick up entire piece; center and pin to 37x54-inch blue felt. Stitch around edges. Sew remaining blue strips around this edge as final border. Trim edges.

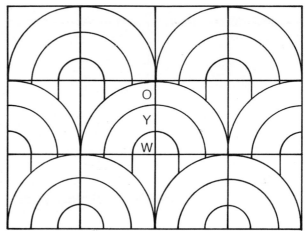

1 SQ = 2½ INCHES

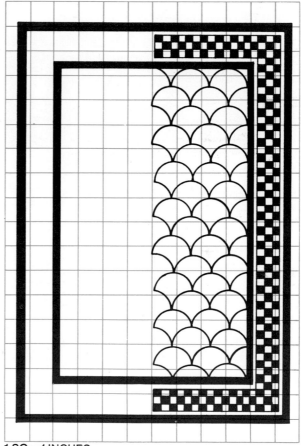

1 SQ = 4 INCHES

Sew wide blue yarn fringe to the outermost blue border at either end of the rug, setting the longest stitch on your sewing machine and using matching thread.

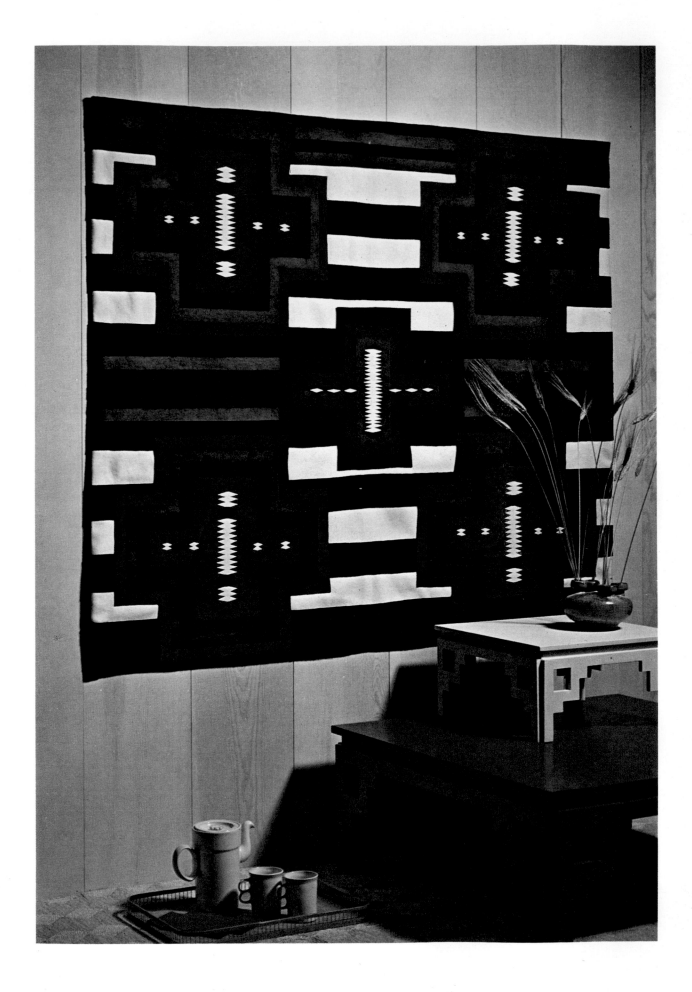

48

Appliquéd Navaho Design Wall Hanging

This handsome reproduction of a 100-year-old Navaho rug, will add American Indian flavor to any room in your house. Display it in the family room, where everyone can enjoy the bold colors and dramatic lines.

The entire project is made of felt, with striking cross designs in purple, red, and green. The crosses are cut, then glued or stitched to a large background piece.

The overall size of the appliquéd wall hanging is 54x62 inches.

Materials
- 1⅔ yards white felt
- 1⅓ yards black felt
- 2 yards red felt
- 1⅓ yards green felt
- 1 yard purple felt
- 1 57x63-inch piece of lining material
- 1 1x2x62-inch pine strip
- Picture hangers
- White glue

Directions
Lay the white felt out and cut a rectangle measuring 54x62 inches.

From the black felt, cut two 5x62-inch strips, one 12x62-inch strip, and four 3¼x62-inch strips. Glue one 5-inch wide strip to the top of the white background felt and one 5-inch wide strip to the bottom. Make sure all the edges are flush. Next, glue the 12-inch wide strip to the central 12 inches of the white

background. (To find the central 12 inches, measure 27 inches down from the top and mark this point. Then measure 6 inches up and 6 inches down from this point.) To the white area above and below the center black strip, evenly space and glue two 3¼-inch black strips—two to the top and two to the bottom.

Cut four 1¼x62-inch strips from the green felt. Evenly space and glue two of the green strips to the top black strip and two to the bottom black strip.

Refer to the central cross pattern. From the purple felt, cut out a cross with side bars extending 26 inches. Cut four 1¼x20-inch green strips and two 1¼x20-inch black strips. Glue them to the side bars as shown—green at

(continued)

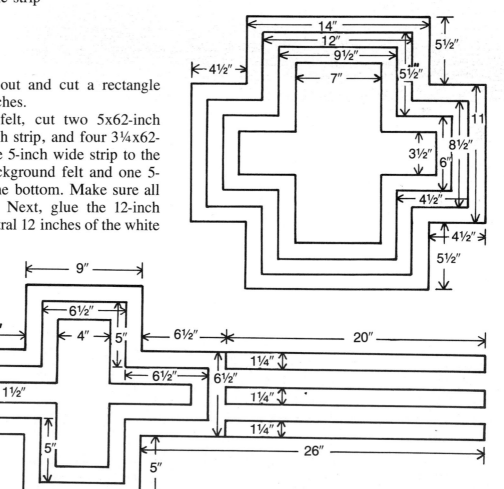

49

the top and bottom edges of the side bars, black at the center, and purple strips between.

Cut out the red and green crosses for the center cross as follows: Cut a 14x19½-inch red piece and an 11½x17-inch green piece. From all corners of both pieces, cut a 5x6½-inch rectangle. (The 5-inch side is the width.) Center and glue the green cross to the red cross. Center and glue the red cross to the purple cross. Allow to dry. Glue the entire purple cross to the center black strip of the background piece. Allow to dry.

Refer to the outer cross pattern. Cut the crosses as follows: Cut four 22x23½-inch red rectangles, four 19½x21-inch green rectangles, four 17x18½-inch purple rectangles, and four 14½x16-inch red rectangles. From all corners of each rectangle, cut a 4½x5½-inch rectangle. (The 5½-inch side is the length and the 4½-inch side is the width.)

Center and glue a small red cross to a purple, a purple to a green, and then a green to a large red cross. Repeat this for the three other crosses. When all have dried, position them and glue them on the background piece. Allow to dry.

To make the triangular motif strip for the four crosses, cut a 1¾-inch wide piece of white felt (it can be any length). Fold the strip in half lengthwise and mark evenly spaced intervals along the cut edge for the apex of each triangle. Cut out the triangle piece. If you wish, cut out some black triangles and intermingle them. For the triangular motif strip of the center cross, use a ⅞-inch wide strip and repeat the procedure. Make triangular strips of different sizes for the side bars.

Sew the lining material to the background material, turning the side and bottom edges under ½ inch. At the top, turn material under 2½ inches to make a casing for the pine strip. Insert the strip.

Attach picture hangers according to manufacturer's directions.

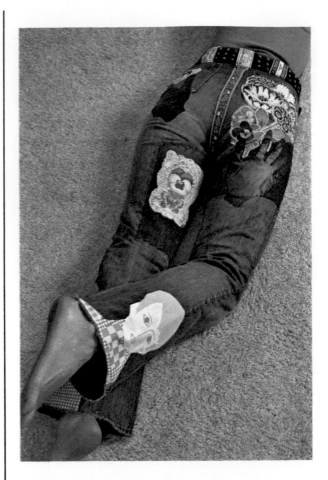

Appliquéd Jeans

Never throw away old jeans, and always save fabric scraps from old garments and leftovers. Here's why: You can create fascinating designs by appliquéing patches on blue jeans. In fact, don't be surprised when friends ask you to "repair" their new jeans. Old or new, appliquéd jeans are great.

Materials
- Pair of jeans
- Fabric scraps and pieces of braid or trim
- Thread or embroidery floss to match

Directions
Cut out fabric scraps and arrange them on jeans in an interesting design. Turn each piece under ¼ inch. Whipstitch (see page 77) each piece or embroider in your favorite stitch (see pages 28-29).

Sew braid or trim to back seam. Embroider side seams or attach braid. Cut smaller fabric pieces and seam to waist for belt loops.

Red Hen Appliquéd Quilt

Delight a small child with this bright addition to his or her bedroom. Once you've quilted the 41x65-inch coverlet, simply enlarge the pattern pieces, cut out the shapes, and stitch them onto the background. Use the red hen or any other colorful character that your child enjoys.

Materials
- 2 yards red-orange polyester blend fabric (45 inches wide)
- 2 yards white polyester blend fabric
- 1 yard red-orange washable velveteen
- 1 roll ½-inch polyester batting
- Blanket binding
- Yellow-orange and white fabric scraps
- Tailor's chalk
- Dressmaker's carbon paper
- Tracing wheel
- Black and red thread

Directions
Place the polyester batting between the red and white fabric, matching the corners, and pin the three layers together. Baste, radiating circles from the center outward, and stitch around all four sides. Trim the batting. Make chalk marks for every inch along the top and bottom edges, and every 1⅛ inch along the sides. Draw in lines. Starting at the center and working out, make small running stitches over lines in black thread.

Enlarge the hen pattern and transfer it to the red velveteen, using carbon and tracing wheel. Cut out the hen; center and pin it to a piece of batting that is 1 inch larger than the hen's circumference. Baste the two pieces together and trim the batting. Sew in the feather detail with straight, even hand stitches.

Cut two ¾-inch white oval pieces of fabric for the eyes and two corresponding pieces of batting (slightly larger). Baste the two together and trim batting. Position ovals on hen and baste. Use satin zigzag stitch around the edges to attach.

Cut out a yellow-orange beak that is 7 inches long and 6 inches wide and a corresponding piece of batting. Baste together, and trim batting. Pin beak onto hen and attach with satin zigzag. Sew in pupils and nostrils with machine satin stitch.

Remove the basting stitches and position the hen on the quilt. Baste and then satin zigzag around the edge to attach. Make yellow straw with satin zigzag.

Cut two white ovals, each 6x8 inches, for eggs. Turn under ¼ inch, and stitch to quilt, stuffing with batting as you stitch.

Attach binding around the four edges.

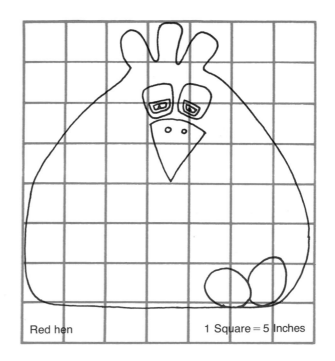

Red hen   1 Square = 5 Inches

51

Appliquéd Headboard with Floral Motif

Keep that old headboard, and don't waste time searching for a "new style" or "look" for your bedroom. A delicate floral design appliquéd to your existing headboard may be just what the room needs. For added charm and elegance, appliqué in satin.

Materials
- 1 1½x1½-yard of eggshell satin
- Scraps of dark green, light green, dusty rose, and pink satin
- 1 1½x1½-yard piece of batting
- 1 36x43-inch piece of plywood (¼-inch)
- 3 yards muslin or inexpensive fabric
- Staple gun and staples or tacks
- Fusible webbing

Directions
Enlarge the design pattern and cut out along the outline. Place pattern on plywood and trace the top sloping edge. Cut out wood.

Transfer floral petal pattern onto cardboard and cut. Do the same for each three-leaf grouping on left side of pattern. Make a pattern for each individual leaf below flower. Be sure to include bordered area around each shape. (Border serves as guide for stitching.) Make cardboard pattern for each stem.

Position flower petal pattern on dusty rose satin; trace, and cut out. Repeat for the three individual leaves and the three-leaf groupings, cutting from light green satin. Cut out the reverse of each grouping for the right side of the design by placing each pattern face down on satin and then tracing. Follow the same procedure for stems, cutting from dark green satin.

Cut dusty rose and light pink border strips; position on eggshell satin, about 9 inches down from the top and 6 inches in from either side. Hold eggshell satin against the plywood headboard, double checking position of border strips.

Cut a small piece of fusible webbing for each piece of the design. Place webbing under each piece and position on eggshell satin. The fusing should not show around the edges. Fuse together with a steam iron. The webbing will keep designs from slipping when you applique them.

Cut a 54x60-inch piece of muslin. Sandwich batting between muslin and eggshell satin; baste all three layers together.

Stitch around all parts of the design with your sewing machine. Use the border area of each design as a guide.

Position eggshell satin on headboard. Staple or tack the excess satin around the back at sides, top, and bottom. Keep the material taut, and staple it at least 2 inches away from the edges. Trim the excess satin close to staples.

Form the remaining muslin, cut a piece to fit the back of the headboard. Turn under 1 inch at the hem. Position muslin on the back so that it is about 1 inch short all around. Whipstitch it to satin around edges.

Color Code:	
	R = dusty rose
D = dark green	P = pink
L = light green	E = eggshell

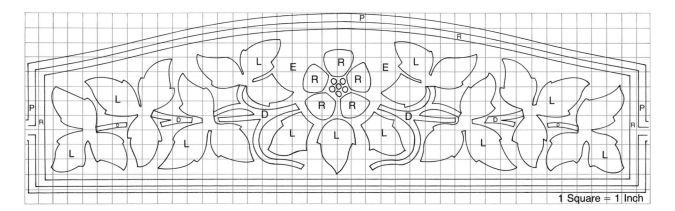

1 Square = 1 Inch

Appliquéd Table Accessories

Create an impressive table setting with appliqued place mats, napkins, and napkin rings. The flower motif was inspired by the dinnerware pattern. Borrow a motif from your dinnerware pattern, or select a different design that complements your table setting.

Materials
- 4 natural-color linen place mats
- 4 purple linen napkins
- 24x24-inch piece of blue fabric
- 18x18-inch piece of white fabric
- 6x12-inch piece of purple fabric
- 6x6-inch piece of pink fabric
  (Choose fabrics that will not fray easily)
- ⅔ yard, ¾-inch wide pink grosgrain ribbon
- ⅔ yard, ¼-inch wide blue grosgrain ribbon
- Thread to match or contrast
- White embroidery floss
- Dressmaker's carbon paper
- Tracing wheel
- Cardboard tube

Directions
Place mats and napkins: Using dressmaker's carbon paper and tracing wheel, trace outline of pattern A onto white fabric. Repeat until you have 12 flowers—three for each place mat. Cut flowers carefully.

In same manner, trace petal sections of pattern A on blue fabric. Make 12 four-petal groupings and cut.

Pin a four-petal grouping in place on each of the 12 white flowers. Attach by machine-sewing around edges with zigzag stitching. Next, pin white flowers to place mats. Place one in lower right-hand corner and two diagonally at upper left-hand corner on each place mat. Sew in place with zigzag stitching around edges.

In same manner, trace outline of pattern B on blue fabric. Trace twelve flower outlines — three for each place mat.

Next, trace petals of pattern B on purple fabric, making 12 four-petal groupings. Cut out all pieces. Position petal pieces on flowers as before and zigzag stitch.

Position blue flowers on place mat, one at top left-hand corner and two diagonally across lower right-hand corner. Sew in place with zigzag stitch.

Follow same procedure for pattern C. Trace flower outline on white fabric and make four flowers — one for each napkin.

Trace petal outline of pattern C on blue fabric and make 4 four-petal groupings. Also, trace 4 small pink and white centers each on pink and white fabric. Cut out all pieces. Position white circles on top of pink circles and sew together. Place circles in center of flowers and zigzag stitch.

Position and pin flowers on napkins and zigzag stitch in place. Refer to embroidery stitches on pages 28-29. Make cross stitches and chain stitch with white embroidery floss (see photo).

For contrast, zigzag stitch around edges of napkins in a color of your choice.

Napkin rings: Cut a 3x24-inch strip of blue fabric. Center and pin pink grosgrain ribbon to it. Zigzag in contrasting or matching color. Center and pin blue grosgrain ribbon on pink ribbon and sew in place. Cut strip into four 6-inch lengths, one for each napkin. With a sharp knife, cut four 2-inch

wide sections of cardboard tube. Wrap the 6-inch length of fabric around tube, inside-out. Seam sides together. Turn the right side out, and slip over ring. Clip edges ¼ inch. Spread white glue inside ring, fold edges of fabric to inside, and glue.

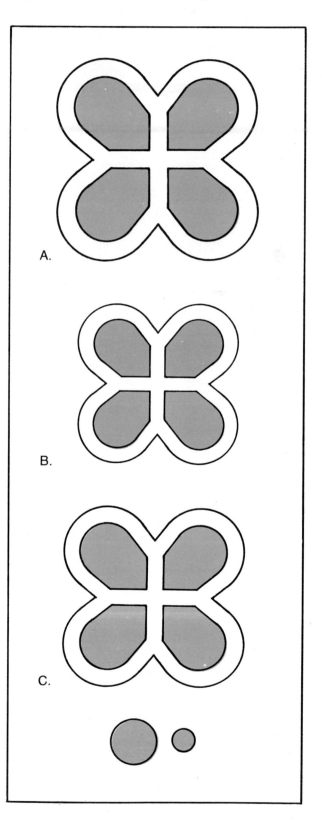

A.

B.

C.

Giant Appliquéd Christmas Sock

Make a stocking large enough to hold Christmastime gifts for the whole family! Just cut out the design on pink felt; back it with red felt; appliqué heart, flower, and leaf shapes onto the stocking, and then hang it by the fireplace. The overall height of the stocking is about 2 feet so there will be plenty of room for lots of stocking stuffers. As an added treat, gather some fabric scraps, yarn, embroidery floss, knit fabric, and some polyester stuffing to make the little dolls. For added surprises, make a doll to represent each member of the family. Stock it to 'em this Christmas!

Materials

Stocking
- ½ yard pink felt
- ½ yard red felt
- ¼ yard orange felt
- Scraps of yellow felt
- 4-ply crewel yarn in matching colors
- Thread to match
- Dressmaker's carbon paper
- Tracing wheel
- Embroidery or decoupage scissors

Dolls
- Natural or white knit fabric scraps
- Polyester stuffing
- Assorted fabric scraps
- Embroidery floss to match
- Yarn for hair

Directions

Stocking: Enlarge the pattern for the appliquéd stocking, making sure that each square equals 2½ inches. Using a dressmaker's carbon and tracing wheel, transfer the outline of the stocking pattern onto the piece of pink felt twice. Cut out the two pink pieces. These two pieces will become the outer part of the stocking. Transfer the outline of the stocking onto red felt twice. Cut out two red stockings. These will become the inner lining for the stocking.

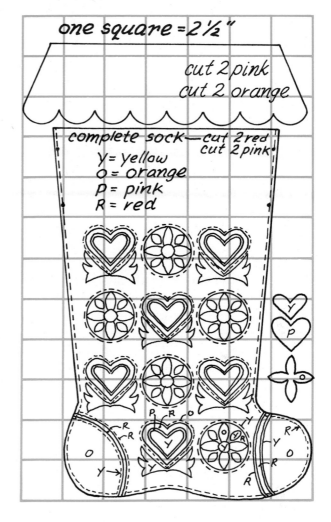

Transfer the outline of the stocking cuff onto the pink felt twice and then onto the orange felt twice. Cut out two orange pieces and then two pink pieces.

Transfer the design detail of the pattern onto one of the pink stocking pieces using dressmaker's carbon and tracing wheel. Carefully cut out all hearts and circles, as well as the heel and toe areas. Use embroidery or decoupage scissors for cutting. Pin this pink piece to one of the red liner pieces, being careful to match all edges.

With red yarn, make running stitches across the stocking under each row of motifs. Be sure to go through both layers of felt. Outline the heel and toe areas and the circles with yellow yarn (see photograph). With orange yarn, outline the hearts. Always make sure you are stitching through both layers of felt so it will hold its shape.

(continued)

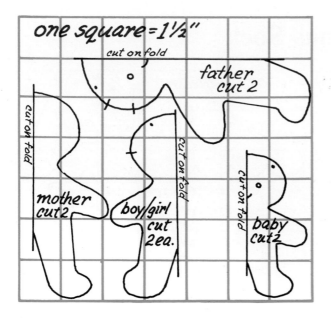

one square = 1½"

cut on fold

father cut 2

cut on fold

mother cut 2

cut on fold

boy/girl cut 2 ea.

cut on fold

baby cut 2

Transfer the small pink hearts shown on the pattern to pink felt. Cut out six small pink hearts altogether. Notice that they are just slightly smaller than the heart-shaped cutout area on the pink stocking. Center a heart in each cutout heart area, pin in place, and whipstitch around the edges with pink embroidery floss.

Transfer the smallest hearts shown on the pattern to the yellow felt and cut out six small yellow hearts. Center each yellow heart on a pink heart, pin and then whipstitch in place with yellow thread.

Next, transfer the leaf-like shapes that are below the hearts onto yellow felt. Cut out six of them. Position them on the stocking, and whipstitch in place with yellow thread.

Last, transfer the orange and yellow flower petals and the yellow centers to the orange and yellow felt respectively. Cut out all pieces and position them on the red cutout circle areas. The bottom circle should have no yellow petals. Whipstitch in place with yellow and orange thread.

Seam one of the pink stocking cuffs to the top back side of one of the red liner pieces. Repeat for the other pink cuff and the front red liner piece. Next, place an orange cuff over each of the pink cuffs and pin in place; be very careful to match all edges and scallops. Stitch around the edges through both layers, with red yarn.

With the red liners on the inside and the pink pieces on the outside (the cuff should be straight up and out of the way), pin all layers together along the two sides and the bottom. Seam with red yarn, following the dashed lines. Seam the top of the back liner piece to the top of the back pink piece and the top of the front liner piece to the top of the front pink piece, sewing close to the top so that the stitches will be hidden when the cuff is down.

Turn the cuff over and whipstitch its sides together with orange thread. Make small stitches that will not show.

Cut two strips of red felt, each 1½x6 inches. Fold each strip in half lengthwise and make ½-inch seams. Turn the strips right side out and press open. Fold each strip into a loop for hanging. Pin each to the top inside of the liner with ends together; the loops should be about 2 inches in from either side. Sew in place.

Dolls: Enlarge doll patterns and transfer to cardboard. Cut out cardboard patterns. Fold knit fabric in half and place cardboard patterns on fabric, along fold. Trace around cardboard, cut out, and unfold. Repeat this procedure so you have two complete fabric figures (front and back) for each doll.

Place the two pieces of fabric right sides together. Seam the two pieces together with a ¼-inch seam, leaving a small opening in the head. Turn doll right side out. Stuff legs, then stitch by hand across body at crotch. Stuff arms, and sew by hand from underarm to shoulder. Stuff body and head, turn in seam allowance at top of head and sew opening closed.

Embroider the eyes and mouth with embroidery floss (see pages 28-29) and make the hair with different colors of yarn. Wrap the yarn several times around a piece of cardboard (in the same way that you would to make tassels) to get hairs the same length.

Sew dresses, shirts, and pants for doll with different scraps of leftover fabric.

Aztecan Motif Appliquéd Yoke

This yoke design is suitable for use with commercial patterns. Use it on a dress, shirt, or a blouse (see drawing on page 60). To make this decorative yoke, with its Aztecan motif, you will use a form of appliqué that is called reverse appliqué.

Instead of cutting out the designs and stitching them on top of the background fabric as you normally do with appliqué, cut out the yoke from the garment fabric, and pin the fabric pieces of contrasting colors to the back of the yoke piece. Then, turn under and sew down the edges of the cutout areas on the main fabric to reveal the contrasting fabric motifs beneath.

The design includes a border across the bottom of the yoke, which you may omit. Also, you may prefer to use small buttons down the center front of the yoke instead of the small circle designs. To emphasize the tiny hand stitches, and to add texture to the yoke, use embroidery floss instead of sewing thread for the whipstitching.

Because this particular design is of Aztec origin, be sure to reproduce it in warm, vibrant colors, in keeping with the theme.

Materials
- Pattern with jewel neckline (dress, shirt, or blouse)
- Fabric and notions as specified by pattern
- Cerise, red, vermilion, gold, and turquoise fabric scraps
- Embroidery floss to match
- Dressmaker's carbon paper
- Tracing wheel

Directions
From the center of the front of the yoke to the edge of the armhole, measure the width of the yoke on the pattern you plan to use (see

(continued)

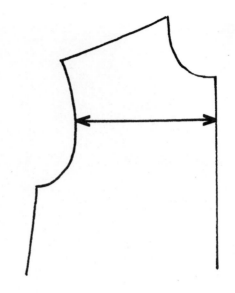

the diagram on the next page). Divide this measurement by four. Then, enlarge the pattern on page 61 on paper, making each square equal to the result of the division. In other words, if the width of the yoke from the center to the armhole is 6 inches, each square of your enlarged design paper pattern should equal 1½ inches.

Cut out the fabric pieces according to the pattern instructions. Keep in mind that appliqué work has a tendency to draw the fabric slightly. To compensate for this, leave 1 inch extra all around the front piece. Later on, when you are making the garment you can trim off any excess material from the edges.

Pin the enlarged pattern to the left side of the garment front. Using dressmaker's carbon and a tracing wheel, transfer the design onto the fabric. Remove the pattern and prepare to transfer it to the right side of the material. Remember that you are going to be transferring the reverse of the pattern because there is a right and left to the design as you can see in the photo. To reverse the pattern, place the carbon paper beneath the pattern, carbon side up, and go over the lines with a pencil. Turn the pattern over; the pattern will ap-

pear in reverse on the back of the paper. Now, simply use this reverse pattern the same as you would the pattern itself—that is, place the dressmaker's carbon between the pattern and the fabric to the right side of the yoke front and go over the lines with the tracing wheel.

You are now ready to start cutting out the design from the fabric. First, start with the large coil shape in the center of the design. Begin to cut it out ¼ inch in from the actual outline. The purpose of this ¼-inch allowance is that it allows for turning under when you stitch the fabric in place.

Cut out a piece of turquoise (W) fabric that is large enough to completely cover the area you just cut out. Pin it to the back of the yoke fabric. Carefully make tiny slits in the ¼-inch allowance on the coil shape design. Next, turn the edges of the coil shape under ¼ inch and whipstitch it to the turquoise fabric. (See whipstitch on page 77.) Be sure to make whipstitches small and even. Turn the yoke to the wrong side and trim the turquoise fabric evenly ¼ inch outside the whipstitching.

Repeat this same procedure for all of the areas marked W on the pattern—that is, cut

FOLD

Color Code:
S = cerise
T = red
U = vermilion
V = gold
W = turquoise

out the area (leaving a ¼-inch allowance for folding under), pin a piece of turquoise fabric to the back of the yoke, make tiny slits in the ¼-inch allowance, turn under, and whipstitch. Don't forget to trim the excess from the turquoise fabric from the underside each time or the appliqué design will start to get bulky and uneven in areas.

Follow this same procedure for red (T), vermilion (U), and gold (V) areas. As you finish each color, be sure to trim away the excess fabric on the wrong side before starting with the next color.

For the areas marked as cerise (S), the procedure is slightly different. With dressmaker's carbon paper and a tracing wheel,

trace the outline of the shape onto the cerise fabric. Cut out the shape and pin it to its proper position (see pattern). Whipstitch it to the fabric beneath it, making small inconspicuous whipstitches.

When you have completed the entire appliqué design, place the garment pattern over your appliquéd yoke and trim away any excess fabric from the edges of the yoke. Now, you are all set to sew the garment according to the pattern instructions.

Appliquéd Bedspread

A bold appliqué design turns an ordinary bedspread into the focal point of a bedroom, as in the above picture.

This particular motif is a contemporary adaptation of an old patchwork design. It will harmonize either with a traditional or a modern decor. Even though the appliqué design is oversize, its neutral tones have pleasing eye appeal, and they complement the room's furnishings and accessories.

Make the bedspread and the appliqué motifs from a sturdy, ravel-resistant fabric. If you wish to make the job still easier, you can purchase a readymade throw-style bedspread instead of making your own. If this is your choice, the instructions for the appliqué design remain the same.

Materials
- 9⅔ yards 36-inch material for double-bed size bedspread
- 10⅓ yards 45-inch material for queen-size bedspread
- 10⅓ yards 45-inch material for king-size bedspread
- 1½ yards 48-inch white fabric
- ⅓ yard 45-inch tan fabric
- 1 yard 45-inch black fabric
- Matching thread

Directions

First, make the throw-style brown bedspread, then appliqué the patchwork pinwheel design on the completed bedspread.

Each of the three sizes of bedspreads requires three lengths of fabric. Cut each length of fabric the finished length of the bedspread plus 6 inches to allow for 3-inch hems at the top and bottom. Use a full-width panel for the center of the bedspread. To figure the width of each side panel, subtract the width of the center panel from the overall width measurement. Divide the remainder in half, then add 4 inches (3 inches for side hem and 1 inch for joining the side piece to the center panel).

Remove the selvage from the fabric panels and pin the center panel and side panels together right side to right side. Seam the sections together with ½-inch seams. Use a French seam, a self-bound seam, or a flat-fell seam to enclose the raw edges.

At the bottom edge of the spread, round the corners gracefully so the spread doesn't gather on the floor because of excess fabric. Turn under ½-inch all the way around the spread. Press. Then, turn a 2½-inch hem. Press

and stitch — either a straight or blind stitch on the machine or hand-sew if you prefer.

To make the large, white circle, spread the white fabric out on a large surface and fold it in quarters. Tie a string to a pencil, and cut the string to 24 inches. Use a thumbtack to hold the end of the string in place, and draw a quarter-circle arc. Cut out the 48-inch diameter circle.

Enlarge the patterns for the tan and black motifs. Cut out the pieces, and arrange them on the white fabric circle. Pin them in place, then zigzag-stitch around each motif or fold under ¼ inch and whipstitch, using small, even stitches.

Place the spread on the bed and center the wheel between the pillows and the bottom edge of the bed. Pin the round appliquéd section securely in position.

Run basting stitches from the center of the wheel to the edges to remove any bubbles. Zigzag stitch around the circle, or fold under ¼ inch and whipstitch by hand. In order for the patchwork wheel to remain secure, turn to the wrong side and take small, hand stitches in several places evenly spaced throughout the wheel.

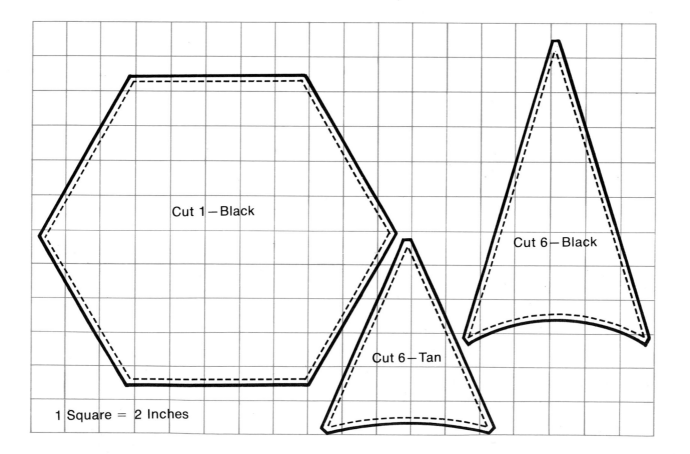

Cut 1 — Black

Cut 6 — Black

Cut 6 — Tan

1 Square = 2 Inches

Sewing

Join the throngs of people who take pride in their sewing expertise, and who are seeking new ideas. Sewing machines, fabrics, notions, and sewing aids available today, help you turn out truly professional projects. Once you master basic sewing techniques, you'll feel a sense of accomplishment and of thriftiness—you'll find it's fun and rewarding.

King-Size Pillow Sofa

Don't let your leisure hours go to waste. Instead, put your sewing talent to work and enjoy life atop this gigantic patchwork pillow surrounded on three sides by a firmly packed cylinder pillow.

The pillow shown measures 5x6 feet, and the tubular pillow is 18 feet long. Alter the measurements according to your space limitations.

For a conventional sofa (see drawing on page 66), make three 36-inch-square pillows surrounded by a 15-foot-long cylinder on three sides. Use the same techniques given for the larger version.

Materials
Patchwork pillow
- 4 yards 60-inch-wide patchwork print (sturdy cotton fabric)
- 2 twin-size sheets for liner
- 36-inch zipper
- Polyester filling or pellets for stuffing (amount depends on firmness desired)

Cylinder pillow
- 14⅔ yards 48-inch-wide velveteen
- 2 king-size sheets for liner
- 2 36-inch zippers
- 6 yards of cord for welting
- polyester filling or pellets for stuffing

Directions
Patchwork pillow: Cut length of fabric in half; each piece will measure 60x72 inches. Place right sides together and machine-stitch (use heavy-duty thread) a ½-inch seam around edges, leaving a 36-inch opening on one side to accommodate zipper. Stitch twice for added strength. Turn to right side and press under ½-inch seam allowance of opening. Baste and sew zipper in opening.

For the liner, cut a 59x71-inch piece from each twin-size sheet. Place on piece on top of the other and stitch a ½-inch seam, leaving a 24-inch opening on one side. Turn liner to right side, stuff with filling to desired plumpness, and hand sew opening closed. Insert muslin-covered pillow form inside patchwork cover and zip it closed.

Cylinder pillow: Cut two 6-yard lengths of velveteen, and two 16x96-inch strips for pillow ends. From remaining fabric, cut 2-inch-wide bias strips and join them together to make a strip 6 yards long for welting.

(continued)

To make welting, fold bias strip around cord, right side out, encasing it completely. Then, using an adjustable cording or zipper foot, stitch close to cord without crowding it. Stretch bias strip slightly as you are stitching it over cord.

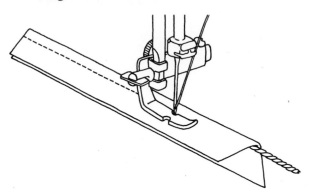

Next, insert cording between the two strips of velveteen in the following manner. Pin cording to right side of one seam allowance, placing the cording's stitching along the seam line. Stitch, using a cording foot. Then pin the corded edge right side down, over the other seam allowance. Stitch between the first row of stitching and cord.

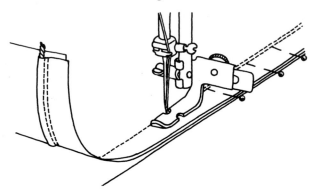

With the right sides together, stitch a ½-inch seam at the other side of the velveteen strips, forming a long tube; leave a 72-inch opening at the center back. Turn to the right side and insert the two 36-inch zippers with the open ends together in the opening at the center back.

To make the gathered endpiece, stitch the ends of each of the 16x96-inch strips together. With the right sides facing, join one edge of the strip to the tube with a ½-inch seam. Gather the other edge of the strip by hand. Draw the gathers tightly and tie the thread. Finish the other end in the same manner. On the right side, attach a covered button over the center gathers.

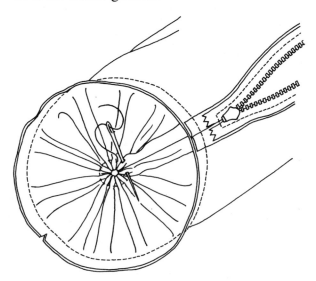

For liner, cut two king-size sheets into 95-inch strips; join strips and cut to 215-inch length. Fold in half lengthwise and stitch a ½-inch seam, leaving open 36 inches in center of strip to insert stuffiing. Use scraps of sheets joined together to make two 16x96-inch strips and make gathered endpieces same as outside cover. Turn to right side, and stuff cylinder to desired firmness. Hand sew opening, and insert cylinder in velveteen cover.

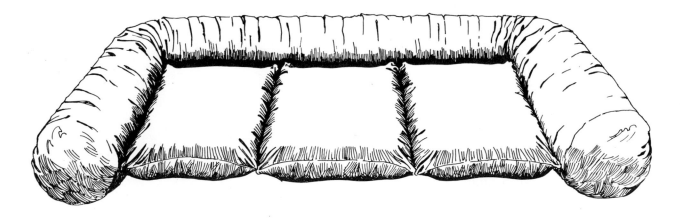

Two-Faced Comforter

Use this plump, warm comforter as a bed-spread and let it do double duty as a bed cover on a chilly night. Add the matching dust ruffle for a totally coordinated look.

Made of bandanna-print handkerchiefs, blue on one side and red on the other, the classic print will add zest to any bedroom with complementing decorating scheme.

Whenever you are in the mood for a change, reverse the comforter and enjoy a complete change of color, such as cool blue in the summer and warm red during bleak, cold days.

Materials
• 4 90x108-inch-size polyester quilt batting
• 1 skein washable red knitting worsted
Twin-bed size
• 18 22x24-inch red bandannas
• 18 22x24-inch blue bandannas
Double-bed size
• 24 22x24-inch red bandannas
• 24 22x24-inch blue bandannas

Directions

Preshrink and press the bandannas; wash the red ones and blue ones separately so the colors will not run together. Bandannas may vary slightly in size, so arrange similar sizes and dye lots before you begin stitching them together.

The twin size comforter requires three bandannas across and six down; the double bed size comforter requires four bandannas across and six down.

Stitch the blue bandannas together in rows of three for the twin size bed; stitch them in rows of four for the double bed size, using a ¼-inch seam for either size. Next, stitch six rows together and press the seams open. Follow this same construction procedure for the red bandannas on the reverse side of the comforter.

Cut out the four layers of polyester batting the same size as the seamed bandannas. Lay the red bandanna section right side down on the floor; place the four layers of polyester batting one on top of another on top of it, and cover it with the blue bandanna side, right side up. Pin or baste the bandannas and batting together to prevent the layers from shifting while you are working on the finishing details.

Fold under ¼ inch of the outer blue and red edges separately and pin all around the four edges. Place the pins close enough to keep the folded edges in place. Using a large stitch on your sewing machine and two colors of thread — red for stitching on the red side, and blue for stitching on the blue side — stitch all the way around the comforter close to the edge.

Tie the comforter at evenly spaced intervals with red knitting worsted yarn to keep everything in place. Clip the ends of yarn so that all the ties are uniform.

Use a ready-made dust ruffle, and stitch a wide band of navy or red fabric two inches from the bottom, all the way around.

Patchwork for Dining

Introduce a time-honored quilt pattern to the contemporary scene. Instead of using it in the bedroom, place it on the dining table. Your family and friends can enjoy it when you entertain.

As you can see, the delicate stripes, old-time blocks, and triangles lend country flavor to a dining table set with contemporary dinnerware, flatware, and an off-center decorative arrangement.

Use easy-care, permanent press fabric. Then you can machine wash and tumble dry. The overall size is 80½x93.

Materials
- 3½ yards 35-inch or 2¾ yards 45-inch white cotton fabric for strips
- 3¼ yards 35-inch or 2¼ yards 45-inch cotton print fabric (includes triangles, squares, and border strips)
- 2 yards 35-inch or 1⅜ yards 45-inch solid blue fabric (includes triangles, squares, and border strips)
- ¾ yard 35-inch or ½ yard 45-inch solid red border fabric
- 1 full-size white sheet

Directions
Cut the white sheet for backing to measure 81x93½ inches. Cut five vertical strips of white cotton 4x87 inches, and 36 horizontal strips of white cotton 4x10 inches.

You will need 42 9x9-inch (finished) patchwork blocks. For each block cut: four print squares, 3½x3½ inches; one blue square for center, 3½x3½ inches; and eight triangles each of blue and print fabric, 3½x2¼x2¼ inches.

For the border strips, cut the following: two 2x72-inch and two 2x84½-inch strips of blue; two 2x75-inch strips and two 2x90½-inch strips of print; and two 3½x78-inch strips and two 3½x93½-inch strips of red. If necessary, seam the fabric to get the proper length. Make ¼-inch seams throughout.

To make each block, stitch four print triangles to the sides of the blue center square. Stitch two adjacent blue triangles to each print square. Right sides together, pin the blue triangles on each square to the print triangles on each side of the center square. Stitch. Sew the four remaining print triangles to the blue triangles to complete the block. Press.

Sew seven blocks to 4x10-inch white strips from top to bottom, alternating blocks with fabric strips. You will now have six long strips. Join strips by stitching them to the five white 4x87-inch vertical strips. See drawing for arrangement of strips and blocks.

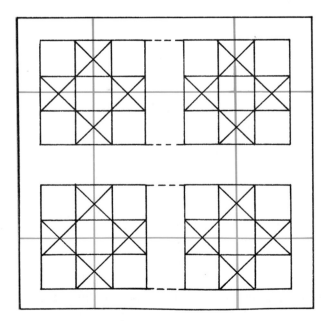

Pin on the blue border strips, forming butt corners; stitch. Repeat for print border strip. Baste the sheet to the patchwork top along the outer edges.

Press under ¼ inch on the long sides of each red strip. Enclose the edges of the table cover with the red strips as you would bind a blanket, stitching close to the edges. Slip-stitch the corners.

print   white   blue   red   ▢ : 9 inches

69

Baskets Lend Themselves to Adornment

Here, a common wicker hamper turns into a very special, fitted picnic basket with an attractive colorful, printed lining. Stitched-down pockets are sized to hold dinner plates and flatware in a well-organized fashion, and fabric ties keep the inexpensive wine glasses in place.

The lining design is repeated in the blue-bordered tablecloth, and motifs cut from the fabric adorn the corners of the napkins. If place mats or table runners are your preference, make them instead of the table cover. Eat in style, anytime.

Materials

- 12x18x7-inch wicker hamper with hinged lid
- 3 yards print fabric (for lining and tablecloth)
- 2½ yards solid blue fabric (for four napkins and border for tablecloth)
- 1 yard polyester batting
- 14 Velcro snaps
- fusible webbing
- white glue
- sturdy poster board

Directions

Cut a 11½x17½-inch rectangle of cardboard to fit snugly inside top of hamper. Spread white glue liberally on one side of cardboard and press it in place inside of the lid. Weight with books until the glue dries. Next, cut out a rectangle of the print fabric so that it is large enough to fit inside the lid of the hamper and extend down the inside edges (approximately 20½x15 inches).

Cut another piece of the print fabric 20x6 inches for the pocket strip. Stitch a ¼-inch hem on one long side of the strip; stitch a ½-inch hem on the three remaining sides. Mark off 10½-inch, 4¼-inch, and 4¼-inch spacing on the strip for plates and two silver-ware pockets. Pin the pocket strip about two inches from the bottom edge of the lining and stitch it in place. Glue the lining inside of the hamper lid, turning the raw edges under at the rim and clipping the corners so they will lie flat.

To line the bottom, cut two pieces of the fabric and a piece of the polyester batting as shown in the diagram below.

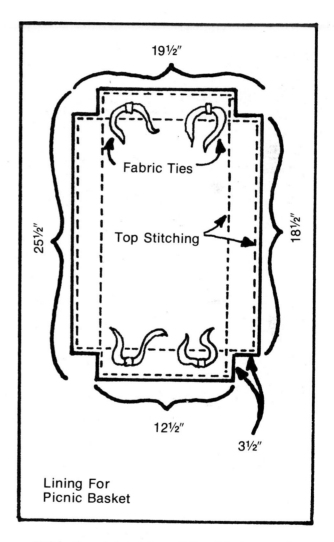

19½"

Fabric Ties

Top Stitching

25½"

18½"

12½"

3½"

Lining For
Picnic Basket

With the right sides of the fabric together, pin and stitch the two pieces of lining fabric, with a ½-inch seam. Leave one long side open for turning. Clip the corners, turn to the right side and press. Trim ½ inch off the batting and slip it into the lining.

(continued)

71

Turn the raw edges under and slip-stitch the fourth edge closed. Topstitch ¼ inch in around the edges of the lining piece and along the horizontal and vertical flap edges (see diagram on page 71).

Cut four 12x2-inch strips from the border fabric. Fold each one in half lengthwise (right sides together), pin, and stitch. Turn to the right side and press. Slip-stitch the ends closed. Position the two strips on each short flap of the padded bottom lining piece and tack them in place (see diagram). These strips are for tying the wine glasses in place.

Glue the Velcro snaps along the sides of the basket bottom (four each on the long sides, and three each on the shorter sides). Glue matching halves of snaps to basket lining. Let glue dry for 24 hours before using basket. Bottom liner of hamper may be removed for laundering.

Tablecloth: Cut a piece of the printed fabric 45 inches square; cut two strips of the border fabric 45x6 inches, and cut two strips 50x6 inches. Stitch the two shorter border strips to the opposite sides of the printed square, right sides together, using a ½-inch seam allowance. Pin and stitch the two remaining edges of the tablecloth.

Press the seams open, and snip the border fabric seam allowance to ⅛ inch. Fold the printed fabric seam allowance under ¼ inch in and over onto the border seam allowance. Pin and stitch along all four sides (flat-fell seams). Double-fold the raw edges of the borders under ¼ inch and stitch along all four edges.

Napkins: Cut four 15-inch squares from border fabric. Double-fold raw edges under ¼ inch and hem. Snip the floral motifs from the print fabric and iron onto one corner of each napkin with fusible webbing.

Dinner Napkins Recycled

If you have access to damask dinner napkins that are no longer being used, convert them into an exciting table cover.

Materials
- Damask napkins (20-, 22-, or 24-inch size)
- 1½-inch wide lace insertion
- Matching thread

Directions
Hand launder and iron the napkins if they have not been in use for some time. For an average size dining table, make three strips of four napkins each.

Join the napkins in each strip by top-stitching the lace insertion to the edges of the napkins. Join the strips by top-stitching the lace insertion to the edges of each strip. If the edges of the table cover are not all even when you have joined the strips, trim them evenly and re-hem.

Ruffled Table Cover

Disguise a small round table that has a scarred top and poorly designed legs by covering it with a long, ruffled, table cover that cascades to the floor. This simple sewing project has the designer touch.

Materials
- 4½ yards print fabric for table cover top and bottom ruffle
- 2⅓ yards red and white polka dot fabric for first and third ruffles
- 1½ yards print fabric for second ruffle
- Matching thread

Directions
These directions and material requirements are based on a table 20 inches in diameter and 27 inches high. The material requirements are figured on 36-inch-wide fabric.

For the tablecloth top, cut a circle of print fabric that measures 29 inches in diameter. This allows for a 4-inch overhang, plus ½-inch to fold under.

For the first ruffle, cut 6-inch strips of the red and white polka dot fabric; join strips together with a ½-inch seam to form a strip 136 inches long. Join the two ends of the strip together with a ½-inch seam. Run a gathering stitch along one edge of the strip. Pull up the stitches so that the strip measures about 91 inches (approximate circumference of the table cover top. Place the folded-under edge of the top piece over the gathered edge, and topstitch around the circular piece (space gathers evenly).

To make the second ruffle, cut 6-inch strips of print fabric; join strips in the same manner as you did with the first one, but make the strip 204 inches long. Gather in the same manner, and pull up the gathering stitches so that the strip measures 136 inches. Place the folded edge of the first strip over the gathered edge of the second strip and topstitch around the strip.

For the third ruffle, cut 6-inch strips of red and white polka dot fabric; join strips in the same manner as the previous ones, but make the strip 306 inches long. Gather in the same manner, and pull up gathering stitches so the strip measures 204 inches. Topstitch the third ruffle in position as you did the first two. Make the fourth ruffle in the same manner, using the same print fabric as the top of the table cover. Cut enough 6-inch strips to measure 460 inches. Gather the strip, and pull up the gathering stitches so the strip measures 306 inches. Topstitch the ruffle in position, and finish with a ½-inch hem around the bottom.

If you wish to make a ruffled table cover for a table with other dimensions, just make the ruffles wider or narrower, so long as total measurements add up to floor length. The larger the tabletop measures, the longer each strip should be to have adequate fullness.

Chamois Pillows and Hassock

Although chamois skins are the all-time favorite for polishing cars, use them in a completely different way, adding comfort and beauty to your home. Make beautiful, soft pillows and cushions with a variety of designs, and in different sizes and shapes.

Find chamois skins in auto supply stores, supermarkets, discount stores, and car wash centers. Also, buy them in leather goods stores—but expect to pay a higher price.

This soft and supple material is fun and easy to handle. It's easy to cut, stitch, decorate, paint, or dye. Chamois is a natural material, and the sizes of the skins vary. An average piece is about 7 square feet, and irregularities and imperfections often occur. However, these slight variations add character and charm to the projects you undertake, rather than distracting from their beauty.

Once you make the pillows, there's no limit to the decorations you can add. Sew on feathers, beads, washers, buttons, shells, or other materials. Paint exciting designs with indelible marking pens, or color them with fabric dyes. Embroider trapunto patterns, such as the swirl design on the large square pillow shown at the right on the opposite page where a piece of clothesline is coiled between the chamois and a piece of burlap and then outline-stitched to achieve a sculptured effect. The raw edges are equally attractive, cut to one length and fringed or left in their natural shapes and lengths.

Discover the joy of working with these pliable skins. Experiment with many shapes, sizes, and designs. Provide comfortable seating in your own home, and surprise your family and friends with these unique hand-crafted furnishings when gift-giving occasions occur. They're so much fun.

Materials

- Chamois skins
- Muslin covered pillow forms
- Old hassock
- 2 yards 45-inch muslin for doughnut and tube pillows
- Polyester stuffing for doughnut and tube pillows
- Corduroy for underside of pillows
- Wax linen thread or any upholstery weight thread
- Feathers
- Buttons
- Beads
- Shells
- Indelible marking pens
- Small amount of clothesline
- 12x12-inch piece of burlap
- Upholstery needle
- 3-inch rubber fingers (from stationery store)

Directions

Note: There are a few basic instructions to be aware of when you are working with chamois. It has lots of give and should always be pinned in place before sewing. Wear "rubber finger tips" to protect your fingers while pushing pins and needles through the chamois. The skins are washable in mild soap and warm water.

Paint chamois with indelible marking pens, or color the skins with fabric dye. In either case, color a small sample of leather and wash it to test for bleeding before you dye or paint a large piece.

Be sure to sew with an upholstery needle, and to use waxed linen thread or upholstery weight thread.

Square pillows: To make the square pillow in the foreground of the photo on the opposite page, use a 26x26-inch-square muslin-covered pillow form. Cut a 27x27-inch-square piece of corduroy and cover the bottom of the pillow, sewing the corduroy tight-

(continued)

ly to the muslin base, using an overcasting stitch. (See drawing of overcasting stitch at the bottom of this page.)

Drape a 7-sq.-ft. piece of chamois over the top of the pillow, pin it in place, and saddle stitch (see drawing of saddle stitch on page 77) around the pillow through the chamois, the corduroy, and the muslin.

To decorate your pillow top, first draw the design on paper. Then, trace it onto the pillow top, and paint the design with indelible marking pens.

Fringe the material that extends beyond the saddle stitching. When you cut the fringe, be careful not to cut too close to the saddle stitching—leave at least ¼ inch of space.

To make the square pillow with the raised design, you will need a 21x21-inch-square muslin-covered pillow form. Cut a 22x22-inch-square piece of corduroy and cover the bottom of the pillow, sewing the corduroy tightly to the muslin base using an overcasting stitch.

Cut a 12x12-inch-square piece of burlap and tack a piece of clothesline to it in a swirl design. (Leave enough space between the swirls for the outside saddle stitching on the chamois.) Pin the piece of burlap to the center of the chamois skin with the clothesline swirl design sandwiched between the two. With the wax thread or heavy up-

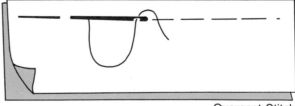

Overcast Stitch

76

holstery thread, saddle stitch around both sides of the clothesline design to give the attractive raised effect.

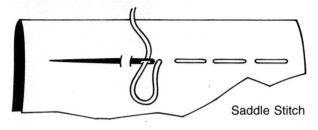

Saddle Stitch

Cut a piece of chamois 12 inches long and 1 inch wide. Fringe it ¾ inch deep; run a basting stitch along the unfringed edge, and gather the strip to form a small circle. Tack it in place at the end of the swirl design and fasten a shell in the center of the fringed circle.

Next, drape the chamois skin over the pillow and saddle stitch around the edge of the pillow, leaving several inches of the natural edge exposed.

Round pillow: Use a 14-inch-diameter round muslin-covered pillow form. Cut a 16-inch-diameter piece of corduroy and cover the pillow back, sewing it tightly to the muslin base using an overcasting stitch.

Cut a circular piece of chamois 16 inches in diameter and saddle stitch it to the pillow top, leaving a 1-inch border. Cut fringe around the edge, but don't cut in closer than ¼ inch from the saddle stitching.

For the feather trim, glue ready-made feather motifs (available at millinery supply shops) or glue individual feathers (available at craft shops) on petal-shaped pieces of fabric. Hand sew the designs in place and attach shells in the center.

Doughnut pillow: Stitch a muslin tube 65 inches long and 22 inches around. Stuff the tube with polyester batting and join the ends to form the doughnut.

Cut the chamois skin in half lengthwise, and cut four notches halfway up the skin to allow for the curve of the pillow. Wrap the skin around the doughnut pillow form,

and sew it together with a whipstitch (see drawing of the whipstitch below) in whatever random pattern results. Be sure to whipstitch all the raw edges of the chamois skin.

Tubular pillow: Stitch a muslin tube 24 inches long and 20 inches around. Stuff the tube with polyester batting and join the ends, pulling the thread tightly to form a rounded effect.

Drape the chamois skin around the tube, leaving about 6 inches extending at each end Whipstitch the chamois in a random pattern, then draw a cord tightly around each end of the pillow and fringe the extended pieces.

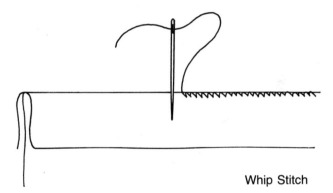

Whip Stitch

Hassock: You will need two skins for this project. Use an old hassock for a base and cut one skin in half lengthwise; drape each half of the skin around the bottom half of the hassock and whipstitch in place.

Take a whole chamois skin and drape it over the top of the hassock with the skin centered over the hassock. Pin it in place, and whipstitch around the top edge of the hassock. Let the rest of the chamois fall gracefully around the sides.

First, plan your design for the top of the hassock on paper; trace the design onto the hassock, and then paint it with indelible marking pens.

Suede Patchwork Throw and Pillows

If you haven't worked with leather since your days at camp, the colorful montage created for this dramatic throw and pillows will spur you to return to this fascinating hobby. Size of patchwork throw is 42x58 inches (without the fringe). Square pillow measures 13½x13½; oblong pillow is 10½ x14 inches.

Materials
  • Eyelet or leather punch
Patchwork throw
  • Suede scraps (tan, yellow, red, brown, dark brown, and rust)
  • Small amounts of matching yarn
  • 1 skein of rust knitting worsted
  • 3 skeins black knitting worsted

Sizes F and G crochet hooks
Patchwork pillows
  • Suede scraps
  • Black knitting worsted for square pillow
  • Polyester batting
  • 1 yard velveteen or corduroy
  • Size F crochet hook

Directions
Patchwork throw: Make cardboard patterns 2 inches square and 2x4½ inches. Lay patterns on back of suede and trace around with felt-tip pen. Cut 35 squares and 140 rectangles. On wrong side of each piece, mark dots ½ inch apart and ¼ inch from

all edges. Punch out dots with a ¹⁄₁₆-inch eyelet or leather punch. Crochet around edges of all pieces with matching yarn. Work loosely and use size F crochet hook. Start in one corner; tie in yarn and work 2 sc in same corner. Ch 1, 2 sc in same sp, * 2 sc in each hole to next corner, 2 sc, ch 1, 2 sc in same sp; repeat from * around, sl st to beg sc; end off. (For crochet abbreviations, see page 150.)

To assemble a five-piece square, lay out pieces as sketch shows. Whipstitch each five-piece square together with black yarn. Work row of 1 sc in each sp around square (at corners work 2 sc, ch 1, 2 sc in same sp); end off. Make 35 squares in same manner.

To assemble, place five squares across and seven down. Whipstitch together in black. With size G hook, work 1 sc in each sp around throw (work 1 sc, ch 1, 1 sc in each corner). End off. Tie on rust yarn and work row of sc around throw. Tie on black and work a row of sc around throw; end off.

To make fringe, wind yarn around 5½-inch-wide piece of cardboard and cut one end to make 11-inch strands. Use four strands for each fringe knot. Attach knots in every other crocheted space across end of throw.

Oblong pillow: Use sketch above as a guide and follow same directions as for throw as far as cutting pieces, punching holes, and crocheting around edges. Colors used here are blue, dark brown, orange, green, gold, red, purple, brown, and maroon.

To assemble, whipstitch together with black yarn. Work a sc edge with black around all sides (1 sc, ch 1, 1 sc at corners); end off. Make a pillow cover with two 11x14½-inch pieces of fabric. Stitch right sides together in ½-inch seams; leave opening to stuff. Turn right side out, stuff, and slip-stitch shut. Whipstitch suede patchwork piece to pillow.

Square pillow: Make square pillow in same manner as oblong version, but follow sketch for placement of pieces and use only black yarn. Colors used here are tan, maroon, gold, blue, brown, purple, and blue green.

Cut fabric cover 14 inches square and construct same as oblong pillow. Whipstitch suede patchwork to top with black thread.

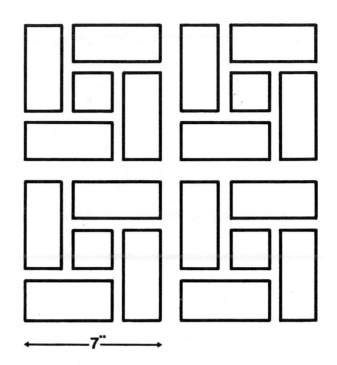

← 7" →

BL	DB	O	GR
G	R	P	B
B	GR	G	M

← 14" →

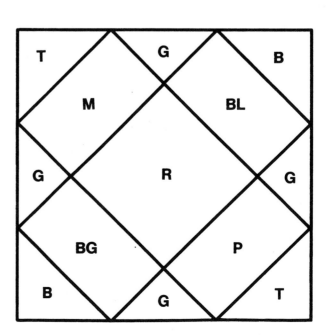

Fanciful Haven For A Teen-ager

Artistically grouped flower and butterfly plaques in a favorite color inspired the decor of this young teen's room. All of the fabrics used to decorate the room are wash-and-wear sheets and pillowcases from a color-coordinated bedding collection.

The furnishings and accessories have been carefully chosen to meet a teen's needs. The room not only provides a place to sleep, but a study area, and plenty of room to entertain friends.

Materials
- 2 full-size striped sheets
- 1 queen-size plaid sheet
- 2 twin-size plaid sheets
- 2 full-size polka dot sheets (based on a 10x12-foot room)
- 1 ready-made pillowcase
- Polyester comforter batting
- 13 yards of sturdy cording (such as Venetian blind cord)
- 16x24-inch sheet of fiberboard (for bulletin board)
- Plywood cornice board
- Cellulose non-staining adhesive for gluing fabric to wall below dado
- Collection of flower and butterfly plaques in various sizes (by Burwood Products)
- Button-covering kit.

80

Directions

Comforter: Cut the two full-size striped sheets to measure 61x91 inches; be sure to have one stripe centered down the middle of the bed so that all of the stripes will be uniformly spaced. Cut the comforter batting to measure 60x90 inches.

Place one sheet (right side down) on the floor; place the layer of batting on top of it, leaving a ½-inch margin of fabric all around the edges; and place the second sheet on top (right side up). Pin or baste around the edge about 1½ inches from the outer edge. Fold under ½ inch all around the edges of both sheets; baste, and then topstitch close to the edge.

Using scraps of orange from the remainder of the sheets, cover 12 buttons (using button-covering kit) and sew them through all three layers at evenly spaced intervals. This adds a decorative touch as well as holding the three layers in position securely. The finished size will be 60x90 inches, which allows for ample tuck-in allowance around the mattress. The bed is merely a twin-size box spring and mattress combination resting on a metal bed frame.

Instead of a conventional headboard, fasten a cluster of large and small floral plaques to the wall. Add several butterflies in the same color to intensify the carefree grouping.

Dust ruffle: Cut four 13-inch-wide lengthwise strips from one of the polka dot sheets. Seam the strips together in a continuous strip. Stitch a 1-inch-wide hem along both edges. Cut the 13-yard length of cord into two pieces and run one piece through each hem. Draw the two cords to gather the fabric after you have placed it around the box spring to conceal both the sides and ends. Adjust the dust ruffle gathers so they are evenly spaced.

Cornice board, draperies, and pillows: Use the remnants of the dust ruffle sheeting fabric to cover the cornice board and to make the pillows. Purchase a plywood cornice board and first cover it with a layer of padding; staple for best results. Then, cover it with the plaid fabric, bringing the material around the edges to the underneath side of the cornice board. Keep the material smooth and taut, and staple it from the wrong side of the cornice board.

Use each twin-size plaid sheet to make one drapery panel. Simply hem the panels so they are floor-length and shirr the panels onto an ordinary curtain rod mounted behind the cornice board. Make the fabric tiebacks of the same plaid sheeting, and attach the floral plaques to them.

Make use of the plaid scraps by making two small pillows — one round and one square. Buy the pillow forms ready-made and cover them with the fabric, or make your pillow forms of muslin stuffed with polyester fiberfill.

Dado, chair cushion, lamp shade drape, and bulletin board: Before you apply the fabric to the wall, paint the molding to match the background of the polka-dotted sheets. Then, cut the sheets into 24-inch-wide strips and attach the fabric dado to the wall. When you use fabric as wall covering, use cellulose non-staining paste. Apply the paste to the wall, rather than to the fabric, as you would in the conventional wallpaper method. If you don't have a molding such as shown in the picture, create your own by using wide braid and gluing it on in the same manner as the fabric.

Cover the wicker chair cushion with more of the polka-dot fabric, and hem a square of it to drape over the lamp shade.

Cover the 16x24-inch fiberboard bulletin board with the same polka dot fabric. Draw the edges around to the back of the board and staple it in position.

Study nook wall treatment: On the far wall of the study nook, alternate prim rows of posy plaques with wide band of the same color. You can either paint the bands of color or use strips of decorative vinyl-coated tape. The study nook is a former walk-in closet with the doors removed. This little alcove can serve as a study, or a dressing room.

Rickrack Wall Hanging

Instead of using paints, brushes, and pallette, express your talents and tastes by creating colorful wall hangings with rickrack and simple hand stitching.

This quick and easy needlecraft produces a three-dimensional, textured appearance. The wall hanging shown here has a pleasing arrangement of garden flowers in vibrant colors on a black background. The avocado frame adds the perfect accent. This technique of shirring rickrack is just as relaxing

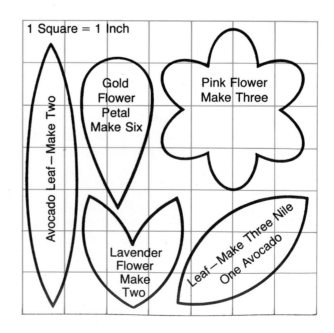

1 Square = 1 Inch

Avocado Leaf—Make Two

Gold Flower Petal Make Six

Pink Flower Make Three

Lavender Flower Make Two

Leaf—Make Three Nile One Avocado

as needlepoint, knitting, or crocheting. Give it a try. The artistic creations that develop from such familiar notions as rickrack, and brush and ball fringe are lovely.

Materials
- 16x20-inch piece of black posterboard or cardboard covered with black paper
- 42 yds. black jumbo rickrack (14 pkgs.)
- 6 yds. orange jumbo rickrack
- 6½ yds. bright pink medium rickrack
- 2⅓ yds. lavender medium rickrack
- 6⅓ yds. gold medium rickrack
- 4 yds. avocado medium rickrack
- 4 yds. nile green medium rickrack
- 1⅓ yds. avocado brush fringe
- ½ yd. scarlet brush fringe
- ½ yd. orange ball fringe
- Matching thread
- White glue

Directions
General instructions: Shirr the rickrack by hand-stitching in and out at each "V." Draw the thread up and spread the points evenly to one half the original length (unless indicated otherwise). Have the stitches longer on the underside and overlap the rows about one-third—shingle-style—when you are gluing them in place. Make patterns of paper in colors similar to the rickrack colors.

Shirr 40 one-yard lengths of black rickrack to 20 inches each. Glue the strips to the cardboard background, one at a time, by running a strip of glue across the board and applying the shirred rickrack.

For the orange flowers, cut out paper circles, one 4 inches in diameter, one 3½ inches, and one 3 inches. Cut strips of orange rickrack 2 yds. 17 inches; 1 yd. 32 inches; and 1½ yds. Follow the directions given under general instructions for shirring the rickrack to one half its original length. Glue the shirred rickrack to the paper circles, starting at the outer edge and working inward to the center. Trim the centers with orange ball fringe pompons, one in the center of the smallest flower, three in the center of the medium-size flower, and four in the largest size flower.

For the other flowers and leaves, enlarge the patterns on the opposite page and cut actual size patterns of paper.

For each pink flower, cut 2 yds. 3 inches of pink rickrack. Shirr the rickrack, then glue it to the paper pattern at one of the indentations, continuing to the center of the flower. Coil 4½ inches of scarlet brush fringe and sew it to each flower center.

Make the lavender flowers in the same manner as the pink flowers, using 1 yd. 1 inch shirred for each one. Start gluing at the indentation, working around the outer edge and in toward the center.

For the six-petal gold flower, you will need three lengths of rickrack for each of the six petals: 16 inches, 12 inches, and 10 inches. Shirr the gold rickrack strips. Start at the point of the petal and glue the longest piece around the outside of the paper pattern. Work toward the center, using progressively smaller pieces. Glue the six points of the petals to a 1¼-inch paper circle. Coil and glue 10 inches of avocado brush fringe to the center of the flower.

Using the patterns, make the leaves in the same manner as the gold flower petals. For the two long avocado leaves, use 24- and 22-inch lengths of rickrack. Make one avocado and three nile green leaves of the smaller size pattern using 17½ inches, 14 inches, and 12 inches of rickrack for each.

Position the flowers and leaves with pins on the black background as shown in the photo. Glue in place. Add a "V" of jumbo orange rickrack at the indentation of each lavender flower. Make a flower of three orange fringe balls and place on the long avocado leaves. Place the hanging in a 16x20-inch wood frame painted avocado.

Easy Sewing With Print Borders

Even those of you who aren't pros with needle, thread, and thimble can convert an average room into a designer's delight by applying decorative braid imaginatively to draperies, slipcovers, cushions, bedspreads, and window shades. Choose a pattern and colors that enhance your decor.

Be sure the trim is colorfast, preshrunk, and of the no-iron variety so the decorative braid is compatible with the fabric you are trimming.

Materials
- 26½ yards of rose-patterned border
- 53 yards yellow gimp
- Fabric glue

(The amounts will vary according to the size and number of items you plan to trim in your room, so measure carefully before you purchase trim. It's always better to have a little extra rather than to run short.)

Directions
Whether you purchase or make the French blue draperies, fitted bedspread, dust ruffle, and slipcover for the chair seat, follow the same method for applying the decorative braid trim. Most importantly, measure accurately so all of the rows are evenly spaced and properly aligned. When measuring for positioning the trim, mark the exact location with a ruler and make dots with a pencil every few inches. When you are stitching the trim in place, be sure to cover the marks with the decorative braid.

Always use matching thread for top stitching. If the braid has multicolor designs, use colorless or transparent thread which does not show. Polyester thread gives good results on any fabric because it doesn't shrink when the item is laundered, as cotton thread might.

The added thickness of a trim makes the sewing machine stitches tighter, so be sure to adjust the tension accordingly. Keep the trim in a relaxed position when you are stitching, so it does not cause the fabric to pucker after it is applied. Work from the full length of trim, and cut it after stitching. This way you will never end up with too short a piece.

For the fitted bedspread, stitch a row of the border around the bottom edge of the bedspread; and another row around the top of the bedspread, evenly spaced 4 inches from the corded seam. (Miter the corners at the foot of the top of the bedspread for a neat, tailored look.) Stitch a row of yellow gimp on each side of the braid at the very edge to give it a finished look.

For the chair seat, apply the braid as you did for the bedspread top, mitering all four corners uniformly. Stitch a row of the yellow gimp to both edges of the decorative band.

Treat the two windows as a single unit in this window rejuvenation. Cover a narrow, horizontal board and a flat, facing board with the same French blue fabric used for the draperies and top the entire window frame and wall to the point where it conceals the shade brackets and rollers. This establishes color continuity without the addition of a heavy valance. Hang a long, narrow mirror between the two windows to camouflage what would otherwise be an awkward area.

Use lemon yellow room-darkening window shades to control light and privacy, and trim them with the braid, whose rose design repeats the same shade of yellow as the shade material. Apply the braid with fabric glue so the shade will remain flexible when it is rolled up and down. First, mark the location for the trim, then apply glue in dots to the marking. Next, place trim over the glue. Work in small areas to avoid messiness. Miter the corners and make a neat fold on the diagonal where the strip ends. Glue a row of yellow gimp around entire banding.

Stitch a row of the decorative braid across each drapery panel 12 inches from the top. Then stitch three rows across the bottom of each panel, starting 4 inches from the bottom and spacing them 4 inches apart. Stitch a row of yellow gimp on top of each edge of all rows of braid.

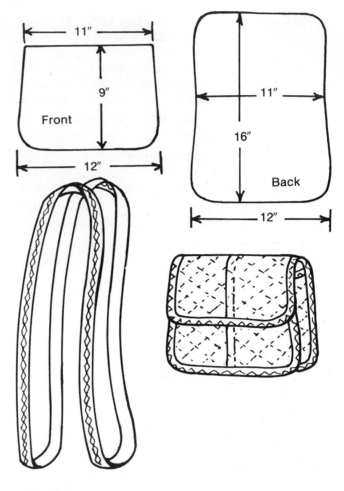

Quilted Shoulder Bag

This diagonally-quilted denim shoulder bag is another popular recycling project, requiring only an old pair of blue jeans and a few yards of decorative woven braid. This doesn't cost a fortune, and the stylish purse is a bargain in more ways than one.

Its sturdy construction and handsome, casual appearance make it a favorite in a teenager's wardrobe. Its roominess allows for stashing many items, and the recycled material makes it a natural matchmate for denim jeans, jackets, skirts, and shirts.

Materials
- 1 pair of old blue jeans
- 1 package of polyester quilt batting
- 1 yard medium-weight interfacing
- 6½ yards wide decorative banding

Directions
Cut off both of the legs from a pair of jeans. Slit each leg open and press. Quilt the two large pieces before you cut the pattern pieces. Sandwich a layer of the polyester batting between the denim and the interfacing and stitch through all three layers. Experiment with a sample first to see if the needle thread tension and bobbin tension need to be adjusted to accommodate the three layers of materials.

Use a large stitch setting on your sewing machine and two strands of thread in the sewing machine needle for a pronounced stitchery look. If you prefer hand quilting, use small, even stitches. When you are satisfied that the sample stitching looks just right, start quilting the two large sections of material.

Quilt the straight lines diagonally, and measure so the lines are spaced two inches apart. Do the entire piece in one direction first, then stitch the entire piece in the opposite direction, forming the diamonds.

Cut out the pattern pieces, following the drawings on the opposite page, and make each one about an inch larger than the shapes shown. In addition to the pieces shown, cut out a boxing strip approximately 30 inches long and 4 inches wide to insert between the back and front sections of the bag.

Pin the boxing strip to the front of the bag with the wrong sides facing, and the pins placed on the right side; machine-stitch the seam on the outside. Follow this same procedure and fasten the boxing strip to the back section of the bag. Press a 3½ yard strip of the decorative banding in half lengthwise. Slip the banding over all the seams and raw edges and stitch as a decorative binding, being sure to catch both edges of the binding in the stitching.

Hold the wide band trim in a relaxed position when applying it to the bag. Pulling the braid taut while stitching causes it to relax after application, resulting in puckering of the denim fabric.

Stitch together the ends of 3 yards of the same braid to form the shoulder bag handles. Pin the strip in position so the bands will be equidistant from each side, looping the strip as shown. Hand-sew the handles to the bag, starting just below the flap on the front, underneath (the boxing strip), and up to the center back of the bag.)

Hand-sew the ball half of the large snap to the underside of the flap at the center about one inch from the edge. Make the location of the socket half by positioning the flap as when fastened; sew the socket half of the large snap in place.

Be Kind to Your Sewing Machine

• *Cleaning and oiling:* If you keep your sewing machine clean and well-oiled, it will perform for many years. Lint has a way of collecting without your being aware of it. Remove the lint from under the throat plate and around the bobbin area. Also, apply a few drops of fresh oil at the proper oiling locations. You'll be surprised how they will keep your machine running more smoothly.

• *Needles:* If your needle is dull or bent, replace it with a new one. Be sure that it is placed correctly in the needle clamp and at the proper height. Use the right type of needle for the fabric you are sewing: for example, use a ball-point needle for knit fabrics, leathers, and vinyls.

• *Thread:* Check to see that your machine is threaded correctly. Select thread that is suitable for the fabric weight, purpose, and color. Match the color of the thread to the fabric, or use a color that is slightly darker.

• *Thread tension:* Because correct thread tension is so important in achieving professional sewing results, it is wise to familiarize yourself with this function. Before starting on a new garment, test the tension and stitch length by practicing on a small swatch of the fabric you plan to use. The ideal tension is obtained when both top and bottom threads are drawn equally into the fabric.

• *Bobbins:* Keep several bobbins wound with the colors of thread you use most frequently. Also, have a few additional ones available so you can avoid winding one color on top of another.

• *Special attachments:* Familiarize yourself with the attachments that come with your sewing machine, and learn how to use them. Practice with small amounts of fabric until you have mastered each technique.

Are Jeans Your Hangup?

Never discard outgrown or worn blue jeans. Use a little ingenuity and make something super like this carryall to hang on a wall or on a closet door.

Not only is it functional, but it also adds a touch of whimsy to the decor of a young person's room.

If you are a veteran at the sewing machine, you probably have a collection of decorative braids and trims tucked in with fabric remnants and sewing supplies. If not, your favorite notions department has a vast selection from which to choose.

Trim the multi-pocket blue jeans as simply or as dramatically as you wish. Use trim colors and designs to fit your fancy. For that personal touch, substitute a three letter monogram for the numbers 1, 2, and 3. The results are great!

Materials
- Pair of blue jeans
- Regular and jumbo rickrack
- Gingham check rickrack
- Tape measure band trim
- Several other decorative woven tape trims
- Wire coat hanger

Directions
Slit the seams on the outer and inner sides of the jeans. Use the front section of the jeans for the background piece; use the back of the jeans to cut the various sizes of pockets.

Cut eight pockets of various sizes, allowing for a ½-inch fold under on the two sides and bottom, and a deeper 1-inch hem across the top. Fold under the top hem allowance and make a double row of stitching. Fold under ½ inch on the other three sides of the pockets and make a single row of stitching, except for the three pockets on the right side which have the numerals placed where a double row is needed.

Draw the #1, #2, #3 numerals on three of the pockets and stitch gingham check rickrack directly over the markings. Fold under about ½ inch at the ends of each piece of rickrack to ensure a neat finish. Ease the trim around the corners and curves so that it lays flat.

Pin all the pockets in position. Stitch the numbered pockets first. Place the trim of your choice over the edges of the other pockets and simultaneously stitch the trim and the pockets to the jeans.

Stitch rows of rickrack down both sides of both legs, and floral tape across the bottom of both legs.

Add four 1½-inch-long floral tape loops to the top of the jeans, spacing them evenly and looping each one over the base of a wire coat hanger. Stitch a wide band of decorative woven tape across the top of the jeans to look like a belt.

blue rickrack. Hand-tack daisies in the corners and in some spaces at the edge.

Place the strip of eyelet ruffling over the top, having the heading parallel with the edge and extra fullness at the corners. In the sketch below, you can see how to add fullness just before you get to the corner — an amount equal to 1¼ times the width of the ruffle. Stitch inside the heading on the seam line.

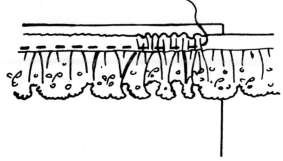

Denim with Frills

Here's positive proof that not all denim falls into the casual, heavy-duty category. This delightful 12x12-inch square denim pillow can be made from denim fabric or worn jeans. Even though the lavish trim is a total contrast to sturdy denim, the combination bears out the adage, "opposites attract."

Materials
• ½ yard blue denim or worn jeans
• 1⅛ yard wide floral banding
• 1½ yard narrow floral banding
• 3 yards blue rickrack
• 2½ yards white rickrack
• 1½ yards eyelet ruffling
• 12-inch-square pillow form

Directions
Cut two pieces of denim to fit the 12-inch-square pillow form, and allow ⅝-inch allowance for seams. Stitch three rows of the wide floral banding across the pillow top, evenly spaced. At each edge of each strip, stitch a row of white rickrack.

In the opposite direction, stitch four rows of the narrower banding evenly spaced. At both edges of these rows, stitch a band of

Add the same amount of fullness — 1¼ times the width of the ruffle — after you turn the corners of the pillows, as shown in the sketch below. Stitch inside the heading on the seam line.

Stitch the eyelet ruffling completely around the pillow, overlapping the ends on one side. Seam the front section to the back with the right sides together, leaving one side open. Turn the pillow to the right side, insert the pillow form, and hand-tack the opening closed.

89

Awake-Asleep Doll

This soft cuddly doll has an element of surprise that will tickle the fancy of little children. Turn the doll in one direction and it is wide awake, in a dress and apron. Reverse the doll and she's sound asleep in a flower-sprigged flannel nightgown.

Materials
- ¼ yard flesh-colored muslin
- ¼ yard flowered flannel nightgown fabric
- ¼ yard tiny checked dress fabric
- 1 6x9-inch piece of white pique
- 1½ yards 1-inch-wide ruffled eyelet trim
- 1 package ruffled flexi-lace
- 12 inches woven band for nightgown
- 12 inches woven band for dress
- 1 red, 1 black felt-tip marker (permanent)
- 3 yards rust-colored brush fringe for hair
- 1 package of polyester batting

(All trims are from Wright's.)

Directions
Enlarge the patterns below, and cut out two body shapes of muslin, four arms of flannel nightgown fabric, and four arms of dress fabric.

With felt-tip markers, draw facial features on one piece of body. Draw open-eyed version at one end, and sleepy-eyed face at other end. Use black for eyes and red for mouth.

Stitch bodies with right sides together, leaving an opening on one side. Clip curves and turn to right side. Stuff with batting. Stitch opening closed.

Make the nightgown by cutting one 8x10-inch piece for the bodice and a 10x20-inch piece for the skirt. Cut same size pieces from dress fabric. Use white pique for apron.

For both the dress and the nightgown, fold the bodice in half lengthwise as shown in

(continued)

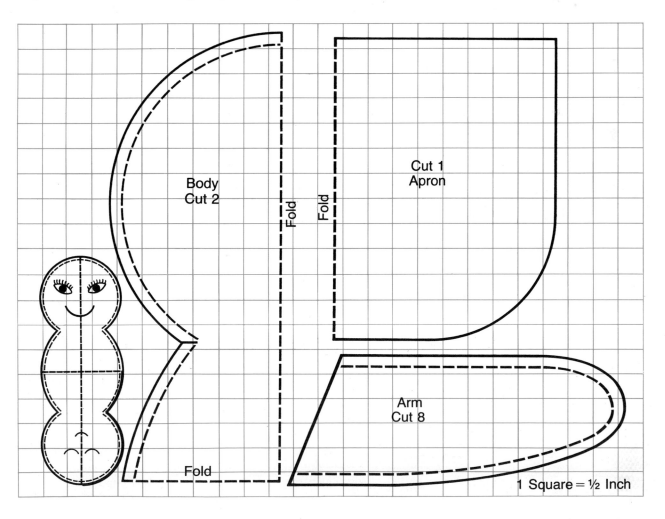

Body
Cut 2

Cut 1
Apron

Fold

Fold

Fold

Arm
Cut 8

1 Square = ½ Inch

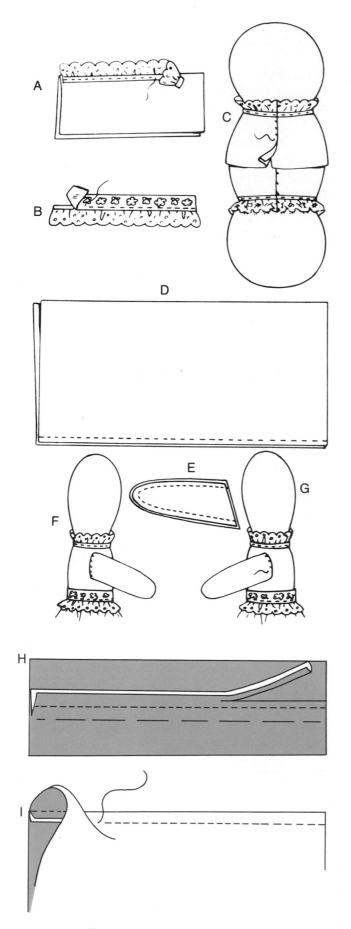

drawing A at left. Stitch eyelet trim to upper fold for dress neckline, and sew flexilace on upper fold of nightgown collar. Stitch ruffled eyelet to edge of woven band for dress waistline, and sew ruffled flexilace to woven band at nightgown waistline (see drawing B).

Stitch ruffled eyelet around sides and bottom of apron, and baste top side of apron to top of dress skirt. Center apron on the 20-inch skirt strip. Stitch flexilace ruffling at bottom of nightgown.

Place dress bodice on the doll's wide-awake end. Handstitch center back as shown in drawing C. Repeat the procedure with nightgown bodice, sewing it to the doll's sleepy-eyed end.

With right sides facing, sew the two skirts together along bottom edge, as shown in drawing D. Turn to right side, and press the two layers as one piece. Gather upper edge of skirt. Seam skirt down center back, using a French seam, as shown in drawings H and I. This makes the skirt reversible.

Place skirt on doll, matching bodice to skirt. Pull up gathers so skirt top fits doll; hand-sew skirt in place. Place woven waistband with ruffled trim over gathered edge and handstitch in place. Reverse the skirt so the other side with its matching bodice is on the right side. Handstitch the other waistband in place.

Stitch sleeves, right sides together, leaving ends open as shown in drawing E. Clip in seam allowance around curves and turn to the right side. Stuff the arms with batting, and hand-sew them to the doll, securing well (see F, G). Fold under the raw edges as you sew.

Handstitch the rust colored brush fringe to the heads for hair. Start at the outer edge, and work in a circular fashion. Sew the fringe in place as you work inward toward the center of the head until the entire hair area is covered.

Sock Dolls for Little Ones

These pint-size dolls made from infant-size socks are soft and squeezable, and will nestle comfortably in the corner of a baby's crib. Discover how quick and easy it is to create these snuggly toys. Make an assortment of them in various sizes and colors. But the fun you have making the dolls can't compare to the fun a child will have playing with these soft, lovable dolls.

Materials
- Sock for each doll (small-size socks with fold-down cuffs
- Scraps of trims
- Embroidery floss
- Buttons for eyes
- Polyester stuffing

Directions
First, stuff the toe of the sock firmly with polyester stuffing to form a ball for the head; then, tie around the neck with a piece of yarn or cord.

Continue stuffing past the heel section. Stuff this part of the sock very firmly so that the doll will sit up. Cut off the cuff. Slit the lower part of the body to form the two legs. Stuff the legs lightly, and slip-stitch the leg openings shut.

Use part of the cuff to make the hat, and the remaining piece to make the arms. Stitch the side and the end of the tube to make each arm. Turn the arms to the right side, stuff them with batting, and whipstitch them to the body. Attach the arms so they reach forward or upward.

Pencil in the facial features and other details; embroider them with embroidery floss. Use buttons for eyes, being especially careful to attach them securely.

Use bits and pieces of ribbon, edging, and daisy trim to decorate the dolls, as shown in the photo. Gather the raw edge of the cuff and pull the stitches tight. Pull the ribbed cuff over the head for the stocking cap.

Knitting

Enter the fascinating world of needlework. In it find the pleasurable and relaxing art of knitting. Here's the opportunity to fashion clothing and home accessories with distinctive good looks. Choose from a wealth of colored yarns in natural and synthetic fiber.
(See page 122 for knitting abbreviations and basic knitting stitches.)

Chinese Folk Art Afghan

Be proud to show off this glamorous afghan that falls into graceful folds when draped casually over a chair or sofa. It is studded with Chinese folk art motifs that look difficult to duplicate, but present no problem to even a beginning knitter.

Simply knit the entire afghan in stockinette stitch, except for the bands of seed stitch that define the individual squares and border the outer edges. Then, embroider the oriental designs, following the pattern on page 96.

Materials
(Unger's, Roly Poly, 3½-oz. balls)
• 7 color A
• 1 color B (for embroidery)
• Size 8 14-inch knitting needles
• Tapestry needle
• Tissue paper

Gauge
5 sts = 1 inch; 6 rows = 1 inch.

Measurements for blocking
44x56 inches.

Directions
Note: Afghan is knitted in one piece, and embroidered when piece is completed.

Seed st: Even number of sts. Row 1: * k 1, p 1; repeat from * across. Row 2: * p 1, k 1; repeat from * across. Repeat these two rows for seed st on an even number of sts. Always k on a p, and p on a k.

With A, cast on 220 sts. ** Work seed st for 2-inch border. Change to pattern st.

Row 1: * seed st for 10 sts, k 60; repeat from * across; end with 10 seed sts.

Row 2: * seed st for 10 sts; p 60; repeat from * across; end with 10 seed sts.

Repeat rows 1 and 2 for pattern for 12 inches from top of 2-inch border (count rows so all other squares are the same). Repeat from ** three times more (four stripes, each with three stockinette st squares), end with 2 inches of seed st. Bind off.

Finishing — Steam lightly on the wrong side. *Do not press.* Trace the design onto 12

(continued)

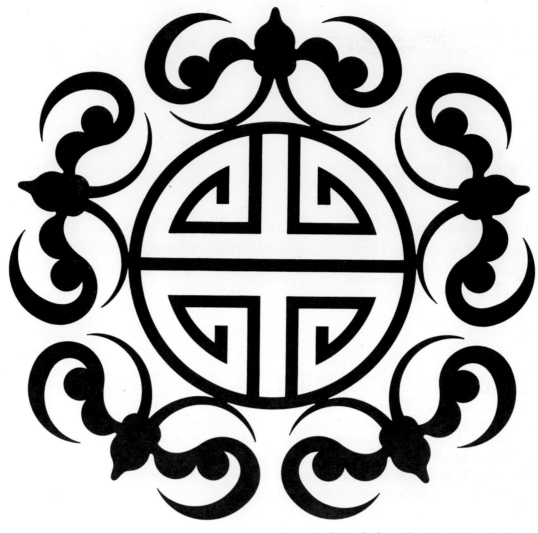

Actual size of embroidery design

pieces of tissue paper. Place a tissue pattern onto each of the 12 squares; then baste in place.

With B, embroider the design in each of the 12 squares, using the outline stitch for the center design and satin stitch for the outside motifs. When the design is completed, tear away the tissue paper.

Satin stitch: Satin stitch is composed of straight over-and-over stitches taken side by side close together, as shown in the drawing at the right. It is used to fill in a given space of a certain shape.

Outline stitch: Work from left to right, as shown in the drawing at the right. Always keep the thread on the same side of the needle—either above or below. Take a back stitch, bringing the needle out where the last stitch went in, and following the line which can be either curved or straight.

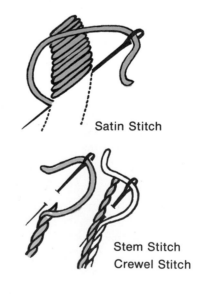

Satin Stitch

Stem Stitch
Crewel Stitch

96

Flowing Stripes Shawl

Shawls are known for their versatility, and every fashion-conscious woman should have one or more in her wardrobe. The rectangular, square, triangular, and circular wraps are ideal for traveling, because they can be folded and packed and emerge without a wrinkle. They are an eye-appealing fashion accessory, and an additional fashion bonus in chilly weather.

Don't be trapped by convention. Make them lacy or tailored; use one or more colors of yarn; and wear your shawl with everything from blue jeans to the most sophisticated evening wear.

The shawl pictured here has wavy stripes in a flattering color combination of bone and mink brown. It is finished at both ends with deep, luxurious fringe. The yarn is soft and supple, easy to work with on large size knitting needles, and drapes casually. If you enjoy crocheting more than knitting, there are also many shawl patterns available for crocheting.

Materials
(Columbia-Minerva, Amy, 1-oz. balls)
- 6 bone, color A
- 4 mink, color B
- Size 8 knitting needles
- Size G crochet hook

Gauge
1 pat measures 2½ inches.

Measurements for blocking
Approximately 21x70 inches plus fringe.

Directions
With color A, cast on 103 sts loosely. Row 1: Right side, k. Row 2: K 2, p to last 2 sts, k 2.

Row 3: K 2, p 2 tog twice, (pick up horizontal strand before next st and k it, k next st) 3 times, pick up horizontal strand before next st and k it, * p 2 tog 4 times, (pick up horizontal strand and k it, k next st) 3 times, pick up horizontal strand and k it, repeat from * to last 6 sts, p 2 tog twice, k 2.

Row 4: K2, p to last 2, k 2. Drop A. Repeat these 4 rows for pat, working 4 rows each of colors B and A to about 70 inches from start, end with an A stripe, k 1 more row. Bind off.

Fringe—Cut eight 17-inch-long strands of color A. Fold each one in half and draw the fold through st at edge of one end of the shawl. Draw ends through loop and tighten. Space 18 more fringes across end, equally spaced. Fringe other end. Trim ends of fringe to same length.

Ribbed Tweed Jacket and Scarf Duo

In warm tones borrowed from mother earth, tweed-textured yarn provides the perfect source for this longer-length, body-hugging jacket, slightly nipped at the waist. The jacket and its matching fringed scarf are ideal for frontline and sideline sports action. Wherever and whenever you model it, this outfit will bring many compliments.

Instructions are for size 8-10 (small), with changes for size 12-14 (medium) in parentheses.

Materials
(Unger's Campo, 1-oz. balls)
• Sizes 10, 10½, and 11 knitting needles
• Size H aluminum crochet hook
Jacket
• 14 (15) balls
• 6 buttons
Scarf
• 4 balls

Gauge
Size 10½ needles, 7 sts = 2 inches

Directions
Jacket: Back—With size 10½ needle, cast on 65 (69) sts. Work pat as follows: Row 1: * K 3, p 1; repeat from *, end k 1. Repeat row 1 for pattern. Work even until 20 inches from beg, or desired length to underarm. Shape armholes—Bind off 4 sts beg next 2 rows—57 (61) sts. Work even until armhole measures 7¼ (7¾) inches. Shape shoulders—Bind off 4 sts beg next 6 rows, then 5 (6) sts beg next 2 rows—23 (25) sts. Bind off rem sts for back of neck.

Left front—With size 10½ needles, cast on 39 (43) sts. Work pattern, keeping 6 sts at front edge in garter st (k every row). Work to underarm as for back. Shape armhole and neck—At arm edge, bind off 4 sts, complete row. At front edge, bind off 9 (11) sts, complete row. Dec 1 st at neck edge every other row 9 (10) times—17 (18) sts. Work even to shoulder as for back. Shape

shoulder—At arm edge, bind off 4 sts every other row 3 times, 5 (6) sts once. Mark for 6 buttons evenly spaced, placing first 1 inch from lower edge and last ½ inch below neck shaping.

Right front—Work to correspond to left front, reversing shaping and working in buttonholes opposite markers for buttons. Buttonhole—At front edge, k 2, bind off 2, complete row. Next row—Cast on 2 sts above bound off sts of previous row.

Sleeves—With size 10 needles, cast on 30 (30) sts. Work in k 2, p 2, ribbing for 3 inches, increasing evenly across last row to 53 (57) sts. Change to size 10½ needles and pattern. Work evenly until 19 inches from beg, or 2 inches more than desired length to underarm. Bind off.

Collar—With size 10 needle, cast on 98 (102) sts. Row 1: K 1, p 1, * k 2, p 2; repeat from *, end p 1, k 1. Row 2: K 2, p 2; repeat from *, end k 2. Repeat these 2 rows until 6 inches from beg. Bind off in ribbing.

Finishing—Sew shoulder seams. Weave straight edge of sleeve to straight edge of armhole (omit armhole bind-off). Weave side edge of sleeve to each 4 st armhole bind-off. Sew undersleeve and side seams. With H crochet hook, work 2 rows of sc around neck, taking in slightly to fit. With H hook, work 1 row of slip st along each front edge. Buttonhole st around buttonholes with a tapestry needle. Sew on collar to within each 6 garter st front border.

Note: *Do not block or press.* Wet block jacket by dampening with cold water. Lay on a towel and shape to measurements. Dry away from heat and sun. Sew on buttons.

Scarf: With size 11 needle, cast on 25 sts. Work garter st for 66 inches, or desired length. Bind off.

Finishing (Fringe)—Cut 15-inch strands. Fold 3 strands to form a loop. Insert crochet hook in st from wrong side and pull loop of 3 strands through st. Pass all loose ends through loop and knot. Work a fringe in every other st along each short end of scarf. Trim fringe.

100

His and Hers Patterned Sleeveless Sweaters

These sleeveless slipovers are perfect for people who like the layered look. They are equally suited for wear over ribbed turtlenecks and tailored shirts. Both have instructions for size 8-10, with changes for size 12-14 in parentheses for women; and size 36-38, with changes for size 40 in parentheses for men.

Materials

Fair Isle Slipover
(Unger's Nanette, 1¾-oz. balls)
• 2 (2-3-3) dark green (A)
• 2 (2-2-3) light aqua (B)
• 2 (2-2-3) French blue (C)
• Sizes 4 and 6 knitting needles

Indian Design Sleeveless Sweater
(Unger's Natuurwol, 1⅝-oz. balls)
• 2 camel (A)
• 2 (2-3-3) light gray (B)
• 1 brown (C)
• Sizes 5 and 6 knitting needles

Gauge (for both sweaters)
5 sts = 1 inch

Note: Carry yarns loosely across back of work when working with two or more colors, to prevent drawing in.

Directions:

Fair Isle Sleeveless Slipover: Back—With size 4 needles and A, cast on 81 (85-91-95) sts. Work in k 1, p 1 ribbing for 4½ (5-5½-5½) inches, increasing 4 (5-4-5) sts evenly spaced across last row, 85 (90-95-100) sts. Change to size 6 needles. Follow chart for pattern in stock st (32 row repeat). When second row 24 is completed, shape armholes. Bind off 5 sts beg next 2 rows, 75 (80-85-90) sts. Continue in pattern until armhole measures 7½ (8-9-10) inches.

Shape shoulders—Bind off 6 (6-7-7) sts beg next 6 (2-6-2) rows, then 0 (7-0-8) sts beg next 0 (4-0-4) rows, 39 (40-43-44) sts.

Back neckband—Change to size 4 needle and A. K 1 row, decreasing 1 st for small and large size, 39 (39-43-43) sts. Work in k 1, p 1 ribbing for 5 rows. Bind off in ribbing.

Front—Work the same as for back until the first row 12 above armhole shaping is completed, 75 (80-85-90) sts. Shape square neck—Work 18 (20-21-23) sts, slip the rem sts to a holder. Work even on these sts to shoulder, as for back.

Shape shoulder—At arm edge, bind off 6 (6-7-7) sts every other row 3 (1-3-1) times, then 0 (7-0-8) sts 0 (2-0-2) times. Leave center 39 (40-43-44) sts on holder, slip rem 18 (20-21-23) sts onto needle. Attach yarn at neck edge and work to correspond to other side, reversing shaping.

Finishing (front neckband)—With size 4 needles, A, starting at left shoulder, pick up and k 1 st in every row to first corner of neck, place a marker, k sts from front neck holder, decreasing 1 st for small and large size only—39 (39-43-43) sts on front neck edge, place a marker at next corner, pick up and k same amount of sts to shoulder as on other side. Work in k 1, p 1 ribbing for 5 rows, decreasing 1 st each side of markers on every row. Bind off in ribbing, decreasing 1 st before and after each marker. Sew shoulder and neckband seams.

Armband—With size 4 needles, A and right side facing, pick up and k 87 (93-101-111) sts along straight edge of armhole, omitting 5 st bind-off on each side. Work in k 1, p 1 ribbing for 5 rows. Bind off in ribbing. Sew side edges of armband to each 5 st armhole bind-off. Sew side seams.

Do not block or press. Dampen garment with cold water. Lay on a towel and shape to measurements. Let dry away from heat and sun.

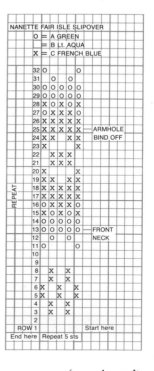

(continued)

Indian design sleeveless sweater: Back—
With size 5 needles and A, cast on 78 (86-90-98) sts. Work in k 2, p 2 ribbing for 2½ (2½-3-3) inches, increasing 7 (5-7-5) sts evenly across last row, 85 (91-97-103) sts. Change to size 6 needles and B. Work stock st (k 1 row, p 1 row) for 8 (8-10-10) rows with B. Attach C. Follow chart for pat 1 in stock st. Fasten off C. Starting with a p row, work 5 rows B in stock st. Attach A (Note: Have 2 balls A ready for pattern). Work 6 rows A in stock st.

Start pat 2 as follows—Row 1: K 29 (32-35-38) A, attach B, k 27 B, attach another A, k 29 (32-35-38) A. Continue in stock st, following chart for pat 2 on center 27 sts and keeping sides as established. Fasten off all balls of yarn. Attach B and work stock st for 4 rows. Start pat 3 as follows—(*Note:* Prepare 3 balls each of B and C and 2 balls A). Row 1: K 18 (21-24-27) B, attach C, k 1 C (row 1 of pat 3), with second ball B, k 47 B; attach C, k 1 C (row 1 of pat); attach third ball B, k 18 (21-24-27) B.

Continue in pat 3, following chart in stock st for 3 more rows with 1 pat on each side and sts between patterns in B. Row 5: K 14 (17-20-23) C, k 9 A (pat 3), k 39 C, k 9 A (pat 3), k 14 (17-20-23) C. Continue following chart for pat 3 for 7 more rows, with sts between patterns worked with C. Row 13: Continue pat 3, having sts between patterns in B and pattern sts in C. Work until the 16 rows of pat 3 are completed.

Break off all balls of yarn, leaving the first B ball only. Work even 4 rows with B. Attach A and work 6 rows even. Work pat 2 as before for 6 rows. Work 6 (6-8-8) rows with B. Work pat 1 for next 3 rows. Starting with a p row, work 1 (1-3-3) rows B.

Shape armholes—With B, bind off 7 sts beg next 2 rows. Fasten off B; attach A. With A, work 6 rows, decreasing 1 st each end every row twice, every other row twice. Fasten off A; attach B. Work 4 rows B, decreasing 1 st each end every other row twice, 59 (65-71-77) sts. Attach C and work 2 rows C, 2 rows B, 2 rows C. Fasten off C and

complete remainder of back with B. Work even until armhole measures 7½ (8-9-10) inches.

Shape shoulders—Bind off 5 (5-6-6) sts. beg next 6 (2-6-2) rows, then 0 (6-0-7) sts beg next 0 (4-0-4) rows, 29 (31-35-37) sts. Back neckband—Change to size 5 needles and A. K 1 row, increasing 1 st on row. Work in k 2, p 2 ribbing for 7 rows. Bind off in ribbing.

Front—Work same as back until armholes measure 2½ (3-3½-4¼) inches, 59 (65-71-77) sts. Shape neck—Work 23 (25-26-28) sts, slip rem sts to a holder. At neck edge, bind off 2 sts once, then dec 1 st every row 4 times, every other row twice, 15 (17-18-20) sts. Work to shoulder as back.

Shape shoulder—At arm edge, bind off 5 (5-6-6) st every other row 3 (1-3-1) times, then 0 (6-0-7) sts 0 (2-0-2) times. Leave center 13 (15-19-21) sts on holder, slip rem 23 (25-26-28) sts onto needle. Attach yarn at neck edge and work to correspond to other side, reversing shaping.

Front neckband—with size 5 needles, B and right side facing, pick up 74 (78-82-90) sts around entire front neck. (This includes sts on holder.) Fasten off B; attach A. P 1 row A. Work in k 2, p 2 ribbing until band is same as back. Bind off in ribbing.

Finishing—Sew shoulder and neckband seams. Armband—With size 5 needle, B and right side facing, pick up 102 (106-114-122) sts around entire armhole. Fasten off B and attach A. P 1 row A, then work in k 2, p 2 ribbing for 5 rows. Bind off in ribbing. Sew side seams. Block lightly on wrong side.

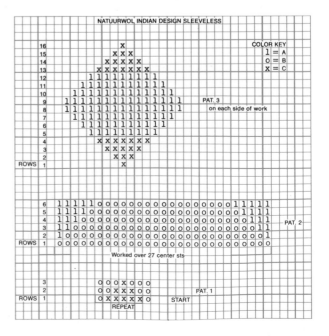

Ribbed Turtleneck

This classic turtleneck pullover has an epaulette topped with three gold buttons.

Instructions are given for size 6-8, with sizes 10-12, and 14-16 in parentheses.

Materials

(Columbia-Minerva Feather-Down yarn, 2-oz. pull skeins)
• 6 (7-8)
• Sizes 6 and 8 knitting needles
• 3 small gold buttons

Gauge

5 sts = 1 inch, 6 rows = 1 inch.

Directions

Back—With size 6 needles cast on 82 (90-98). Row 1 (right side): K 2, * p 2, k 2; repeat from * across. Row 2: P 2, * k 2, p 2; repeat from * across. Repeat these 2 rows for pat, working 4 more rows. Change to size 8 needles. Continue in pat to 19 inches from start. Width: 16½ (18-19½) inches.

Armholes—Bind off 3 (4-4) at beg of next 2 rows. Dec 1 each side every other row 5 (6-7) times. Work on 66 (70-76) sts to 7 (7½-8) inches straight above underarm. Width is 13¼ (14-15¼) inches.

Shoulders—Bind off 7 at beg of next 4 rows, then 4 (6-7) at beg of next 2 rows. Sl rem 30 (30-34) sts to holder for neck.

Front—Same as back to 5½ (6-6½) inches straight above underarm. Neck and shoulder—Work 22 (24-25) and sl to holder, work center 22 (22-26) and sl to 2nd holder for neck, work to end. Dec 1 at neck every other row 4 times. At same time when armhole matches back armhole, bind off 7 sts at armhole twice then 4 (6-7) at same edge once. Starting at opposite neck edge, work other side.

Sleeves—With size 6 needles cast on 34 (38-42). Work in rib pat as on back for 3 inches. Change to size 8 needles. Continue in pat, increasing 1 st each side every 6th row 12 times working added sts in pat. Work on 58 (62-66) sts to 17 inches or desired length from start to underarm. Width is 11¾ (12½-13¼) inches. Sleeve cap—Bind off 3 (4-4) at beg of next 2 rows. Dec 1 each side every other row until 28 (28-30) sts rem. Bind off 2 sts at beg of next 4 rows. Bind off.

Turtleneck—Sew left shoulder seam. On right side with size 6 needles, starting at open shoulder, work in ribbing across 30 (30-34) back sts, pick up and k 18 on left neck edge, work in ribbing on 22 (22-26) front sts, pick up and k 18 on other side. Work ribbing on 88 (88-96) sts for 2 inches. Change to size 8 needles and continue to 5 inches. Bind off in ribbing. Sew open shoulder, joining turtleneck, reversing seam for turn. Sew in sleeves; sew side and sleeve seams.

Epaulette—With size 6 needles cast on 13. Row 1: K 1, * p 1, k 1; repeat from * across. Row 2: P 1, * k 1, p 1; repeat from * across. Repeat these 2 rows for 3 inches. Dec 1 each side every row until 3 sts rem. K 3 tog. Fasten. Trim with buttons and sew to shoulder.

Fluffy Cable Stitch Cardigan

Cable stitch sweaters are always in vogue and this soft and fluffy yarn cardigan is no exception.

Instructions are given for size 8, with changes for sizes 10, 12, and 14 in parentheses.

Materials
(Unger's Fluffy, 1¾-oz. balls)
• 7 (8-8-9)
• Sizes 4 and 6 knitting needles
• 1 cable (double-pointed) needle

• Size 0 steel crochet hook
• 8 plastic rings for buttons

Gauge
6 sts = 1 inch

Directions
Back—With size 4 needles, cast on 99 (103-109-115) sts. Row 1: Wrong side. P 1, *

k 1, p 1; repeat from * across. Row 2: K 1, * p 1, k 1; repeat from * across. Repeat these 2 rows for ribbing for 2 inches, ending with row 1, and increasing 3 sts evenly spaced — 102 (106-112-118) sts. Change to size 6 needle and pattern. Row 1: P 1 (3-6-9), k 4 (small cable), * p 6, k 8 (large cable), p 6, k 4 (small cable); repeat from *, end p 1 (3-6-9).

Rows 2, 4, 6, and 8: K 1 (3-6-9), p 4, * k 6, p 8, k 6, p 4; repeat from *, end k 1 (3-6-9). Row 3: P 1 (3-6-9), slip next 2 sts to dp needle, hold in back, k 2, k 2 from dp needle (C 4), * p 6, k 8, p 6, C 4; repeat from *, end p 1 (3-6-9). Row 5: P 1 (3-6-9), k 4, * p 6, slip next 4 sts to dp needle, hold in back of work, k 4, k 4 from dp needle (C 8), p 6, k 4; repeat from *, end p 1 (3-6-9). Row 7: Repeat row 3. Row 9: Repeat row 1. Row 10: Repeat row 2. Repeat rows 3 through 10 for pattern. Work even until 16 inches from beg.

Shape armholes — Bind off 6 sts beg next 2 rows. Dec 1 st each end every other row 4 (5-6-7) times — 82 (84-88-92) sts. Work even until armholes measure 7¼ (7½-7¾-8) inches.

Shape shoulders — Bind off 7 (8-9-9) sts beg next 2 rows, 8 (8-8-9) sts beg next 4 rows — 36 (36-38-38) sts. Place rem sts on holder for back of neck.

Left front — With size 4 needles, cast on 57 (59-62-65) sts. Row 1: Wrong side. P 1, * k 1, p 1; repeat from * across. Work border as for back, ending with row 1 and increasing 1 st at end of last row — 58 (60-63-66) sts. Change to size 6 needle and pat. Row 1: P 1 (3-6-9), k 4, p 6, k 8, p 6, k 4, p 6, k 8, p 6, work ribbing on rem 9 sts as established for front border. Work pat and 9 rib sts for front border to underarm as for back.

Shape armhole — At arm edge, bind off 6 sts once, dec 1 st every other row 4 (5-6-7) times — 48 (49-51-53) sts. Work even until armhole measures 5 (5¼-6-6¼) inches.

Shape neck — At front edge, work 16 (17-18-18) sts and slip onto a holder, complete row. Dec 1 st at neck edge every row 6 times, every other row 3 (2-2-2) times — 23 (24-25-27) sts. Work to shoulder as for back.

Shape shoulder — At arm edge, bind off 7 (8-9-9) sts once, 8 (8-8-9) twice. Mark for

8 buttons evenly spaced, placing the first 1 inch from the lower edge and the last one in the center of the neckband.

Right front — Work to correspond to left front, reversing shaping and pattern and working in buttonholes opposite markers for buttons. Buttonhole — At front edge, rib 4 sts, bind off next 3 sts, complete row. Next row: Cast on 3 sts above those bound off on previous row.

Sleeves — With size 4 needles, cast on 39 (41-45-47) sts. Work in k 1, p 1 ribbing for 3 inches, increasing 19 sts evenly across last row — 58 (60-64-66) sts. Change to size 6 needles and pattern. Row 1: P 1 (2-4-5), k 8 (large cable), * p 6, k 4 (small cable), p 6, k 8 (large cable); repeat from * across, end p 1 (2-4-5). Work pattern as established for 2 inches. Inc 1 st each end of next row, then every 2 inches for 5 times more (work all inc sts in p on right side, and k on wrong side) — 70 (72-76-78) sts. Work even until 17 inches from beg, or desired length to underarm.

Shape cap — Bind off 6 sts beg next 2 rows. Dec 1 st each end every row 4 times, every other row 17 (18-19-20) times. Bind off 2 sts beg next 4 rows. Bind off. Finishing — Sew shoulder, side and sleeve seams. Sew in sleeves.

Neckband — Slip 16 (17-18-18) sts from right front holder onto size 4 needle, attach yarn and pick up and k until there are 89 (93-97-101) sts around neck (including sts on holders). Work in ribbing 7 rows, keeping front borders in rib as established and working in 8th buttonhole in center of neckband.

Buttons — Make 8. Sc over plastic ring until completely covered. Fasten off, leaving a long strand. Turn outer edge to inside and weave center tog. Sew on buttons.

Trim — Attach yarn at right front neck edge. With right side facing, working backwards from left to right, sc along front edge, making sure work lies flat. Work left front to correspond, starting at lower left front edge. *Do not steam press.* Wet garment with cold water. Lay on towel and shape to measurements. Dry away from heat.

Sleeveless Jacket Banded in Seed Stitch

This sleeveless jacket, with large patch pockets, belongs in every woman's wardrobe. The body pattern is a simple combination of knit and purl stitches, and bands around edges and across pockets are in seed stitch.

The directions are given for small size (8-10), with changes for medium size (12-14) and large size (16-18) in parentheses.

Materials

(Bernat-Carioca, 1-oz. tubes)
- 14 (14-15)
- Size 5 knitting needles

Gauge

6 sts = 1 inch, 8 rows = 1 inch

Pattern stitch

Rows 1 and 5: Knit
Rows 2 and 6: Purl
Row 3: K 2, * p 2, k 2, repeat from * across row.
Rows 4 and 7: P 2, * k 2, p 2, repeat from * across row.
Row 8: K 2, * p 2, k 2, repeat from * across row.
Repeat these 8 rows for pattern.

Directions

Back — Cast on 108 (120, 132) sts. Row 1: * K 1, p 1; repeat from * across row. Row 2: * P 1, k 1; repeat from * across row. Repeat these 2 rows 4 times more. Work in pat st. On next row, inc 1 st each end of needle — 110 (122, 134) sts. Continue to work in pat st until piece measures 3 inches. Dec 1 st each end of needle and repeat dec every 3 inches twice more. Work even in pat st on 104 (116, 128) sts until piece measures 19 inches, ending with a wrong side row.

Shape armholes — At the beg of each of the next 4 rows, bind off 5 (6, 7) sts. Dec 1 st each end of needle every other row 8 times. Work even in pat st on 68 (76, 84) sts until armholes measure 7½ (8, 8½) inches.

Shape shoulders — At the beg of each of the next 2 rows, bind off 8 (9, 11) sts. At the beg of each of the next 2 rows, bind off 7 (9, 10) sts. Bind off rem 38 (40, 42) sts.

Left front — Cast on 54 (60, 66) sts. Row 1: * K 1, p 1; repeat from * across row. Row 2: * P 1, k 1; repeat from * across row. Repeat these 2 rows 4 times more. Work even in pat st on 46 (52, 58) sts; put a marker on needle, (p 1, k 1) 4 times (8 sts in seed st for front-band). Work in seed st pat to marker, then work in pat st to end of row. Keeping 8 sts for frontband in seed st, work rem sts in pat st for 3 inches. On the next row dec 1 st at arm edge and repeat this dec every 3 inches twice more. Work even in pat st on 51 (57, 63) sts until piece measures 16½ inches, ending at arm edge.

Shape neck — Work in pat st to 2 sts before marker, dec 1 st, work to end of row. Continue to dec 1 st at neck edge every sixth (sixth, fourth) row 14 (16, 18) times more, and at the same time, when piece measures 19 inches, ending at arm edge.

Shape armhole — Bind off 5 (6, 7) sts, work to end of row. Dec 1 st at same edge every other row 8 times. When all decs have been completed, work even on 23 (26, 29) sts until armhole measures 7½ (8, 8½) inches.

Shape shoulder — At arm edge bind off 8 (9, 11) sts once and 7 (9, 10) sts once. Continue in seed st on rem 8 sts for 2½ (2½, 2¾) inches. Bind off.

Right front — Work to correspond to left front, reversing placing of frontband and all shaping.

Pocket — Make 2. Cast on 34 sts. Work even in pattern st for 5 inches, then work even in seed st for 10 rows. Bind off in seed st.

Armbands — Make 2. Cast on 8 sts. Work even in seed st until piece measures 15 (16-17) inches. Bind off in seed st.

Finishing — Sew underarm and shoulder seams. Seam armbands and sew to armholes. Seam neckband and sew to back of neck. Sew pockets in place 1½ inches above lower edge and 3 inches from front edge. Steam seams.

Nubby V-Neck Slipover Features Wide Ribs

Worn with a tailored shirt and colorful patterned scarf, this V-neck pullover will complement your wardrobe of slacks and skirts.

The yarn, with its tweed-like, nubby texture, knits up very rapidly on large-size knitting needles. The pattern is simply ribbing on a large scale.

Sweaters such as these are great for weekends in the country, or for any occasion calling for an air of casual elegance.

Instructions are given for size 8, with changes for sizes 10, 12, and 14 in parentheses.

Materials

(Unger's Lots of Pebbles, 1¾-oz. balls)
• 10 (11, 12, 13)
• Sizes 10½ and 11 knitting needles

Gauge

5 sts = 2 inches

Directions

Back — With size 10½ needle, cast on 41 (43, 45, 47) sts. Work in k 1, p 1 ribbing for 3 inches, increasing 1 st at end of last row for sizes 10, 12, and 14 only — 41 (44, 46, 48) sts. Change to size 11 needles and pat st. Row 1: K 9 (10, 10, 10), p 7 (7, 8, 9), k 9 (10, 10, 10), p 7 (7, 8, 9), k 9 (10, 10, 10).

Row 2: P 9 (10, 10, 10), k 7 (7, 8, 9), p 9 (10, 10, 10), k 7 (7, 8, 9), p 9 (10, 10, 10). Repeat these 2 rows for pattern. Work even until 15½ inches from beg.

Shape armholes — Bind off 3 sts beg next 2 rows. Dec 1 st each end of next row — 33 (36, 38, 40) sts. Work even until armholes measure 7 (7½, 8, 8½) inches. Shape shoulders — Bind off 4 sts beg next 2 rows, then 4 (5, 6, 6) sts beg next 2 rows — 17 (18, 18, 20) sts.

Back neckband — Change to size 10½ needle. Work in k 1, p 1 ribbing for 4 rows. Bind off in ribbing.

Front — Work same as for back to within 2 rows before armhole shaping. Shape V neck and armholes — Work 20 (21, 22, 23) sts, slip next 1 (2, 2, 2) sts to a pin (center of V); attach another ball and work 20 (21, 22, 23) sts. Working both sides at same time, work 1 row even. Next row: At arm edge, bind off 3 sts; work to within 2 sts from neck edge, k 2 tog (neck dec), with 2nd ball of yarn, k 2 tog (neck dec), complete row.

Next row: Bind off 3 sts at arm edge, complete row. Dec 1 st at each arm edge, at the same time, dec 1 st at each neck edge every 3rd row 6 times more, every other row 1 (1, 1, 2) times — 8 (9, 10, 10) sts. Work even to shoulder shaping as for back.

Shape shoulders — At each arm edge, bind off 4 sts once, 4 (5, 6, 6) sts once. Front neckband — With size 10½ needle, right side facing, starting at left shoulder, pick up and k 28 (30, 32, 34) sts to center of V, k 1 (2, 2, 2) sts from pin and mark for center, pick up and k 28 (30, 32, 34) sts along other side of V neck.

Row 1: K 1, p 1 ribbing for 26 (28, 30, 32) sts, k 2 tog, p 1 (2, 2, 2), k 2 tog, p 1, k 1 ribbing to end of row. Work 2 more rows of ribbing as established, decreasing 1 st each side of the 1 (2, 2, 2) center sts on each row. Bind off in ribbing.

Sleeves — With size 10½ needle, cast on 21 (23, 25, 25) sts. Work in k 1, p 1 ribbing for 3 inches. Change to size 11 needles and stock. st. Inc 1 st each end of first row, then every 4 (4, 4, 3½) inches for 3 (3, 3, 4) times more — 29 (31, 33, 35) sts. Work even until 17 inches from beg.

Shape cap — Bind off 3 sts beg next 2 rows. Dec 1 st each end every 4th row 4 times, every other row twice, every row 2 (3, 4, 5) times. Bind off.

Finishing note — Use a straight yarn or strong sewing thread in the same color to sew seams. Sew shoulder and neckband, side and sleeve seams. Sew in sleeves. *Do not block or press.*

Matching Sweaters for the Family

Instructions for this trio of sweaters are for size 32-34, with changes for sizes 36-38, 40-42, and 44-46 in parentheses. The child's sweater is for size 4-6, with changes for sizes 8-10, and 12-14 in parentheses.

Materials

(Bernat Krysta, 2-oz. skeins)
- Size 10 circular knitting needle
- Size 8 dp knitting needles
- Size 10 dp knitting needles

Adult sizes
- 8 (10-11-12) Main Color (MC)
- 2 (2-2-3) Color A
- 1 (1-1-2) Color B

Children's sizes
- 5 (6-7) Main Color (MC)
- 1 (2-2) Color A
- 1 Color B

Gauge

7 sts = 2 inches, 5 rows = 1 inch

Note: When changing colors, hold color which has just been worked to left and pick up new color from underneath to twist yarn and avoid holes. Carry yarn not in use loosely across wrong side of work.

Directions

Adult sweaters: Body—Using color A and circular needle, cast on 120 (132-144-156) sts. Join, being careful not to twist sts and mark beg of round, carrying marker up. K 1, p 1 ribbing 2 inches. Following chart, k st st until chart has been completed. Using MC only, continue st st until piece measures 17 (18-18-19) inches or to underarm.

Shape armholes—Starting at beg of rnd bind off 2 (2-3-3) sts, k until 56 (62-66-72) sts are on needle after last bound off st, and sl sts onto holder for back; bind off next 4 (4-6-6) sts, k until 56 (62-66-72) sts are on needle after last bound off st and sl sts onto holder for front, bind off 2 (2-3-3) sts.

Sleeves—Using M C and smaller dp needles, cast on 36 (36-42-42) sts. Join, being careful not to twist sts and mark beg of round, carrying marker up. K 1, p 1 ribbing 2 inches. Change to larger dp needles and k st st, inc 1 st each side of marker every 2 (1½-2-1½) inches 6 (8-6-9) times. Work even on 48 (52-54-60) sts until piece measures 18 (18½-19-19½) inches.

Shape underarm—Starting at beg of rnd bind off 2 (2-3-3) sts, k until 44 (48-48-54) sts are on needle after last bound off st and sl sts onto holder; bind off rem 2 (2-3-3) sts.

Raglan shaping—Using MC and circular needle, k 54 (60-66-72) sts of back, put marker on needle, k 44 (48-48-54) sts of one sleeve, put marker on needle, k 54 (60-66-72) sts of front, put marker on needle, k 44 (48-48-54) sts of other sleeve, put marker on needle— 196 (216-228-252) sts. Work as follows: Rnd 1: Join, * k to 2 sts before next marker, sl 1, k 1, psso, k 2 tog; repeat from * 3 times more —8 sts dec. Rnds 2, 3, and 4: K. Repeat last 4 rnds 4 (3-4-2) times more.

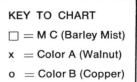

KEY TO CHART

☐ = M C (Barley Mist)

x = Color A (Walnut)

o = Color B (Copper)

(continued)

Repeat rnds 1 and 2 only 10 (13-13-18) times —76 (80-84-84) sts.

Turtleneck—Change to larger dp needles and k next rnd, dec at even intervals to 68 (68-72-72) sts. K 1, p, ribbing 7 (8-8-9) inches. Bind off.

Finishing—Weave bound off sts of underarm tog. Steam lightly.

Child's sweater: Body—Using color A and circular needle, cast on 90 (96-114) sts. Join, being careful not to twist sts and mark beg of rnd, carrying marker up. K 1, p 1 ribbing 2 inches. Follow chart on page 111; k st st until chart is completed. Continue in M C st st until piece measures 10½ (12½-14) inches or length to underarm.

Shape armholes—Starting at beg of rnd bind off 2 (2-3) sts. K 41 (44-51) sts and sl sts onto holder for back; bind off next 4 (4-6) sts, k until 41 (44-51) sts are on needle after last bound off st and sl sts onto holder for front; bind off rem 2 (2-3) sts.

Sleeves—Using M C and smaller dp needles, cast on 24 (24-30) sts. Join, being careful not to twist sts and mark beg of rnd, carrying marker up. K 1, p 1 ribbing 2 inches. Change to larger dp needles and k in st st, inc 1 st each side of marker every 1½ (1½-2) inches 5 (7-6) times. Work even on 34 (38-42) sts until piece measures 11 (12¾-13¾) inches or desired length to underarm.

Shape underarm—Starting at beg of rnd bind off 2 (2-3) sts, k until 30 (34-36) sts are on needle after last bound off sts and sl sts onto holder, bind off rem 2 (2-3) sts.

Raglan shaping—Using M C and circular needle, k 41 (44-51) sts of back; put marker on needle, k 30 (34-36) sts of one sleeve; put marker on needle, k 41 (44-51) sts of front; put marker on needle, k 30 (34-36) sts of other sleeve; put marker on needle—142 (156-174) sts. Work as follows: Round 1: Join, * k to 2 sts before next marker, sl 1, k 1, psso, k 2 tog, repeat from * 3 times more—8 sts dec. Rounds 2, 3 and 4: Repeat last 4 rounds 0 (0-2) more times. Repeat rnds 1 and 2 only 10 (11-10) times—54 (60-70) sts. Change to larger dp needles; k 1, p 1 ribbing 7 inches. Bind off.

Finishing—Weave bound off sts of underarms tog. Steam lightly.

All-Occasion Topper

This stunning, easy-to-knit coat looks well with a pantsuit, a street-length dress, or an after-five outfit. Even though it combines only garter stitch and ribbing, its push-up puffed sleeves, slash pockets, and three-quarter length give it style. Instructions are given for size 8-10, with sizes 12-14 and 16-18 in parentheses.

Materials
(Bernat Krysta, 2-oz. skeins)
• 17 (18-19)
• Size 9 circular knitting needle

Gauge
4 sts = 1 inch in garter st.

Directions

Back—Cast on 73 (77-81) sts. Work even in garter st until piece measures 17 inches. Shape armholes—At the beg of each of the next 2 rows bind off 4 sts—65 (69-73) sts.

Yoke—Row 1: K 1, * p 3, k 1, repeat from * across row. Row 2: P 1, * k 3, p 1, repeat from * across row. Repeat these 2 rows until yoke measures 3 inches, ending with row 2. First dec row (small and large sizes): K 1, * p 3, k 1, p 1, p 2 tog. k 1, repeat from * across row. Medium size: K 1, repeat from * to last 4 sts, p 3, k 1. Work in new ribbing pat until yoke measures 5½ inches, ending with wrong side row. Second dec row (small and large sizes): K 1, * p 1, p 2 tog, k 1, p 2, k 1, repeat from * across row. Medium size: K 1, repeat from * to last 3 sts, p 2 tog, k 1. Work in new ribbing pat until yoke measures 9 inches, ending with wrong side row.

Third dec row (small and large sizes): K 1, * p 2, k 1, p 2 tog, k 1, repeat from * across row. Medium size: K 1, repeat from * to last 3 sts, p 2, k 1. Work in new ribbing pat until yoke measures 10 inches. Fourth dec row (small and large sizes): K 1, * p 2 tog, k 1, p 1, k 1, repeat from * across row. Medium size: K 1, repeat from * to last 3 sts, p 2 tog, k 1. Work in k 1, p 1 ribbing on 33 (35-37) sts until yoke measures 11 inches, ending with wrong side row. Sl 33 (35-37) sts onto holder.

Pocket lining—Make 2. Cast on 22. Work in garter st for 4½ inches. Sl sts onto holder.

Left front—Cast on 40 (44-48) sts. Work in garter st for 7½ inches. Form pocket opening: K 12 and sl these sts onto holder. K next 2 sts tog (inner pocket edge). K to end of row. Continue in garter st, dec 1 st at same edge every other row 15 times more, ending at inner pocket edge. Sl rem 12 (16-20) onto holder. With right side facing, sl 12 from holder onto needle, join yarn at inner edge and k 22 sts of one pocket lining onto same needle.

Work garter st on 34 sts for 33 rows, ending at arm edge. On next row k 28 sts, sl 12 (16-20) from holder onto a spare needle and hold in front of 6 sts on left-hand needle; k tog 1 st from spare needle and

left-hand needle 6 times, k to end of row. Continue garter st on 40 (44-48) until piece measures 17 inches, ending at arm edge. Shape armhole—At beg of next row bind off 4, k to end of row, k 1 row and sl rem 36 (40-44) sts onto holder.

Right front—Work to correspond to left front until piece measures 7½ inches. Form pocket opening—K 26 (30-34) sts, k 2 tog, sl rem 12 sts onto holder. Finish to correspond to left front, reversing all shaping.

Sleeves—Cast on 24 (26-28) sts. K 1, p 1 ribbing 4 inches. K next row, inc to 72 (76-80). Continue garter st until piece measures 14 inches. Shape cap—At beg of each of next two rows, bind off 4. Sl rem 64 (68-72) onto holder.

Left front yoke—With right side facing, sl sts of left front and one sleeve onto needle—100 (108-116) sts. Join yarn at sleeve edge. Row 1: * P 3, k 1, repeat from * to last 4 sts, k 4 (front-band). Row 2: K 4, * p 1, k 3, repeat from * across row. Keep 4 sts at front edge in garter st; work rem sts in ribbing as established. Work between *'s of dec rows for back; dec 4 times same as back. Work in pattern as established on 52 (56-60) sts until yoke measures 11 inches, ending with wrong side row. Sl sts onto holder.

Right front yoke—Work to correspond to left front yoke, reversing placing of front band, ending at front edge. Do not break off yarn. Neckband—Row 1: With right side facing,· k across sts of right front yoke, k across sts of back yoke, k across sts of left front yoke. Row 2: K 2 tog across row—69 (75-79) sts. Work in garter st 8 rows more. Bind off. Sew underarm, yoke, and sleeve seams. Sew pocket linings in place. Pocket bands—With right side facing, pick up 28 sts along shaped edge of pocket opening. K 1, p 1 ribbing for 4 rows. Bind off. Sew bands in place. Steam seams.

Sweater and Cap for Active Youngsters

This rugged, matching sweater and cap set is an ideal outfit for children who like to play outdoors. It has raglan sleeves, a big front pocket to tuck hands in for warmth, and a stocking cap whose brim can be pulled up or down according to the temperature.

These matchmates are knit of heavy yarn that knits up rapidly on large needles. The simple stockinette stitch edged with knit 2, purl 2 ribbing is a timeless knit pattern that never goes out of style.

Instructions are given for small size (4-6), with changes for medium size (8-10), and large size (12-14) in parentheses.

Materials
(Bernat Krysta, 2-oz. skeins)
• 7 (8-8)
• Sizes 8 and 10 knitting needles

Gauge
7 sts = 1 inch, 5 rows = 1 inch

Directions

Pullover: Back — using smaller needles, cast on 44 (48-56) sts. K 2, p 2 in ribbing for 3 inches, inc 0 (1-0) st at each end of last row — 44 (50-56) sts. Change to larger needles and work even in st st until piece measures 10 (12-13) inches or desired length to underarm, ending with a p row.

Shape full-fashioned raglan armholes — At the beg of each of the next 2 rows bind off 2 sts. Row 3: k 1, sl 1, k 1, psso, k to last 3 sts, k 2 tog, k 1. Row 4: Purl. Repeat the last 2 rows 11 (12-15) times more. Sl rem 16 (20-20) sts onto a holder.

Front — Work to correspond to back.

Sleeves — Using smaller needles, cast on 24 sts. K 2, p 2 in ribbing for 3 inches. Change to larger needles and working in stock st, inc 1 st each end of needle every 1½ (1½-1) inches 5 (6-9) times. Work even on 34 (36-42) sts until piece measures 11 (13-14) inches or desired length to underarm, ending with a p row.

Shape full-fashioned raglan cap — At the beg of each of the next 2 rows bind off 2 sts. Dec in same manner as on back sl remaining 6 sts onto a holder.

Pocket — Using larger needles, cast on 32 (36-44) sts. Work even in stock st for 1 inch. Dec Row: K 1, sl 1, k 1, psso, k to last 3 sts, k 2 tog, k 1. Row 2: Purl. Repeat the last 2 rows 4 more times. Work even on 22 (26-34) sts until piece measures 6 (8-9) inches. Bind off. Using smaller needles and with right side facing you, pick up 24 (28-30) sts along shaped edge of pocket to within 1 inch of cast on edge. K 2, p 2 in ribbing for 1 inch. Bind off. Work other edge in same manner.

Finishing — Sew right sleeve to back and front armholes. Sew left sleeve to front armhole. Neckband — Sl sts from holders onto smaller needles — 48 (52-56) sts. With right side facing you, join yarn and k 2, p 2 in ribbing for 3 inches. Sew left back sleeve to armhole including neckband. Sew underarm seams. Fold neckband in half and sew to wrong side. Sew cast on edge of pocket to front and end of ribbing. Sew upper edge of pocket in place. Steam lightly.

Stocking cap: Using smaller needles, cast on 56 sts. K 2, p 2 in ribbing for 5 inches. Change to larger needles and k the next row, dec 1 st each end of needle — 54 sts. Work even in st st until piece measures 8 inches, ending with a k row.

Shape top — Row 1 and all uneven rows: Purl. Row 2: * K 7, k 2 tog, repeat from * 5 times more — 6 sts dec. Row 4: * K 6, k 2 tog, repeat from * 5 times more — 6 sts dec. Continue in this manner to dec 6 sts every other row, having 1 st less between decs on each dec row until 12 sts remain. Break off yarn, leaving a 12 inch end. Draw end through rem sts and pull up tightly. Sew back seam.

Toddlers Jumpsuit with Attached Hood

This delightful one-piece knitted overall with handsome Aran Isle design zips down the front, for easy dressing and undressing. It has an attached hood that protects little ones' ears when the wind blows. The instructions are given for toddler size 2, with changes for toddler sizes 3 and 4.

Materials

(Columbia-Minerva Fisherman Knit Yarn, Nantuk. Sweater and Afghan Yarn, or Featherdown, 2-oz. pull skeins)
• 7 (8-9)
Or (Columbia-Minerva Nantuk 4-ply Knitting Yarn, or Nantuk Knitting Worsted, 4-oz. pull skeins)
• 4 (4-5)
• Sizes 6 and 9 knitting needles
• 1 cable (double-pointed) needle
• Size G crochet hook

Gauge

11 sts = 2 inches; 6 rows = 1 inch.

Directions

Stitches Used: Front twist—Sk next st on left needle, k in front of next st but do not drop from left needle, k the sk'd st, then drop both from left needle. Back twist—Sk next st on left needle, k in back of next st but do not drop from left needle, k the sk'd st, then drop both from left needle. Right twist—Sk next st on left needle, k in front of next st but do not drop from left needle, p the sk'd st, then drop both from left needle. Left twist—Sk next st on left needle, p in back of next st but do not drop from left needle, k the sk'd st, then drop both from left needle.

Jacket: Back—With size 6 needles cast on 60 (64-68). K 1, p 1 in ribbing for 4 rows. K next row for turn. Change to size 9 needles. Work in pattern. Row 1 (right side):

P 1 (2-4), k 4, p 2 (3-3), * k 4, p 3, sl next 2 sts to cable needle and hold in back, k 1 then p 1, k 1 from cable needle for start of diamond, p 3, k 4 *; p 2, [front twist and back twist] twice, p 2, repeat from * to * once, p 2 (3-3), k 4, p 1 (2-4).

Row 2 and all even rows: K the k sts and p the p sts as they face you.

Row 3: P 1 (2-4), sl next 2 to cable needle and hold in back, k next 2 then k the 2 from cable needle for cable, p 2 (3-3), * cable, p 2, right twist, p 1, left twist, p 2, cable *; p 2, [back twist and front twist] twice, p 2; repeat from * to *, p 2 (3-3), cable, p 1 (2-4). Row 5: P 1 (2-4), k 4, p 2 (3-3), * k 4, p 1, right twist, p 3, left twist, p 1, k 4 *; p 2, [front twist and back twist] twice, p 2; repeat from * to *, p 2 (3-3), k 4, p 1 (2-4).

Row 7: P 1 (2-4), cable, p 2 (3-3), * cable, p 1, k 1, p 2, k in front and back of next st twice then pass the 2nd, 3rd, and 4th sts over first st for a popcorn, p 2, k 1, p 1, cable *; p 2, [back twist and front twist] twice, p 2; repeat from * to *, p 2 (3-3), cable, p 1 (2-4). Row 9: P 1 (2-4), k 4, p 2 (3-3), * k 4, p 1, left twist, p 3, right twist, p 1, k 4 *; p 2, [front twist and back twist] twice, p 2; repeat from * to *, p 2 (3-3), k 4, p 1 (2-4).

Row 11: P 1 (2-4), cable, p 2 (3-3), * cable, p 2, left twist, p 1, right twist, p 2, cable *; p 2, [back twist and front twist] twice, p 2; repeat from * to *, p 2 (3-3), cable, p 1 (2-4). Row 12: Repeat row 2. Repeat these 12 rows for pat, working to 7½ (8-8½) inches above turn, end on wrong side. Width is 11 (11½-12¼) inches.

Raglan Armholes—Bind off 2 at beg of next 2 rows. Dec 1 each side on next row then every other row until 22 (24-26) rem. Sl to holder.

Left front: With size 6 needles cast on 36 (38-40). K 1 and p 1 in ribbing for 4 rows. K next row for turn. Change to size 9 needles. Start pattern: Row 1 (right

(continued)

side): P 1 (2-4), k 4, p 2 (3-3), k 4, p 3, sl next 2 sts to cable needle and hold in back, k 1, then p 1, k 1 from cable needle for start of diamond, p 3, k 4, p 2, [front twist and back twist] twice, p 1, k 1.

Row 2 and all even rows: K 1 then p the p sts and k the k sts as they face you.

Row 3: P 1 (2-4), cable, p 2 (3-3), cable, p 2, right twist, p 1, left twist, p 2, cable, p 2, [back twist and front twist] twice, p 1, k 1. Row 5: P 1 (2-4), k 4, p 2 (3-3), k 4, p 1, right twist, p 3, left twist, p 1, k 4, p 2, [front twist and back twist] twice, p 1, k 1. Row 7: P 1 (2-4), cable, p 2 (3-3), cable, p 1, k 1, p 2, popcorn, p 2, k 1, p 1, cable, p 2, [back twist and front twist] twice, p 1, k 1.

Row 9: P 1 (2-4), k 4, p 2 (3-3), k 4, p 1, left twist, p 3, right twist, p 1, k 4, p 2, [front twist and back twist] twice, p 1, k 1. Row 11: P 1 (2-4), cable, p 2 (3-3), cable, p 2, left twist, p 1, right twist, p 2, cable, p 2, [back twist and front twist] twice, p 1, k 1. Row 12: Repeat row 2. Repeat these 12 rows for pat, working to match back to underarm, end on wrong side. Width is 6½ (7-7¼) inches.

Raglan Armhole—Bind off 2 sts at beg of next row. Dec 1 st at same edge every other row until 17 (18-19) sts rem. Sl to holder.

Right Front—Work hem and turn same as left front. Change to size 9 needles. Start pattern. Row 1 (right side): K 1, p 1, [front twist and back twist] twice, p 2, k 4, p 3, sl next 2 to cable needle and hold in back, k 1, p 1, k 1, from cable needle for diamond, p 3, k 4, p 2 (3-3), k 4, p 1 (2-4).

Row 2 and all even rows: K the k sts and p the p sts as they face you to last st, k 1.

Row 3: K 1, p 1, [back twist and front twist] twice, p 2, cable, p 2, right twist, p 1, left twist, p 2, cable, p 2 (3-3), cable, p 1 (2-4). Continue in pat as established to correspond to left front. Sleeves—With size 6 needles cast on 38 (40-42). K 1, p 1 in ribbing for 2 inches. Inc 6 (8-10) evenly spaced across last row. Change to size 9 needles. Start pat on 44 (48-52) sts.

Row 1 (right side): P 6 (6-8), k 4, p 2 (3-3), k 4, p 2 (3-3), [back twist and front twist] twice, [p 2 (3-3), k 4] twice, p 6 (6-8). Row 2: K the k sts and p the p sts. Row 3: P 6 (6-8), [cable, p 2 (3-3)] twice, [front twist and back twist] twice, [p 2 (3-3), cable] twice, p 6 (6-8). Row 4: Repeat row 2. Repeat these 4 rows for pat, working to 9 (10-11) inches or desired length from start to underarm; end on wrong side. Width is 8 (8¾-9½) inches.

Raglan Sleeve Cap—Bind off 2 sts at beg of next 2 rows. Dec 1 st each side on next row then every other row until 6 (8-10) rem. Sl to holder. Sew raglan seams, joining sleeves to back and fronts. Sew side and sleeve seams.

Neckband and Hood—On right side starting at right front edge, sl all sts from holders to size 6 needles: 68 (76-84) sts. P across. Dec to 67 (71-75) sts.

Row 1 (right side): K 1, * p 1, k 1; repeat from * across. Row 2: K 2, p 1, * k 1, p 1; repeat from * to last 2 sts, k 2. Row 3: Repeat row 1.

Eyelet Row—K 2, * k 2 tog, yo, p 1, k 1; repeat from * to last st, k 1. Rows 5, 6, and 7: Repeat rows 1, 2, and 1. Change to size 9 needles. Next row k 1, inc 13 (13-11) evenly spaced, p to last st, k 1. Start pat on the 80 (84-86) sts.

Row 1 (right side): K 1, p 1, [front twist and back twist] twice, p 2; repeat from * to * of row 1 of back, p 2 (3-3), k 4, p 10 (12-14), k 4, p 2 (3-3); repeat from * to * as before, p 2, [front twist and back twist] twice, p 1, k 1. Row 2: K 2, p the p sts and k the k sts, end k 2.

Row 3: K 1, p 1, [back twist and front twist] twice, p 2; repeat from * to * of row 3 of back, p 2 (3-3), cable, p 10 (12-14), cable, p 2 (3-3); repeat from * to * as before, p 2, [back twist and front twist] twice, p 1, k 1. Continue in pat as established until 2nd cable twist has been completed.

Work 40 (42-43); place marker on needle, work to end. Sl marker every row. Continue in pat, inc 1 st each side of marker on next row then every 4th row 4 times more, working added sts in reverse stockinette st. Work on the 90 (94-96) sts to 4½ (5-5) inches above ribbing, end on right side.

Dec row: K 2, p 8, k 2 tog, * p 2 tog twice, k 3, p 1, k 1, p 1, k 3, p 2 tog twice *, k 2 (3-3), p 2 tog twice, k 20 (22-24), p 2 tog twice, k 2 (3-3), repeat from * to *, k 2 tog, p 8, k 2: 14 decs, 76 (80-82) rem.

Work 10 and sl them to holder; bind off next 18 (19-19); work to last 28 (29-29); bind off next 18 (19-19); work to end and sl last 10 to holder. Break yarn. Join yarn and continue in reverse stockinette st on the 20 (22-24) sts to fit across bound-off sts. Bind off. Sew side edge to bound-off sts. Continue in pat on the 10 border sts to fit to center front, sl to holder. Work border on other side the same. Sew or weave sts tog at center front. Sew to edge of hood. With double strand crochet a 34-inch chain. Draw through eyelets. Trim with pompons. Insert zipper. Leggings (right leg)—With size 6 needles cast on 40 (42-44). K 1 and p 1 in ribbing for 3 inches, inc 20 (22-22) sts across last row. Change to size 9 needles. Work on 60 (64-66) sts: Row 1 (right side) —P 14 (14-15) [K 4, p 2 (3-3)] twice, [back twist and front twist] twice, [P 2 (3-3), k 4] twice, p 14 (14-15). Row 2: K the k sts and p the p sts.

Row 3: P 14 (14-15), [cable, p 2 (3-3)] twice, [front twist and back twist] twice, [p 2 (3-3), cable] twice, p 14 (14-15). Row 4: Repeat row 2. Repeat these 4 rows for pat, working to 5 inches from start, end on wrong side. Working added sts in reverse stockinette st, inc 1 each side on next row then every 6th row 8 (8-9) times more. Work on the 78 (82-86) sts to 13 (14-15) inches from start. Mark end of right side row for back edge and start of crotch.

Crotch—Dec 1 st each side every other row 4 times then every 6th row 3 times. Work on the 64 (68-72) sts to 7½ (8-8½) inches above crotch, end at back edge.

Short row 1: Work 32 (34-36), turn. Rows 2, 4, 6, and 8: Sl 1, work to back edge. Row 3: Work 28 (30-32), turn. Row 5: Work 24 (26-28), turn. Row 7: Work 20 (22-24), turn. Row 9: Work 16 (18-20), turn.

Row 10: Sl 1, work to back edge. Change to size 6 needles. K 1, p 1 in ribbing on the 64 (68-72) sts for 1 inch, end on right side. K next row for turn. K 1, p 1 in ribbing for 1 inch more. Bind off in ribbing. Left Leg—Work same as right leg to crotch. Mark beg of right side row for back edge and finish to correspond to right leg. Sew leg seams; sew back and front seams. Sew hem at waist leaving opening to insert elastic.

Caring for Knits

• All yarns are labeled with laundering recommendations—hand or machine-washing.

• For machine-washing, use mild soap or detergent. Machine-dry at regular setting. (Be sure garment is absolutely dry so that it returns to original size and shape.)

• For hand washing, use lukewarm water and mild soap or detergent. Rinse well. Squeeze excess water. Roll in Turkish towel, and squeeze again. Remove from towel, and lay flat until dry.

• To block a knit or crochet garment, pin it to the ironing board, wrong side up with rustproof pins, stretching to the desired measurements. Steam lightly —one way only—with moderately hot iron over a wet cloth, taking care not to let weight of iron rest in any one spot. Steam press seams. Leave garment pinned to board until it is dry.

• Do not steam block 100% acrylic yarns. First, pin garment to padded surface according to blocking measurements. Then, lay a damp cloth over the garment and allow it to dry.

Tots Knit Outfit

Spark up a youngster's enthusiasm for playing in the cold outdoors with this hand-knit outfit. The three-piece knit playsuit features a patriotic red, white, and blue color scheme —a checkered sweater and cap, and solid color pants.

Instructions are given for size 1, with changes for sizes 2, 3, and 4 in parentheses. pants are knit of heavier yarn than sweater and cap for added durability and warmth.

Materials
Sweater and cap
(Columbia-Minerva Nantuk Sports Yarn, 2-oz. pull-out skeins)
- 2 (3-3-3) white (A)
- 2 (2-2-2) navy (B)
- 2 (2-2-2) scarlet (C)
- Sizes 4 and 6 knitting needles

Gauge
13 sts = 2 inches, 13 rows = 2 inches

Pants
(Columbia-Minerva Nantuk 4-ply knitting yarn, 4-oz. pull-out skeins)
- 2 navy (B)
- Sizes 6 and 8 knitting needles

Gauge
9 sts = 2 inches, 6 rows = 1 inch

Directions
Pullover: Back—With size 4 needles and color A—cast on 64 (68-72-76), K 1, p 1 in ribbing for 2 inches, increasing 6 sts evenly spaced across last row. Change to size 6 needles. Work in pat on the 70 (74-78-82) sts. *Note:* When changing colors always pick up next color from under dropped color to prevent a hole.

Row 1: Right side. K 2 A, * k 2 B, 2 A, repeat from * across. Row 2: P with matching colors. Drop A. Row 3: K 2 B, * k 2 C, 2 B, repeat from * across. Row 4: P with matching colors. Repeat these 4 rows for pat working to 8 (8½-9-9½) inches from start, end on wrong side. Width is 11 (11½-12-12½) inches.

Raglan Armholes—Bind off 4 (4-5-5) at beg of next 2 rows. Dec 1 st each side on next row, then every other row until 38 (40-40-42) sts rem, end on right side.

Neck—Work 9 sts and sl them to a holder, work center 20 (22-22-24) and sl them to a second holder for neck, work to end. Dec 1 st at neck every other row 3 times and at the same time continue to dec at raglan until 2 sts rem. P 2 tog and fasten. Starting at opposite neck edge work other side the same.

Front—Work same as back.

Sleeves—With size 4 needles and color A —cast on 32 (34-38-40). K 1, p 1 in ribbing for 2 inches. Inc 14 (16-16-18) sts spaced evenly across last row. Change to size 6 needles. Work in pat on the 46 (50-54-58) sts same as on back to 8½ (9-9½-10) inches from start; end with same pat row as on back at underarm. Width is 7¼ (7¾-8¼-9) inches.

Raglan Sleeve Cap—Bind off 4 (4-5-5) at beg of next 2 rows. Dec 1 st each side on next 2 (2-2-4) rows, then every other row until 4 (6-6-6) rem. Sl sts to a holder. Leaving right back raglan open, sew raglan seams, joining sleeves to back and front.

Turtleneck—On right side starting at open raglan with size 4 needles and color A—pick up and k 76 (84-84-88) sts around neck, including holders. K 1, p 1 in ribbing for 3 inches. Change to size 6 needles. Continue in ribbing to 5 inches from start. Bind off loosely in ribbing. Sew open raglan, joining turtleneck and reversing seam for turn. Sew side and sleeve seams.

Stocking Cap: Small size (1 to 2) and medium (3 to 4). With size 4 needles and color A —cast on 72 (76). K 1, p 1 in ribbing for 2½ inches; inc 6 sts evenly spaced across last row. Change to size 6 needles. Work in pat on the 78 (82) sts as on pullover to 7 inches from start, end on wrong side with pat row 4.

Dec row: With color A only—K 5 (7), k 2 tog, * k 4, k 2 tog; repeat from * to last 5 (7) sts. K to end. P 1 row, k 1 row and p 1 row on the 66 (70) sts. Work in pat for 2 inches, end with row 4. Second dec row: With A only—K 2 (4), k 2 tog, * k 2, k 2 tog, repeat from * to last 2 (4) sts, k to end. P 1 row, k 1 row and p 1 row on 50 (54) sts. Work 2 inches in pat, end with row 4.

Third dec row: With color A only—K 1 (3), k 2 tog, * k 1, k 2 tog, repeat from * to last 2 (4) sts, k to end. P 1 row, k 1 row and p 1 row on the 34 (38) sts. Work 2 inches in pat, end with row 4. With A—K 2 tog across row. P the 17 (19) sts. Cut yarn leaving an end for sewing. With tapestry needle gather rem sts tog tightly, fasten securely, then sew back seam. Trim with tassel of color C.

Pants: Right leg—Starting at ankle, with size 6 needles and color B—cast on 36 (36-38-38). K 1 and p 1 in ribbing for 3 inches.

Inc: K 1 (1-2-2), inc 1 in next st, * k 1, inc 1 in next st, repeat from * across, end sizes 3 and 4 only k 1—18 inc's. Change to size 8 needles. Work on the 54 (54-56-56) sts. Starting with a p row, work in st st; inc 1 st each side every sixth row 5 (6-6-7) times. Work on the 64 (66-68-70) sts to 12 (13-14-15) inches from start. Mark end of k rows for back seam and for start of crotch.

Crotch—Dec 1 st each side every other row 3 times then every sixth row 3 times. Work on the 52 (54-56-58) sts to 7 (7½-8-8½) inches from start of crotch, end at back edge. Short row 1: P 26 (27-28-29), turn. Rows 2, 4, 6, and 8: Sl 1, k to end. Row 3: P 22 (23-24-25), turn. Row 5: P 18 (19-20-21), turn. Row 7: P 14 (15-16-17), turn. Row 9: P 10 (11-12-13), turn. Row 10: Sl 1, k to back edge. Change to size 6 needles. K 1, p 1 in ribbing on all 52 (54-56-58) sts for 1 inch, end on right side. K next row for turn. K 1, p 1 in ribbing for 1 inch more. Bind off.

Left leg—Work to correspond to right leg, marking beg of k rows for back seam and working short rows on k side. Sew leg seams to start of crotch. Sew marked back seam. Sew front seam. Turn in hem at waist, leaving ½-inch opening for elastic cut to fit.

Knitting Abbreviations

k	knit
p	purl
st(s)	stitch(es)
tog	together
pat	pattern
inc	increase
dec	decrease
beg	beginning
sp	space
rnd	round
yo	yarn over
rem	remaining
rep	repeat
sk	skip
st st	stockinette stitch
MC	main color
CC	contrasting color
sl st	slip stitch
psso	pass slip st over
dp	double-pointed

Basic Knitting Stitches

To cast on, make a slip knot around needle at a distance from yarn end that equals one inch for each stitch to be cast on.

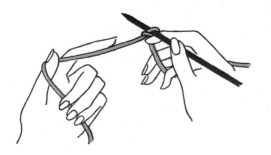

Hold needle that has slip knot in your right hand and make a loop of the short length of yarn around your left thumb.

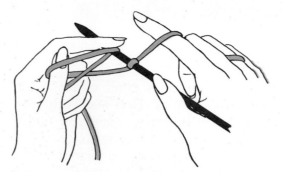

Insert point of needle in your right hand under loop on your left thumb. Loop yarn from ball over fingers of your right hand.

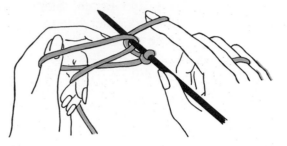

Wind yarn from ball under and over needle and draw it through loop, leaving the stitch on the needle.

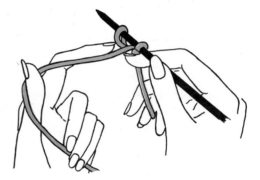

Tighten stitches on needle and bring yarn end around thumb so it is ready for next stitch. Repeat steps C through E until you have desired number of stitches. Switch needle with cast on stitches to left hand.

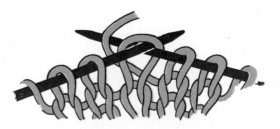

To make a knit stitch, hold needle with stitches in left hand and other needle in right hand. Insert right needle through stitch on left needle from front to back. Pass yarn around point of right needle to form loop.

122

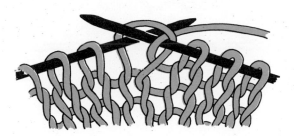

Pull this loop through the stitch on the left needle, and draw the loop onto the right needle.

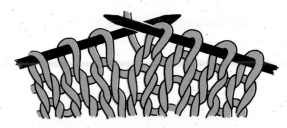

Now, slip the stitch completely off of the left needle. Repeat these steps until you have transferred all of the stitches from the left needle to the right needle. This completes one row of knitting. When you start working on the next row, move the needle holding the stitches to your left hand, and free the needle to your right hand.

To make a purl stitch, hold the needle with the stitches in your left hand and the other needle in your right hand. Insert the right needle through the stitch on the left needle from back to front. Wind the yarn around the point of the right needle to form a loop.

Draw a loop through the stitch on the needle in your left hand, and transfer it to the needle in your right hand.

Slip stitch completely off left needle. Repeat these steps until all loops on left needle have been transferred to right needle. This completes one row of purling. Switch needles and work next row.

In order to increase a stitch, knit or purl as usual, but do not slip it off the left needle. Instead, insert right needle into back of stitch and knit or purl into stitch a second time. Slip both onto right needle, resulting in two stitches.

To decrease, knit or purl two stitches together at the same time.

To slip a stitch, insert the right needle as if to purl (unless directions read to do it as if to knit). Then slip stitch onto right needle without working; be careful not to twist stitch.

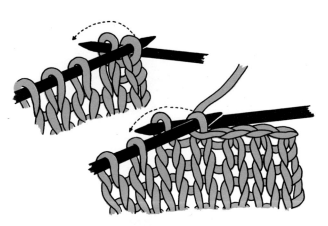

To bind off, work two stitches in pattern loosely. With left needle, lift first stitch over second stitch and off right needle. This binds off one stitch. Repeat this same technique for required number of stitches. If you are binding off an entire row, continue until one stitch remains; break yarn and draw end of yarn through the last stitch.

Crocheting

In this chapter you'll find something you will enjoy creating, whether you crochet for yourself or to surprise those you love with handcrafted gifts. The collection of crochet patterns that appear in the next 20 pages are geared to the average crocheter. Even the designs that appear complicated are a combination of the simplest basic crochet stitches.

Triangular Swedish Shawl

The shawl at the left is a replica of one that a young Swedish bride made for her trousseau when she came to this country 100 years ago. The adult version is worn by the great-granddaughter of the Swedish girl who crocheted the original wraparound shawl, and the child's shawl is worn by her great, great-granddaughter. The latter is of brown wool fabric with crewel embroidery; instructions are on pages 18-19.

Materials
(Coats & Clark's Red Heart Wintuk Sock and Sweater Yarn, 2 oz. skeins)
• 3 chestnut brown (No. 357)
• 1 red (No. 905)
• 1 gold (No. 602)
• 1 turquoise (No. 515)
• 1 amethyst (No. 588)
• Size 1 steel crochet hook

Gauge
8 sts = 1 inch, 7 rows = 2 inches

Blocking measurements
Length up center front (including edging) 21½ inches; length around entire outer edge 86 inches.

Directions
Foundation row (outer edge of shawl): Ch 674 with Br (brown) to measure 86 inches. Dc in third ch from hook and in each ch across—672 dc, counting ch at beg of row as 1 dc. Break off and fasten.

Note: Entire scarf is worked from right side. Do not turn and work back. All dc are worked through back loops of st on preceding rows.

Row 1: Skip first 332 dc (including ch at beg of row as 1 dc). Attach Br to back loop of next dc, sc in same st, dc in each of next 2 dc, 2 dc in next dc, ch 1 (center), 2 dc in next dc, dc in each of next 2 dc, sc in next dc. Break off and fasten.

Row 2: Working on foundation row, attach Br to back loop of third dc before beg of row 1, sc in same st, dc in next 2 dc on foundation row, dc in 5 st of row 1, 3 dc in ch 1, dc in 5 remaining st of row 1, dc in next 2 st of foundation row, sc in next st. (19 st in row). Break off and fasten.

Row 3: Attach Br to third dc before beg of row 2, sc in same st, dc in next 2 dc on foundation row, dc in each st before 3 dc

(continued)

center group. Dc in first dc of group, 2 dc in center st, ch 4, sc in second ch from hook, sc in each of next 2 ch, sc in top of last dc, dc in same center st of 3 dc group, dc in each st of row 2, dc in next 2 st of foundation row, sc in next st. Break off; fasten.

Row 4: Attach Br to third dc before beg of row 3, sc in same st, dc in next 2 st, dc in each st before ch 4, dc in next 2 ch, 2 dc in sc at end, ch 4, sc in second ch from hook, sc in next 2 ch, sc in top of last dc made, dc in same st with last 2 dc, dc in each st of row 3, dc in next 2 st of foundation row, sc in next st. Break off and fasten.

Row 5: Same as row 4. Row 6: Attach Br to twelfth st before beg of row 5, sc in same st, dc across row following directions for row 4, ending with dc in 11 st of foundation row, sc in next st. Break off and fasten. Rows 7, 8, 9: Same as row 6.

Row 10: Attach Br to sixty-seventh st before beg of row 9, sc in same st. Place strand of T (turquoise) along top of row 9. * With Br, working over T (so T is hidden), dc in next 11 st. With Br start a dc in next st, drawing Br through first two loops. Drop Br, pick up T and draw this through last two loops (color change made). With T, start a dc in next st, drawing T through first two loops. Drop T and draw Br through last two loops (another color change made). Repeat from * 11 more times.

Note: When two or more colors are being used in same row, carry colors not in use inside sts as described above, and always change color in last st of group.

With Br, working over T, dc in next 4 st, dc in 2 ch st, 2 dc in sc at end. Drop T and continue with Br only. Ch 8, sc in second ch, 6 sc in ch, sc in top of last dc. Again working over T, dc in same st with previous 2 dc, dc in next 3 sc, dc in next 3 dc, changing to T in last dc, T in next dc changing to Br. * 12 Br dc, changing to T in last st, T in next dc changing to Br. Repeat from * 10 more times, ending with Br 12 dc, sc in next dc. Break off and fasten.

Row 11: Attach Br to twelfth st before last row, sc in same st. Working over T, dc in next 11 st of foundation row and in sts of row 10, changing color in last Br st before first T st. * Make 2 T dc, 2 Br, 1 T,

8 Br. Repeat from * 10 more times; then 2 T, 2 Br, 1 T, 4 Br in next 4 dc with Br dc in next 6 ch, 2 dc in next sc, drop T and with Br only ch 8, sc in second ch from hook and in next 6 ch, sc in top of last dc made, dc in same sc as last 2 dc made. Working over T, dc in next 7 sc and following 3 dc, changing to T in last dc.

Always be careful to see that the same number of dc are on both sides of point and that pattern on return row is an exact reverse of first part of row.

Finish row with reverse of pattern ending with 11 dc on foundation row, sc in next dc. Break off both strands and fasten.

Row 12: Work same as row 11, changing to T in last Br dc. * Make 3 T, 1 Br, 2 T, 2 Br, 1 T, 4 Br; repeat from * 11 more times. With Br, dc in next 4 dc and next 6 ch, 2 dc in next sc, (dropping T) ch 4, sc in second ch from hook and in next 2 ch, sc in top of last dc made, (again over T) dc in same sc as last 2 dc, dc in next 7 sc, dc in next 8 dc, changing to T in last dc. Reverse pattern of first part of row and complete same as row 11.

Row 13: Same as row 11 to first T st. * Make 6 T, 1 Br, 3 T, 3 Br. Repeat from * 12 more times; dc in next 2 ch, 2 dc in next sc. With Br only, ch 4, sc in second ch from hook and in next 2 ch, sc in top of last dc made, dc in same sc as last 2 dc, (over T) dc in next 3 sc, dc in next 2 dc, changing to T in last dc. Reverse pattern and complete row as for row 11. Break off and fasten.

Row 14: Same as for row 11 to first T dc. * Make 3 T, 2 Br, 4 T, 4 Br. Repeat from * 12 more times. Place R (red) over top edge of last row, working over T and R, dc in next 2 dc, changing to R in last dc, 1 R dc changing to Br. With Br working over both colors, dc in next dc and in 2 ch, 2 dc in next sc. With Br only, ch 4, sc in second ch from hook and in next 2 ch, sc in top of last dc. Again over both colors, dc in same sc as last 2 dc, dc in next 3 sc, changing to R in last dc, R dc in next dc, changing to Br. Break off R and fasten. With Br over

T, make 6 dc. Reverse pattern and complete as for row 11.

Row 15: With Br only, work same as for row 11 to within a few sts of first R dc. Working over R and changing R in last Br dc before R, make 2 R, 2 Br, 1 R. With Br over R, dc in each st to point, 2 dc in point sc. With Br only, ch 4 and work point as before, dc over R in next 3 sc, changing to R. Make 1 R, 2 Br, 2 R. Break off R and fasten. With Br, dc in each remaining st on row 14 and in following 11 dc on foundation row, sc in next dc. Break off and fasten.

Row 16: Same as row 15, changing to R in last Br dc before R dc. Make 3 R, 1 Br, 2 R. Continue as for row 15, reversing pattern on other side of point.

Row 17: Attach Br to twelfth dc before last row, sc in same st, dc in next 11 dc. Working over A (amethyst), dc in first 5 sts of row 16, changing to A in last dc. * Make 1 A, 12 Br, repeat from * 18 more times. Break off A. With Br, working over R, dc to first R dc, changing to R in last dc. Make 6 R, 1 Br, 3 R, 1 Br, 1 R. With Br, work along point as in row 15 and reverse pattern through R design. Break off R and fasten. Working over A, continue along row reversing pattern. End with 11 dc in foundation row, sc in twelfth dc. Break off both colors and fasten.

Row 18: Attach Br to twelfth st before row 17, sc in same st. With Br, working over A, dc to first A st, changing to A in last st. * Make 2 A, 2 Br, 1 A, 8 Br; repeat from * 18 more times; break off A. With Br, working over R, dc to first R st, changing to R in last dc. Now working over both Br and G (gold), make 8 R dc, 2 G, 4 R, 1 Br, 1 R. With Br, work over R and G, making point as before and reversing pattern through R design. Break off R and G. With Br, working over A, reverse pattern of first part of row, completing row as before.

Row 19: Same as for row 18 to first A st. * Make 3 A, 1 Br, 2 A, 2 Br, 1 A, 4 Br. Repeat from * 18 more times. Break off A. With Br, working over R, dc to first R dc. With Br, working over R and G, dc in first R dc; then make 5 R, 2 G, 2 Br, 2 G, 6 R, 1 Br, 1 R. Make point as before and complete row reversing pattern as before.

Row 20: Work same as for row 18 to first A st. With A work each motif as for motifs in row 13. Break off A. With Br, working over R and G, work to first R st. Make Br dc over first R dc; then 4 R, 2 G, 2 Br, 2 G, 8 R, 1 Br, 1 R. With Br, work point as before and complete row reversing pattern as directed.

Row 21: Work same as for row 18 to first A st. With A work motifs as for row 14. Break off A. With Br over R and G, dc to first R dc. Make Br dc in first R dc, 5 R, 2 G, 4 R, 2 Br, 7 R, 1 Br, 1 R. With Br work along point as before, completing row by reversing pattern.

Row 22: With Br only work same as for row 18 to first R st. Make 9 R, 2 Br, 7 R, 2 Br, 5 R, 1 Br, 1 R. With Br, work point as before and complete row by reversing pattern.

Row 23: With Br only work as for row 18 to the ch-4 at point, dc in next 2 ch, 2 dc in next sc, ch 11, sc in second ch from hook and in next 9 ch, sc in top of last dc made, dc in same sc as last 2 dc made. Complete row to correspond with first part of row.

Row 24: Attach A to top of first dc of foundation row, ch 3; with A, working over G, dc in next 3 dc, changing to G in last dc. Work in pattern of 3 G, 4 A along entire row and along ch at point. Keeping in pattern, make 3 dc in sc at end of point and dc in each of next 10 sc, and complete row ending in last dc of foundation row, being careful to end with 4 A sts. (If necessary, inc 1 or 2 sts along foundation row). Break off and fasten.

Row 25: Attach Br to top of ch-3 at beg of last row, ch 3. Working over R, dc in next 5 dc, changing to R in last dc. * Make 1 R, 1 Br, 3 R, 1 Br, 1 R and 12 Br. Repeat from * across to last st before 3-dc group ending with any st of repeat. With Br 2 dc in next dc, dc in next dc, ch 4, sc in second ch from hook and in next 2 ch, sc in top of last dc made, dc in same st as last dc

(continued)

made, 2 dc in next dc. Complete row reversing opposite side.

Row 26: Skip first 19 sts at beg of last row, attach Br to next dc, sc in same st; working over R, dc in each dc to one st before first R dc, changing to R in last dc. * Make 4 R, 1 Br, 4 R, 10 Br. Repeat from * across to last dc before the ch-4 point, ending with any st of repeat. With R over Br, dc in last dc made before ch-4, dc in next 2 ch, 2 dc in next sc, with R only, ch 4, sc in second ch from hook and in next 2 ch, sc in top of last dc made; with R over Br, dc in same st as last 2 dc made, dc in next 3 sc. Complete row to correspond with first side, ending with sc in twentieth st from end of last row.

Row 27: Skip first 19 sts at beg of last row; attach Br to next dc, sc in same st; working over R, dc in each dc to one dc before next R dc. * Make 4 R, 1 Br, 1 R, 1 Br, 4 R, 8 Br. Repeat from * across to one st before ch-4 point ending with any st of repeat. With R over Br, dc in top of last dc made before ch-4, dc in next 2 ch; with Br make 2 dc in sc at point, ch 4, sc in second ch from hook and in next 2 ch, sc in top of last dc made, dc in same st as last 2 dc made; with R, dc in next 3 sc. Complete row to correspond with first part, ending as for last row.

Row 28: Skip first 19 sts at beg of last row, attach Br to next dc, sc in same st; working over R, dc in each dc to first R st; with Br dc in first R dc. * Make 4 R, 1 Br, 4 R, 10 Br. Repeat from * to one st before ch-4 point; with R, dc in top of last dc made before ch-4, dc in next 2 ch; with Br make 3 dc in next sc; with R, dc in next 3 sc. Complete row to correspond with first side, ending as before.

Row 29: Work same as last row to first R dc; with Br, dc in first R dc. * Make 1 R, 1 Br, 3 R, 1 Br, 1 R, 12 Br. Repeat from * across to one st before 3-dc group at point, ending with any st of repeat; with R, dc in next dc, 2 dc in next dc; with Br 3 dc in next dc; with R, 2 dc in next dc, dc in next dc. Complete row as before.

Row 30: Attach G to top of ch-3 at beg of foundation row; working over A, make 3 G dc over end of Br row, 4 A in each dc of Br row. Keeping in pattern of 3 G, 4 A, dc in each st to the 3 R — 3 Br — 3 R center sts at point. Still continuing pattern, dc in next dc, 2 dc in next dc four times along point. Continue in pattern to end of row, trying to end with 3 G dc over end of Br row. Sl st to top of last st of foundation row. Break off and fasten.

Row 31: Attach Br to base of ch st at beg of foundation row. With Br only, dc in st where G is attached, dc in next dc, 2 dc in next dc, three times around end; dc in each dc for entire row, increasing 5 dc evenly spaced along point, ending in last 6 sts with 2 dc, dc, three times. Join to base of last st of foundation row with sl st. Break off and fasten.

Edging — Rnd 1: Attach A to first dc on last row, ch 3. Working over R and G, dc in same st, changing to G. * 1 G dc in next st, changing to A, 2 A in next dc, changing to R, 1 R dc in next dc, changing to A, 2 A dc in next dc, changing to G. Repeat from * once. * Working dc in each st, make 1 G, 2 A, 1 R, 2 A. Repeat from * across last row, increasing 3 dc evenly spaced along point and 4 sts along other end of scarf. Working along starting chain, continue in pattern along neck edge, ending with a R dc (if necessary, inc near end of rnd to complete pattern). Join to top of ch-3 at beg of rnd. Rnd 2: Attach R to first R dc, ch 3, dc in next dc, sc in next 2 dc, * dc in next 4 dc, sc in next 2 dc. Repeat from * around, ending with dc in last 2 dc. (If necessary, inc at center of 4-dc group three times around point and around ends of scarf.) Join to top of ch-3. Break off and fasten.

Tie string (Make two) — For each string, cut 2 strands of each color 45 inches long. Twist all strands together tightly in one direction; fold in half and twist in opposite direction. Tie a knot at loose ends about ½ inch from end. Trim evenly to form tassel. Tack one tie to center of each end of scarf.

To block: Steam lightly, but *do not press*.

Mandarin Slipover

Three harmonious vivid colors interspersed with neutral white are combined in a striking manner in this drop-shoulder, short-sleeved pullover. Except for hugging the hips, this striped, crocheted sweater has a free and easy swing to it. And the boat neckline that is a natural foil for exposing the shirt collar underneath is an old-time favorite in the world of fashion.

With a design influenced by the Oriental-look, this casual style slipover is equally effective worn over a turtleneck slipover, or worn simply with a scarf that matches one of the yarn colors. It will be a handsome addition to the wardrobe of anyone who appreciates handmade garments with classic good looks.

Instructions are given for size 6-8 (small), with changes for sizes 10-12 (medium), and 14 (large) in parentheses.

Materials

(Columbia-Minerva Nantuk Sweater & Afghan Yarn, 2 oz. pull skeins)
- 2 (2-3) color A
- 1 (1-2) color B
- 1 (1-2) color C
- 1 (1-2) color D
- Size H crochet hook

Gauge

8 sc and 7 ch-1 spaces = 4 inches, 7 rows = 2 inches.

Directions

Back—With color A-ch 54 (58-62). Row 1: 1 sc in 2nd ch from hook, * ch 1, skip 1 ch, 1 sc in next ch, repeat from * across, ch 1, turn: 27 (29-31) sc and 26 (28-30) ch-1 spaces.

Row 2: 1 sc in next sc, * ch 1, 1 sc in next sc, repeat from * across, change to color B, ch 1, turn. Repeat row 2 for pat, working * (2 rows each of B and A) twice, (2 rows each of C, D, C, and A) twice, repeat from * for stripe pat, working to 11 inches from the start. Place a marker at each side for the start of the armholes. Work pat to 8 (8½-8½) inches above the markers.

Shoulders—Work 8 (8-9) pats, ch 1, turn. Work 1 more row, fasten off. Skip the center 11 (13-13) sc on the last long row, join in the next space, and work to the end of the row. Ch 1, turn and work 1 more row. Fasten off.

Front—Work the same as for the back. Seam the shoulders.

Sleeves—Join color C on right side at armhole marker and work 35 (37-37) sc and 34 (36-36) ch-1 spaces to other marker, ch 1, turn. Work in pat for 1 more row of C, then 2 rows each of D, C, A, C, D, C, A, (B and A) twice. Fasten off. Sew the side and sleeve seams.

Sunny Yellow Pullover

A crocheted sweater in sunny yellow is a natural as a topper for this flower-sprigged shirt-waist dress. The yarn is easy to work with, soft and fluffy, and the crochet pattern has a slightly open weave appearance that almost resembles fine lace.

Worn with a turtleneck slipover and a pair of tailored slacks, or over a classic shirt and a flared or pleated skirt, this sweater will appeal to everyone. Also, it has an air of understated elegance when it is teamed with a long, flowing evening skirt and a casually draped neck scarf.

This sweater will be a favorite, regardless of whether you wear it at a vacation spot, at the office, or at school.

Directions are given for small (8-10), with changes for medium (12-14) in parentheses.

Materials
(Unger's Fluffy, 1¾ oz. balls)
- 7 (8)
- Sizes E, F, and G aluminum crochet hooks

Gauge
G hook; 2 patterns = 1 inch

Directions
Back—With size E hook, ch 69 (73). Row 1: Dc in 4th ch from hook, * dc in next ch; repeat from * — 67 (71) dc. Ch 1, turn.

Row 2: Dc in first st, * back post around the next st (back post—yo hook, insert the hook in the space before the next st, bring the hook across the front of the st and out in the next space from front to back, draw up a loop, work off as a dc), dc in next st; repeat from * across. Ch 1, turn.

Row 3: Dc in the first st, * front post around next post st (front post—yo hook, insert the hook in the next space before st from front to back, bring hook across the back of the st and out in the next space from back to front, draw up a loop and work off as a dc), dc in the next st; repeat from * across. Repeat rows 2 and 3 alternately for 5 inches, ending with row 3.

Work 1 row of sc, increasing at even intervals to 72 (76) sts. Ch 2, turn. Change to size G hook and pattern.

Row 1: Draw up a loop in the 2nd ch, retain it on hook, skip the first st, draw up a loop in the next st, yo draw through 3 loops on hook, ch 1, * draw up a loop in the last st worked in, retain on hook, skip 1 st, draw up a loop in the next st, yo draw through 3 loops on hook, ch 1 (1 pattern); repeat from * across — 36 (38) patterns. Ch 2 on turn (1 ch of pattern plus 1 extra ch).

Row 2: Draw up a loop in the 2nd ch, retain on hook, draw up a loop in the first st, yo draw through the 3 loops on the hook, ch 1, * draw up a loop in the last st worked, retain on the hook, skip 1 st, draw up a loop in the next st, yo draw through 3 loops on hook, ch 1; repeat from * — 36 (38) patterns. Ch 2, turn (1 ch of pattern plus 1 extra ch). Repeat row 2 for pattern. Work even until piece measures 14 inches from beg.

Shape armholes—Slip st loosely across 4 patterns, work to within 4 patterns from end—28 (30) patterns. Work even until armhole measures 7¼ (7¾) inches.

Shape shoulders—Next row: Slip st loosely across 4 patterns, work to within 4 patterns from end. Next row: Slip st across 4 (5) patterns, work to within 4 (5) patterns from end—12 patterns. Fasten off.

Front—Work same as for back until 13 inches from beg, or 1 inch less than back to underarm—36 (38) patterns.

Left side—Work 15 (16) patterns. Ch 2, turn. Work on these sts only. At neck edge, dec 1 pattern on 6th and 7th row 3 times (to dec 1 pattern—on 6th row work to within 2 patterns from front edge, do not go back in last st worked, work a sc in next st of pattern, work last pattern. Ch 2, turn. On next row, skip over the sc of previous row).

At the same time, when the front measures the same length as the back to the underarm, at the arm edge, leave off 4 patterns—8 (9) patterns. Work to shoulder same as you did for the back.

Shape shoulder—At the arm edge leave off 4 patterns once, 4 (5) patterns once. Right side: Go back to the last full row. Leave out the center 6 patterns for the neck, attach yarn and work to correspond to the left side, reversing the shaping.

Sleeves—With E crochet hook, ch 47 (49). Row 1: Dc in 4th ch from hook, dc in each ch—45 (47) dc. Ch 1, turn. Work rib the same as for the lower back border for 2 inches, ending with row 3. Work 1 row of sc, increasing at even intervals to 56 (60) sts.

Change to size G hook and pattern. Work even on 28 (30) patterns 7½ inches above the border. Fasten off.

Front band—Make 2. With size E hook, ch 9. Row 1: Dc in 4th ch from hook, dc in each ch—7 dc. Ch 1, turn. Work in rib pattern the same as for the border for 6 (6½) inches. Fasten off.

Finishing—Sew the shoulder seams. With E crochet hook and the right side facing, work 1 row of slip st along each side of the neck, being careful not to draw it in. Sew each front band to each side of the neck and to 3 patterns at lower edge of neck opening.

Collar—With the wrong side facing and size E hook, work 63 (67) dc around the neck (this includes a 7 st border at each side of the neck). Work the pattern as for the lower border (make sure the right side of the pattern is on the inside so the collar can turn back). Work 1 row with size E hook, then change to size F hook. Work even until 7 rows of the pattern have been worked. Fasten off.

With size E hook, work 1 row of slip st along each side of the neck (this includes the collar edges). Sew the straight edge of the sleeve to the straight edge of the armhole. Sew the side edge of the sleeve to each 4 pattern armhole bind-off. Sew the side and under-sleeve seams.

Do not block or press. Wet block (Wet the garment with cold water; lay it out on a towel on a flat surface to measurements away from heat and let dry).

Crocheting Tips

• Gauge: At the beginning of each garment there is a gauge that specifies how many stitches per inch you should have with a certain size hook. To check your gauge, work a sample swatch about 3 inches square with the hook and yarn recommended. Block it, then measure the piece to see if the rows and stitches correspond to the required gauge in the instructions. If they do not, use a larger or smaller hook to compensate.

• Measuring work: Spread your garment on a flat surface without stretching it. Measure down the center. When you are measuring the length to the underarm, or the sleeve length, always place a marker, such as a safety pin or piece of colored thread, in the center of the row so that the measuring from that point will be accurate.

Multicolor Patchwork Topper

Patchwork is in vogue, not only for heirloom quilts and comforters, but also for ready-to-wear clothing.

Here's a version that's bound to perk up the spirits of any young teen-ager who has been featuring the popular blue jeans look most recently.

If you're already a crochet or knitting enthusiast, you probably have stored away many small amounts of left-over yarn from other needlecraft projects that will work well in this colorful topper.

Instructions are given for size 8-10 (small), 12-14 (medium), and 16-18 (large).

Materials

(Bernat Berella Germantown, 2 oz. balls)
- 2 main color (MC)
- 1 color A
- 1 color B
- 1 color C
- 1 color D
- 1 color E
- 1 color F
- Size F crochet hook (for small size)
- Size G crochet hook (for medium size)
- Size H crochet hook (for large size)

Gauge

4 sc on size F hook = 1 inch, 7 sc on size g hook = 2 inches, and 3 sc on size G hook = 1 inch.

Directions

Note: All sizes are made with the same number of sts, using the hook suggested for the correct gauge.

Squares: Make 14 color A; 12 color B; 13 color C; 10 color D; 15 color E; 12 color F.

Using color being worked, ch 9. Row 1: 1 sc second ch from hook, 1 sc in each remaining st of ch, ch 1, turn — 8 sc. Row 2: 1 sc in each st, ch 1, turn. Repeat row 2 six times more — 8 rows. Fasten off. Edging — Join M C and work 1 sc in each st and 1 sc, ch 1, 1 sc in each corner st, join. Fasten off.

Finishing — Using M C and always working in back loop only, work as follows: Body — Row 1: With right side facing you and alternating colors, sew 12 squares tog to form a tube. Row 2: Changing placement of colors, repeat row 1. Sew rows 1 and 2 tog to form body of sweater. Yoke back — Row 1: Changing placement of colors, sew 5 squares tog. Row 2: Repeat row 1. Sew rows 1 and 2 tog to form yoke.

Yoke front — Changing placement of colors, work in same manner as yoke back. To join: Back — Holding 5 squares of yoke back over 5 squares of body, sew tog. Front — Skip next square of body and sew 5 squares of yoke front over 5 squares of body in same manner as for back. Fold skipped squres in half to form sides of body.

Shape shoulders — With right side facing you and alternating colors, sew 2 squares tog to form strip. Sew one end of strip to first square of yoke back and other end of strip to fifth square of yoke front to form shoulder. Join 2 squares tog to form strip for other shoulder in same manner and sew in place to body for other shoulder.

Sleeves — Row 1: Alternating colors, sew 7 tog to form a tube. Row 2: Changing placement of colors, repeat row 1. Sew rows 1 and 2 tog to form sleeve. Folding fourth square of sleeve in half and holding fold of sleeve over fold of body, sew in place. Form other sleeve in same manner and sew in place.

Ribbing — Using M C, ch 15. Row 1: 1 sc in second ch from hook, 1 sc in each remaining st of ch, ch 1, turn — 14 sts. Row 2: Working in back loop only, 1 sc in each st, ch 1, turn. Repeat row 2 for ribbing until 78 rows of sc have been completed — 39 ridges. Fasten off. Sew ends tog to form a tube. Sew one edge of tube to lower edge of sweater. Using M C, work 1 row sc around neck and sleeve edges. Fasten off. Steam lightly.

Rugged and Right for Action

This oversize bulky, handmade sweater will make a youngster the envy of his or her buddies. The crocheted design pullover sports an exaggerated turtleneck collar, raglan sleeves, and wavy horizontal stripes.

With this rugged sweater and a pair of matching slacks or skirt, your mod youngster will be ready for every action-packed activity. It will be a knockout at sports events, in the classroom, and it will even fill the bill for dressier occasions.

Even though the crochet pattern that is featured in this sweater looks intricate, it's only an easy-to-master combination of single and double crochet stitches.

Instructions are given for size 6-8 (small), with sizes 10-12 (medium), and 14-16 (large) in parentheses.

Materials

(Columbia-Minerva Nantuk Sweater and Afghan yarn, 2 oz. pull skeins)
- 2 (3-3) dark brown (A)
- 3 (4-4) beige (B)
- 1 (2-2) medium brown (C)
- Size G crochet hook

Gauge

7 sts = 2 inches; 8 rows = 3 inches.

Directions

Pattern stitch—Multiple of 4 ch plus 1. Ch indicated number of sts. Row 1: 1 sc in 2nd ch from hook, 1 sc in next ch, 1 dc in each of next 2 ch, * 1 sc in each of next 2 ch, 1 dc in each of next 2 ch, repeat from * across, ch 1, turn.

Row 2: * 1 sc in each of next 2 dc, 1 dc in each of next 2 sc, repeat from * across, ch 1, turn. Repeat row 2 for pat, working in stripes of 2 rows each of colors A, B, C and B, always working off last st of 2nd row of each stripe with next color.

Back—With color A, ch 49 (57-65). With 48 (56-64) sts across, work in pat for 11 (13-15) inches or desired length from start to underarm. Width is 14 (16-18) inches.

Raglan Armholes—Sl st across 2 (3-3) sts, ch 1, work to last 2 (3-3), ch 1, turn.

Dec Row: Draw up a loop in each of first 2, yo and through all 3 loops for a dec, work to last 2, dec 1 as before, ch 1, turn. Careful to keep in pat, repeat dec each side every row 6 (8-10) times then every other row 7 times. Fasten off, leaving 16 (18-22) sts for back of neck.

Front—Work same as back until 26 (28-32) sts rem, end with a dec row.

Neck—Work 10 sts, ch 1, turn. Dec 1 at neck every other row 3 times and at the same time continue to dec at raglan every other row until 2 sts rem. Dec on the 2 sts, fasten off. Leaving 6 (8-12) sts free on last long row, join and work other side.

Sleeves—With color A, ch 27 (29-33). Starting in 2nd ch from hook, work 1 sc in each ch, ch 1, turn. Rows 2 through 7: 1 sc in each of the 26 (28-32) sc, ch 1, turn. Work 1 more row, inc 2 (4-4) sc across, ch 1, turn: 28 (32-36) sc.

Pat Row 1: With A, * 1 sc in each of next 2 sc, 1 dc in each of next 2 sc, repeat from * across, ch 1, turn. Continue in stripe pat, working to 5 inches from start. With care to keep pat, inc by working 2 sts in 1 st each side on next row then every 4th row 4 times more, working added sts in pat. Work on the 38 (42-46) sts to about 13 (14½-16) inches from start, end with same color row as on back at underarm. Width is 11 (12-13) inches.

Raglan Sleeve Cap—Sl st across 2 (3-3) sts, ch 1, work to last 2 (3-3), ch 1, turn. Dec 1 each side every row 7 (7-9) times then every other row until 6 rem. Fasten off. Sew raglan seams, joining sleeves to back and front. Sew side and sleeve seams, matching stripes.

Turtleneck—On wrong side, with color A, starting at back raglan seam, crochet 64 (68-76) sc around neck. With 1 sc in each sc, work rather loosely around to 6 (6½-7) inches from start. Sl st in next st. Fasten off.

Multicolor Bag and Belt

You only need to know how to make a chain and do the simple single crochet stitch to create this handsome bag and belt set. The riotous rainbow of jewel-tone colors gives this matching set of fashion accessories a spark of individuality.

This pair will team up with clothing of every color, and will be suitable worn with both casual and dressy clothes.

The bag measures 8½x10 inches. Instructions for the belt are given for small (22-23-inch waist), with changes for medium (24-25½-inch), and large (27-29-inch).

Materials
(Coats & Clark's Red Heart knitting worsted, 4 ply "Tangle-Proof" Pull-Out Skeins)
• 2 (3,3) ounces sea tones (No. 432)
• 1 (2,2) ounces deep rose (No. 759)
• 1 ounce amethyst (No. 588)
• 1 ounce deep turquoise (No. 514)
• 1 ounce cantaloupe (No. 434)
• 1 ounce dark gold (No. 602)
• 1 7-inch skirt or neck zipper
• Size H and K crochet hooks
• 1 9x10½-inch piece of lining material, if desired
• 4 button molds, ¾-inch in diameter

Gauge
4 sc = 1 inch, 9 rnds = 2 inches

Directions
Bag: Lower Section — Starting at side edge with sea tones and size H hook, ch 49 to measure 13 inches. Row 1 (right side): Sc in 2nd ch from hook, sc in each remaining ch — 48 sc. Break off and fasten. Turn. Row 2: Attach amethyst to last sc made, sc in same sc where yarn was attached and in each sc across — 48 sc. Ch 1, turn.

Row 3: Sc in each sc across. Ch 1, turn. Row 4: Repeat row 3. Break off and fasten. Turn. Row 5: Using turquoise instead of amethyst, work same as for row 2. Break off and fasten. Turn. Rows 6 and 7: Using deep rose instead of amethyst, work same as for rows 2 and 3. Break off and fasten.

Rows 8 through 10: Using sea tones, work same as for rows 2, 3, and 4. Break off and fasten. Turn. Row 11: Using cantaloupe, work same as for row 2. Break off and fasten. Turn. Continuing in this manner, crochet 1 row dark gold, 1 row amethyst, 3 rows deep rose, 2 rows turquoise, 3 rows sea tones, 2 rows amethyst, 1 row cantaloupe, 1 row sea tones, 3 rows deep rose, 2 rows cantaloupe, 1 row sea tones, 2 rows turquoise, 1 row amethyst, 2 rows dark gold and 1 row sea tones. There are 37 rows in all.

Upper Back Section — With right side facing and size H hook, attach sea tones to first sc on first row of lower section. Row 1: Working along ends of rows, sc in same place where yarn was attached, sc in end st of each of next 3 rows, * skip next row; sc in end st of each of next 6 rows. Repeat from * across, ending with skip next row, sc in end st of each of last 4 rows — 32 sc. Ch 1, turn.

Row 2: Sc in each sc across — 32 sc. Ch 1, turn. Row 3: Repeat last row. Break off and fasten. Turn. Working same as for lower section, crochet 1 row amethyst, 2 rows turquoise, 1 row sea tones, 1 row dark gold, 2 rows cantaloupe, 1 row amethyst, 3 rows deep rose, 1 row turquoise, 3 rows sea tones. There are 18 rows in all.

Upper Front Section — Working along the opposite ends of the rows on the lower section and arranging the colors differently, if desired, work to correspond with the upper back section. If lining is desired, turn back a ¼-inch hem all around the outer edges of the lining material and stitch it to the wrong side of the crocheted piece.

Finishing — Fold the bag in half crosswise, matching the top rows of the upper sections. With sea tones, sew the side seams. Sew the zipper inside the top opening, ¼ inch below the top edges.

Cord — Using 4 strands of sea tones held together and a size K hook, make a chain 42 inches long. Break off and fasten. Starting at the lower edge and holding the wrong side of the chain up, sew the first 10 inches of the chain along one side seam; starting with the opposite end of the chain, sew end 10 inches along the other side seam in the same way; the remainder of the chain forms the shoulder strap.

Bottom Tassels — Holding one strand of each of the 6 colors together, wind the yarn 3 times around a 6-inch square of cardboard. Cut at one edge, thus making 12-inch strands. Hold all of the strands together and double these strands to form a loop. Insert a large hook from back to front through sts at one corner of lower edge of bag and draw the loop of strands through. Draw the loose ends through the loop and pull tightly to form a knot. Make a tassel in the same way on the opposite corner. Trim evenly.

Zipper Tassel — Cut 3 strands of sea tones and one strand each of the 5 other colors, each 10 inches long. With a separate strand, tie strands together at center and fold in half. Starting ½ inch below tied end, wind a 24-inch strand of sea tones (or any color) several times around tassel, covering a 1-inch area, and tie ends together. Trim evenly and tack tassel to zipper.

Belt: Starting at one long edge with sea tones and size H hook, ch 91 (101-115) to measure 23 (25½-29) inches. Having 90 (100-114) sc on each row, work same as for lower section of bag until 20 rows in all have been made. Ch 1, turn.

Edging — With the right side facing and sea tones, make 2 sc in the first sc, sc in each sc across to the last sc, 2 sc in the last sc, along the short edge make 20 sc to the next corner; working along the opposite side of the starting chain, make 2 sc in the next ch, sc in each ch to the next corner, 2 sc on the corner st, make 20 sc along the next short edge. Join with a sl st to the first sc of this rnd. Ch 1, turn.

Button-loop row — Skip joining, sc in the next sc, * ch 4 for the button-loop, skip the next 3 sc, sc in each of the next 3 sc. Repeat from * 2 more times, ch 4, skip 3 sc, sc in the next sc — 4 button-loops in all. Break off yarn and fasten.

Block to measure 5x23 (25½-29) inches, excluding button-loops.

Button (Make 4) — Starting at center with sea tones and size H hook, ch 4. Join with a sl st to form a ring. Rnd 1: 6 sc in ring. Do not join. Rnd 2: 2 sc in each of 6 sc. Rnd 3: Sc in each of 12 sc. Rnd 4: Slip mold inside crocheted piece, * draw up a loop in each of next 2 sc, yarn over hook and draw through all 3 loops on the hook. Repeat from * around. Leaving an 8-inch length of yarn, break off. Using end of yarn, sew sts of last rnd together.

Sew the four buttons to the short edge of the belt opposite the button-loops.

Gauge
4 sts = 1 inch; 9 rows = 2 inches.

Directions

Hat: Ch 37 sts. Row 1: 1 sc in 2nd ch from hook, 1 sc in each remaining st of ch, ch 1, turn, 36 sts. Row 2: 1 sc in each sc, ch 1, turn. Repeat row 2 73 times more. Fasten off. Seam first and last rows to form a tube.

Finishing—Run yarn through one end of tube and pull up tightly to form top of hat. Turn back lower edge to form desired width cuff. Work 1 row sc around lower edge. Fasten off.

Pompon—Cut a 3-inch-wide piece of cardboard. Wind yarn around cardboard 40 times. Slip yarn off cardboard and tie tightly in the center. Cut the loops at each end and shake the yarn vigorously. Trim the ends. Sew to top of hat.

Mittens: Palm—Make 2. Ch 29 sts. Row 1: 1 sc in 2nd ch from hook, 1 sc in each remaining st of ch, ch 1, turn, 28 sc. Row 2: 2 sc in first st (inc), 1 sc in each remaining st, ch 1, turn. Put a marker in work to mark wrist edge. Row 3: 1 sc in each st, ch 1, turn. Repeat rows 2 and 3 three times more, 32 sts. Row 9: 1 sc in each st, ch 1, turn. Row 10: Skip first st (dec) 1 sc in each of next 21 sts, ch 20 for thumb, 1 sc in each of last 10 sts, ch 1, turn.

Row 11: 1 sc in each of first 10 sts, 1 sc in each st of ch for thumb, 1 sc in each of last 21 sts, ch 1, turn, 51 sts. Rows 12, 14, and 16: Skip first st, 1 sc in each remaining st, ch 1, turn. Rows 13 and 15: 1 sc in each st, ch 1, turn. Row 17: 1 sc in each of first 10 sts, skip 20 sts for thumb, 1 sc in each of last 18 sts. Fasten off.

Back—Make 2. Work in same manner as palm until 9 rows have been completed. Row 10: Skip first st (dec), 1 sc in each remaining st, ch 1, turn, 31 sts. Repeat rows 9 and 10 three times more, 28 sts. Row 17: 1 sc in each st. Fasten off.

Finishing—With right side of back touching right side of palm and being sure that thumb is in correct place, sew seams. Sew thumb in same manner. Steam lightly, using a warm setting on your iron.

Cold Weather Twosome

At first glance, you might think the youngster above is overcome with shyness. But, covering his face with his hands is simply a deliberate move to show off his matching crocheted cap and mittens.

This matching set is suitable for both boys and girls and the stretchability of the yarn allows a child to wear it several seasons. The brim of the hat can be rolled down to protect ears from icy blasts.

As an extra safety precaution, always use bold, vivid colors so that your child is easily visible to motorists when crossing streets.

Materials
(Bernat Berella Germantown, 2 oz. balls)
• 4
• Size G crochet hook

Striped Cap and Scarf

This duo is ideal for winter sports, for when you are shuttling children to school activities or waiting on a windy corner.

The head size fits teen-agers and adults, and the scarf can be as long as you wish.

Materials

(Bernat Berella, 4 oz. balls)
- 2 color A
- 1 color B
- 1 color C
- Size F crochet hook

Gauge

4 sc = 1 inch

Directions

Hat: Striping pattern for cuff, 10 rows color A, 2 rows color B, 2 rows color C, 3 rows color A. Striping pattern for top, * 2 rows color B, 2 rows color C, 2 rows color A, repeat from *.

Cuff—Using color A, ch 85 sts. Row 1: 1 sc in 2nd ch from hook, 1 sc in each remaining st of ch, ch 1, turn—84 sts. Row 2: Working in back loop only and working in striping pattern for cuff, 1 sc in each sc, ch 1, turn. Continue to work in this manner until striping pattern for cuff has been completed. Working in striping pattern for top of hat, work even in sc until piece measures 7 inches.

Shape top—Continuing to work in striping pattern for top, work as follows: Row 1 (dec row): * 1 sc in each of next 12 sts, draw up a loop in each of next 2 sts, yo and draw through 3 loops on hook (dec), repeat from * across row—6 sts dec. Work even in pattern st on 78 sts for 4 rows. Row 6 (2nd dec row): * 1 sc in each of next 11 sts, dec 1 st, repeat from * across row— 6 sts dec.

Work even in pattern st on 72 sts for 3 rows. Row 10 (3rd dec row): * 1 sc in each of next 10 sts, dec 1 st, repeat from * across row—6 sts dec. Work even in pattern st on 66 sts for 1 row. Continue in this manner to dec 6 sts every other row, having 1 st less between decs, until 30 sts remain. Fasten off. Sew seam. Turn up cuff. Steam lightly.

Scarf: Striping pattern for scarf, * 2 rows color A, 2 rows color B, 2 rows color C, 4 rows color A, 4 rows color B, 4 rows color C **, 12 rows color A, repeat from ** to * once for striping pattern for scarf.

Using color A, ch 257 sts. Row 1: 1 sc in 2nd ch from hook, 1 sc in each remaining st of ch—256 sts. Row 2: Working in back loop only and working in striping pattern for scarf, 1 sc in each sc, ch 1, turn. Repeat row 2 until striping pattern for scarf has been completed. Fasten off.

Finishing—Cut strands of yarn 8 inches long. Knot 3 strands in every other row across each short end of scarf. Trim the ends of the strands evenly. Steam lightly.

Helmet and Mittens

When it comes time for winter sports, what could be more welcome than a head-hugging helmet with ear flaps and a pair of matching mittens, made up in the neutral tones that are shown here.

This set will be equally fashionable for skiing, snowmobiling, cheering at football games, or for a career girl to wear to work.

Instructions are given for just one size, which will fit both teen-agers and adults.

Materials
(Bernat Berella Germantown, 2 oz. balls or Bernat Sesame, 2 oz. pull pouches)
• 3 main color (M C)
• 2 contrasting color (C C)
• Size F crochet hook
• 1 button

Gauge
4 sc = 1 inch

Directions
Note 1: When changing colors, always draw new color through 2 loops of last stitch. *Note 2:* Do not join rounds. *Note 3:* To make a long dc, work 1 dc in sc in round below ch 1 space of previous round.

Helmet: Using M C, ch 4, join with a sl st to form a ring. Work 2 sc in each st of ch — 8 sts. Work 2 sc in each st until there are 24 sts in round. Put a marker in work to mark beg of rounds (center back) and carry marker up.

Round 1: * Ch 1, skip 1 st, 1 sc in next st, repeat from * around — 12 ch 1 spaces. Drop M C. Round 2: Using C C, * 1 long dc in next st, 2 sc in next st (inc), repeat from * around — 12 long dc's. Drop C C. Round 3: Using M C, 1 sc in each st around — 36 sts. Round 4: * 1 sc in each of next 2 sts, 2 sc in next st (inc), repeat from * around. Round 5: Repeat round 1 — 24 ch 1 spaces.

Drop M C. Round 6: Using C C, * 1 long dc in next st, 2 sc in next st (inc), 1 long dc in next st, 1 sc in next st, repeat from * around — 24 long dc's. Drop C C. Round 7: Using M C, repeat round 3 — 60 sts. Round 8: Repeat round 4 having 4 sc between inc sts. Round 9: Repeat round 1. Drop M C. Round 10: Using C C, * (1 long dc in next st, 1 sc in next st) twice, 1 long dc in next st, 2 sc in next st (inc), repeat from * around — 36 long dc's. Drop C C.

Rounds 11 through 17: Using M C, repeat round 3 — 84 sts. Round 18: Repeat round 1. Drop M C. Round 19: Using C C, repeat round 6, omitting incs — 42 long dc's. Drop C C. Round 20: Using M C, 1 sc in each st around. Drop M C. Round 21: Using C C, repeat round 1. Drop C C.

Round 22: Using M C, * 1 long dc in next st, 1 sc in next st, repeat from * around. Drop M C. Round 23: Using C C, repeat round 3. Drop C C. Round 24: Using M C, repeat round 1. Drop M C. Round 25: Using C C, * 1 long dc in next st, 1 sc in next st, repeat from * around. Drop C C. Round 26: Using M C, repeat round 3—84 sts. Drop M C.

Round 27: Using C C, repeat round 1. Drop C C. Round 28: Using M C, repeat between *'s of round 25—42 long dc's. Drop M C. Round 29: Using C C, repeat round 3. Drop C C. Round 30: Using M C, repeat round 1. Drop M C. Round 31: Using C C, repeat round 19. Drop C C. Round 32: Using M C, 1 sc in each st around, join with a sl st to first st of round—84 sts. Fasten off.

Left Earlap—Using M C and with right side facing you, join yarn in 26th st from marker for center back and work 1 sc in each of 20 sts. Row 1: Turn, skip first st (dec), 1 sc in each st to last st (dec)—18 sts. Continue to dec 1 st each end of earlap every row until 4 sts remain. Fasten off.

Right Earlap—Using M C and with right side facing you, join M C in 6th st from marker for center back and work to correspond to left earlap, but do not fasten off.

Chin Strap—Turn, 1 sc in each st—4 sts. Continue to work 4 sts in this manner until 20 rows have been completed. On the last row, ch 6 sts at end of row, join to other end of same row to form buttonloop. Fasten off.

Finishing: Using C C and with right side facing you, starting at marker for center back, join yarn and working in sc, work 1 sc in each st around helmet, working 6 sc in buttonloop. Fasten off. Sew on button. Steam lightly.

Mittens: Using M C and starting at fingertips, ch 4, join with a sl st to form a ring. Work 2 sc in each st of ch and in each sc until there are 28 sts in round. Put a marker in work to mark beg of rounds and carry marker up.

Round 1: * Ch 1, skip 1 st, 1 sc in next st, repeat from * around—14 ch 1 spaces. Drop M C. Round 2: Using C C, * 1 long dc in next st, 1 sc in next st, repeat from * around—14 long dc's. Drop C C. Rounds 3 and 4: Using M C, 1 sc in each st around —28 sts. Round 5: Using M C, repeat between *'s of round 1. Drop M C.

Round 6: Using C C, * 1 long dc in next st, 1 sc in next st, repeat from * around— 14 long dc's. Drop C C. Rounds 7 through 13: Using M C, 1 sc in each st around. Round 14: Using M C, repeat between *'s of round 1. Drop M C. Round 15: Using C C, repeat round 6. Drop C C. Round 16: Using M C, 1 sc in each st around. Drop M C. Round 17: Using C C, repeat between *'s of round 1. Drop C C.

Round 18: Using M C, repeat between *'s of round 6. Drop M C. Round 19: Using C C, repeat round 16. Drop C C. Round 20: Using M C, ch 5, skip 5 sts (thumb opening), 1 sc in next st, * ch 1, skip next st, 1 sc in next st, repeat from * around. Drop M C. Round 21: Using C C, 1 sc in each of 5 sts of ch, * 1 long dc in next st, 1 sc in next st, repeat from * around. Drop C C. Round 22: Using M C, 1 sc in each st. Drop M C.

Round 23: Using C C, repeat between *'s of round 1. Drop C C. Round 24: Using M C, repeat between *'s of round 6. Drop M C. Round 25: Using C C, repeat round 16. Drop C C. Round 26: Using M C, repeat between *'s of round 1. Drop M C. Round 27: Using C C, repeat between *'s of round 6. Drop C C. Round 28: Using M C, 1 sc in each st around, join to first st with sl st. Fasten off.

Thumb—Using M C, join yarn in any st at thumb opening and work 1 sc in each st around—11 sts. Working round and round, work 1 sc in each st until 11 rounds or desired length has been completed. Fasten off, leaving a 6 inch end. Weave end through top of last row. Draw up tightly.

Cuff—Using M C, join yarn in any st at wrist with a sl st, ch 15. Row 1: 1 sc in 2nd st of ch from hook, 1 sc in each remaining st of ch, sl st in each of next 2 sts at wrist, turn—14 sts. Row 2: Working in back loop only, 1 sc in each st, ch 1, turn. Row 3: Working in back loop only, 1 sc in each st, sl st in each of next 2 sts at wrist, turn. Repeat rows 2 and 3 until cuff has been worked around wrist opening, sl st last row to first row. Fasten off.

Crocheted Pillows Add Beauty and Comfort

Among decorative accessories that you can crochet for your home, pillows rate very high. The two shown here have unusual textures—one looks like popcorn effect, the other shell. Fluffy tassels at the four corners add a finished look.

These pillows will accent the decor in your living room, family room, or bedroom and will make handsome gifts.

The finished size for each pillow is approximately 14x14 inches square.

Materials

(Bernat Berella Germantown, 2 oz. balls)
- 6 (for pillow at top)
- 4 (for pillow at lower right)
- Size G crochet hook
- 14x14-inch pillow forms

Gauge

1 bobble and 2 dc = 1 inch for pillow at top; 4 shells = 6 inches for pillow at lower right.

Directions

Pillow (at top in photo): Make 2 pieces alike (back and front—Ch 57 sts. Row 1: 1 dc in fourth ch from hook, 1 dc in each of next 3 sts, * 5 dc in next st, remove hook from st, insert hook in back loop of first st and draw loop of last st through loop on hook (back loop bobble), 1 dc in each of next 5 sts, repeat from *, ending back loop bobble in next st, 1 dc in last st—9 bobbles.

Row 2: Ch 3, turn, working in back loop only, 1 dc in st of bobble, 1 dc in each of next 2 dc, * 5 dc in next dc, remove hook from st, insert hook in front loop of first st, and draw loop of last st through loop on hook (front loop bobble), 1 dc in each of next 2 dc. 1 dc in st of bobble, 1 dc in each of next 2 dc, repeat from *, ending front loop bobble in next st, 1 dc in next dc, 1 dc in turning ch—9 bobbles. (Bobbles will be on right side).

Row 3: Ch 3, turn, working in back loop only, 1 dc in next dc, 1 dc in st of bobble, 1 dc in each of next 2 dc, * back loop bobble in next dc, 1 dc in each of next 2 dc, 1 dc in st of bobble, 1 dc in each of next 2 dc, repeat from *, ending back loop bobble in next st, 1 dc in turning ch—9 bobbles. Repeat rows 2 and 3 twelve times more. Fasten off.

Finishing—Steam pieces lightly. With right sides touching, sew 3 sides tog. Turn right side out, then insert pillow form and sew fourth side tog.

Tassel—Make 4. Cut a piece of cardboard to measure 4 inches. Wind yarn around cardboard 40 times; tie together at one end; slip off cardboard and wind yarn around loops ¾ inch from top and tie. Cut bottom edge. Trim evenly. Sew one tassel to each corner of pillow.

Pillow (at lower right in photo): Make 2 pieces alike (back and front)—Ch 58 sts. Row 1: 2 dc in fourth ch from hook (half shell), * skip 2 sts, 1 sc in next st, skip 2 sts, 5 dc in next st (shell), repeat from *, ending 3 dc instead of 5 dc in last st (half shell)—8 shells and 2 half shells. Row 2: Ch 1, turn, working in back loop only, * 1 shell in next sc, 1 sc in center st of next shell, repeat from *, ending 1 sc in turning ch—9 shells.

Row 3: Ch 3, turn, working in back loop only, 2 dc in first sc, * 1 sc in center of next shell, 1 shell in next sc, repeat from *, ending 3 dc in turning ch—8 shells and 2 half shells. Repeat rows 2 and 3 only 13 more times. Then repeat row 2 once more. Fasten off.

Finishing—Steam pieces lightly. With right sides touching, sew 3 sides tog. Turn right side out, then insert pillow form and sew fourth side tog.

Tassel—Make 4. Cut a piece of cardboard to measure 4 inches. Wind yarn around cardboard 40 times; tie together at one end; slip off cardboard and wind yarn around loops ¾ inch from top and tie. Cut bottom edge. Trim evenly. Sew one tassel to each corner.

Americana Afghan or Coverlet

This design, steeped in the tradition of historical rooms and four-poster elegance, has been faithfully reproduced so that its beauty may live on in the homes of today.

The pattern can be crocheted as an afghan, or as a cover for a twin bed or double bed. The directions that follow are given first for a 48x62-inch afghan, not including fringe. Then, inside the parentheses, are the size changes for a medium-size coverlet for a twin bed (66x102 inches), not including fringe, and for a large size coverlet for a double bed (76x102 inches), not including fringe. Both coverlets have been fringed all the way around so they will look attractive used with a dust ruffle.

Materials
(Bernat Berella, 4 oz. balls)
• 18 (21-27)
• Size G crochet hook

Gauge
4 dc = 1 inch

Note: Entire afghan is worked in back loop only.

Directions
Pattern stitch for shell — Row 1: 1 dc in 4th ch from hook, 1 dc in same st, skip next 2 sts, 1 sc in next st, skip next 2 sts, * 5 dc in next st (shell), skip next 2 sts, 1 sc in next st, skip next 2 sts, repeat from * across row, ending 3 dc in last st (half shell) — 29 (40-45) shells and 2 half shells.

Row 2: Ch 1, turn, working in back loop only, 1 shell in next sc, * 1 sc in 3rd dc of next shell, 1 shell in next sc, repeat from *, ending 1 sc in top of turning ch — 30 (41-46) shells. Row 3: Ch 3, turn, 2 dc in first st, * 1 sc in 3rd dc of next shell, 1 shell in next

sc, repeat from *, ending 3 dc in top of turning ch — 29 (40-45) shells and 2 half shells. (Always count ch 3 as first dc). Repeat rows 2 and 3 for pattern stitch.

Pattern stitch for dc — Row 1: Ch 3, turn, working in back loop only, 1 dc in each st across row — 181 (247-277) sts. Repeat row 1 for pattern stitch.

Pattern stitch for bobble — Row 1: Ch 3, turn, working in back loop only, 1 dc in each of next 4 dc, * 5 dc in next st, remove hook from st, insert hook in back loop of first st of 5 dc just made and draw loop of last st through loop on hook (back loop bobble), 1 dc in each of next 5 dc, repeat from *, ending back loop bobble in next st, 1 dc in turning ch — 30 (41-46) bobbles.

Row 2: Ch 3, turn, 1 dc in each of next 3 sts, * 5 dc in next st, remove hook from st, insert hook in front loop of first st of 5 dc just made and draw loop of last st through loop on hook (front loop bobble), 1 dc in each of next 5 sts, repeat from *, ending front loop bobble in next st, 1 dc in next st, 1 dc in turning ch. Bobbles will be on right side.

Repeat rows 1 and 2 for pattern st. Ch 184 (250-280) sts. Work in pattern st as follows: 8 rows shell pattern. 8 rows dc pattern. 8 rows bobble pattern. 8 rows dc pattern.

Repeat these 32 rows 3 times more for small size afghan only. Do not fasten off. For medium and large size coverlets only, repeat these 32 rows 4 times more, ending 8 rows shell pattern, 9 rows dc pattern. Do not fasten off.

Edging — For all sizes: With right side facing you, * 5 dc in turning ch of next row (shell), 1 sc in last st of next row, skip 1 row, repeat from * to first corner, working 1 shell in corner st. Work same edging on remaining lower and side edges. Fasten off.

Fringe — Cut strands of yarn 10 inches long, knot 10 strands in space between 2nd and 3rd st of shell st on 3 sides of afghan. Trim ends. Steam lightly.

Crocheted Rug Stems From Shaker Design

The crocheted rug above is an adaptation of a Shaker style, although it is done in contemporary colors, instead of the muted tones that were popular in the Shaker communities.

The overall size of this rug is about 60 x 100 inches, making it an ideal choice for a family room or informal living room. You crochet it with 12 pleasing colors of rug yarn. The stitches are simple, and you will enjoy creating this handmade rug.

Materials
(Rayon and cotton rug yarn, 70-yard skeins)
- 18 white
- 9 turquoise icing
- 9 peacock
- 9 sea blue
- 9 light jade
- 6 light yellow

146

- 6 light avocado
- 6 black
- 6 chartreuse
- 6 evergreen
- 6 antique gold
- 6 wood brown
- Large tapestry needle
- ⅝-inch wood or plastic crochet hook

Note: Use three strands of each color throughout entire rug.

Directions

Center: Using sea blue, ch 5, sl st to make ring. Row 1: Ch 3, dc 11 over ring, sl st into 3rd ch, break off. Row 2: Turquoise ice: sl st, ch 2, dc same st, 2 dc into next 7 sts; light jade: tie in back of last st, 2 dc next 4 sts, sl st 2nd ch, end. Row 3: White: sl st, ch 2, dc 1st st, dc, (2 dc next st, dc) around, sl st in 2nd ch, end.

Row 4: Light yellow: back 2 sts, sl st, ch 2, dc same st, dc, (2 dc, dc 2 across) 6; antique gold: tie on, (2 dc, dc 2) 5, sl st 2nd ch, end. Row 5: Light avocado: skip 6 sts, sl st, ch 2, dc same st, dc 3, (2 dc, dc 3) 5; chartreuse: tie on, (2 dc, dc 3) 6, sl st 2nd ch, end. Row 6: Peacock: skip 4 sts, sl st, ch 2, dc same st, dc 4, (2 dc, dc 4) 7; turquoise ice: (2 dc, dc 4) 4, sl st 2nd ch, end.

Row 7: Sea blue: back 14 sts, sl st, ch 2, dc same st, dc 5, (2 dc, dc 5) 8; evergreen: (2 dc, dc 5) 3. Row 8: White: sl st, ch 2, dc same st, dc 6, (2 dc, dc 6) around, sl st 2nd ch, end. Row 9: Peacock: back 8 sts, sl st, ch 2, dc same st, dc 7, (2 dc, dc 7) 3; light jade: (2 dc, dc 7) 8, sl st 2nd ch, end.

Row 10: Black: skip 15 sts, sl st, ch 2, dc same st, dc 8, (2 dc, dc 8) 4; wood brown: (2 dc, dc 8) 7, sl st, end. Row 11: White: sl st, ch 2, dc same st, dc 9, (2 dc, dc 9) around, sl st, end. Row 12: Antique gold: skip 4 sts, sl st, ch 2, dc same st, dc 10, (2 dc, dc 10) 6; light yellow: (2 dc, dc 10) 5, sl st, end.

Row 13: Light jade: back 2 sts, sl st, ch 2, dc same st, dc 11, (2 dc, dc 11) 4; light avocado: (2 dc, dc 11) 7, sl st, end. Row 14: Turquoise ice: skip 16 sts, sl st, ch 2, dc same st, dc 12 (2 dc, dc 12) 7; peacock: (2 dc, dc 12) 4, sl st, end.

Row 15: White: sl st, ch 2, dc same st, dc 13, (2 dc, dc 13) around, sl st, end. First side. Row 16: Chartreuse: sl st 2 sts, sc 2 sts, ½ dc, 2 dc next st, dc 9 across. (2 dc next st, dc 14 across) 2; light yellow: 2 dc, dc 14, 2 dc, dc 9, ½ dc, sc 2, sl st 2, end. Row 17: Sea blue: skip 6 sts at beginning of row 16, sl st, sc 2, ½ dc, dc, 2 dc, dc 14, 2 dc, dc 7; light avocado: dc 7, 2 dc, dc 14, 2 dc, dc 13, 2 dc, dc, ½ dc, sc 2, sl st, end.

Row 18: White: skip 5 sts, sl st, sc, ½ dc, dc 2, (2 dc, dc 14) 3, 2 dc, dc 8, 2 dc, dc 2, ½ dc, sc, sl st, end.

Row 19: Turquoise ice: skip 4 sts, sl st, sc, ½ dc, dc 2, (2 dc, dc 14) 2; peacock: 2 dc, dc 14, 2 dc, dc 5, 2 dc, dc 2, ½ dc, sc, sl st, end.

Row 20: Light jade: skip 3 sts, sl st, sc, ½ dc, dc 2, 2 dc, dc 10, 2 dc, dc 12; sea blue: (2 dc, dc 12) 2, 2 dc, dc 2, ½ dc, sc, sl st. Row 21: Wood brown: skip 3 sts, sl st, sc, ½ dc, dc 2, 2 dc, dc 9, (2 dc, dc 12) 2; black: 2 dc, dc 12, 2 dc, dc 2, ½ dc, sc, sl st, end.

Row 22: Light avocado: skip 3 sts, sl st, sc, ½ dc, dc 2, 2 dc, dc 8, 2 dc, dc 12; turquoise ice: (2 dc, dc 12) 2, 2 dc, dc 2, ½ dc, sc, sl st, end. Row 23: White: skip 2 sts, sl st, sc, ½ dc, dc 2, 2 dc, dc 15, 2 dc, dc 16, 2 dc, dc 15, 2 dc, dc 2, ½ dc, sc, sl st, end.

Row 24: Light yellow: skip 2 sts, sl st, sc, ½ dc, dc 2, 2 dc, dc 15, 2 dc, dc 16; antique gold: 2 dc, dc 15, 2 dc, dc 2, ½ dc, sc, sl st, end. Row 25: Sea blue: skip 2 sts, sl st, sc, ½ dc, dc 2, 2 dc, dc 15, 2 dc, dc 8; peacock: dc 8, 2 dc, dc 15, 2 dc, dc 2, ½ dc, sc, sl st.

Row 26: White: repeat row 23. Second side. Row 16: Light yellow: skip 14 sts, sl st 2, sc 2, ½ dc, dc 2, (2 dc, dc 14) 2; antique gold: 2 dc, dc 14, 2 dc, dc 2,

(continued)

½ dc, sc 2, sl st 2, end. Row 17: Chartreuse: skip 6 sts, sl st, sc 2, ½ dc, dc, 2 dc, dc 14; sea blue: (2 dc, dc 14) 2, 2 dc, dc 13, 2 dc, dc, ½ dc, sc 2, sl st, end.

Row 18: Same as for first side. Row 19: Peacock: skip 4 sts, sl st, sc, ½ dc, dc 2, (2 dc, dc 14) 2; light jade: 2 dc, dc 14, 2 dc, dc 5, 2 dc, dc 2, ½ dc, sc, sl st, end. Row 20: Turquoise ice: skip 3 sts, sl st, sc, ½ dc, dc 2, 2 dc, dc 10, (2 dc, dc 12) 3, 2 dc, dc 2, ½ dc, sc, sl st, end.

Row 21: Evergreen: skip 3 sts, sl st, sc, ½ dc, dc 2, 2 dc, dc 9, 2 dc, dc 12, 2 dc, dc 6; black: dc 6, 2 dc, dc 12, 2 dc, dc 2, ½ dc, sc, sl st, end. Row 22: Light avocado: skip 3 sts, sl st, sc, ½ dc, dc 2, 2 dc, dc 8, (2 dc, dc 12) 2; chartreuse: 2 dc, dc 12, 2 dc, dc 2, ½ dc, sc, sl st, end.

Row 23: Same as for first side. Row 24: Chartreuse: skip 2 sts, sl st, sc, ½ dc, dc 2, 2 dc, dc 14; light yellow: 2 dc, dc 16, 2 dc, dc 15, 2 dc, dc 2, ½ dc, sc, sl st, end. Row 25: Sea blue: skip 2 sts, sl st, sc, ½ dc, dc 2, 2 dc, dc 15, 2 dc, dc 16; peacock: 2 dc, dc 15, 2 dc, dc 2, ½ dc, sc, sl st, end.

Row 26: Same as first side. Corners (first side, right corner). Row 27: Turquoise ice: skip 2 sts, sl st, sc, ½ dc, dc 2, 2 dc, dc 10, ½ dc 2, sc 2, sl st 2, end. Row 28: Black: skip 2 sts, sl st, sc, ½ dc, dc, 2 dc, dc 6, ½ dc 2, sc 2, sl st, end. Row 29: Peacock: skip 2 sts, sl st, sc ½ dc, 3 dc, 2 dc, dc 2, ½ dc, sc 2, sl st, end.

First side, left corner. Row 27: Turquoise ice: skip 16 sts, sl st 2, sc 2, ½ dc 2, dc 10, 2 dc, dc 2, ½ dc, sc, sl st, end. Row 28: Evergreen: skip 5 sts, sl st, sc 2, ½ dc 2, dc 6, 2 dc, dc, ½ dc, sc, sl st, end. Row 29: Sea blue: skip 4 sts, sl st, sc 2, ½ dc, dc 2, 2 dc, 3 dc, ½ dc, sc, sl st, end.

Second side, right corner. Row 27: Turquoise ice. Row 28: Evergreen. Row 29: Light jade.

Second side, left corner. Row 27: Turquoise ice. Row 28: Black. Row 29: Sea blue.

Border—Begin in 2nd of 3 dc in right corner of first side. Row 1: Light yellow: sl st, ch 2, 4 dc in corner st, dc across to next corner, 5 dc corner, dc 19 across; chartreuse: dc 52 across; antique gold: dc to corner, 5 dc in corner, dc 16; light yellow: dc to corner, 5 dc, dc 10; chartreuse: dc 60; antique gold: dc to end, sl st to join in 2nd ch, end.

Row 2: Light avocado: skip 1 st, sl st, ch 2, 4 dc in corner st, dc 17; chartreuse: dc to corner; light jade: 5 dc in corner, dc 32; turquoise ice: dc 13; light avocado: dc to corner; light jade: 5 dc corner, dc 33, light avocado: dc to corner; turquoise ice: 5 dc corner, dc 38; light jade: dc 17; turquoise ice: dc 23; light avocado: dc to end, sl st, end.

Row 3: White: dc around with 5 dc in each corner. Row 4: Peacock: skip 1 st, sl st, ch 2, 4 dc in corner st, dc 45; sea blue: dc to corner, 5 dc in corner st, dc 32; peacock: dc 32; turquoise ice: dc to corner; sea blue: 5 dc in corner, dc to next corner, 5 dc in corner, dc 27; peacock: dc 46; light jade: dc to end, sl st, end.

Row 5: Turquoise ice: skip 1 st, sl st, ch 2, 4 dc in corner st, dc 35; light jade: dc to corner; peacock: 5 dc corner, dc 17; turquoise ice: dc 25; sea blue: dc 32; peacock: dc to corner, 5 dc in corner, dc to next corner; light jade: 5 dc corner, dc 18; light avocado: dc 27; sea blue: dc 49; turquoise ice: dc to end, sl st, end.

Row 6: Evergreen: skip 1 st, sl st, ch 2, 4 dc in corner st, dc 14; black: dc to corner, 5 dc corner, dc 10; wood brown: dc 43; evergreen: dc to corner; black: 5 dc to corner, dc 25; wood brown: dc 21; evergreen: dc to corner, 5 dc corner, dc 35; wood brown: dc 14; black: dc 42; evergreen: dc to end, sl st, end. Weave in ends with tapestry needle; trim. Block with steam iron. Do not press.

Crocheted Shag Rug

Handmade rugs are noted for their durability, and this one is machine-washable and dryable. With just one simple double-looped stitch you form both the pile and the backing. The finished size is approximately 38 x 54 inches.

Materials
(Rayon and Cotton rug yarn, 70-yard skeins)
- 14 dark orange
- 9 dark pink
- 8 red
- 5 dark red
- 3 gold
- 3 orange
- 3 light pink
- Size K aluminum crochet hook
- Large tapestry needle

Gauge
8 sts = 5 inches; 5 rows = 3 inches. Loops: 1¾-2 inches long.

Directions
Using one strand each of red and dark red, loosely ch 67 (ch should measure about 40 inches). Beginning in second ch from hook, work loop st into ch (66 st across). End off. Following color chart from bottom, work rug.

Weave ends from joinings and color changes into back of rug. Weave loose ends at sides of rug into their row and pull taut before trimming. When washing rug, remove from dryer before dry and position on floor to dry.

Loop stitch: Using two strands throughout, sl st in upper loop of first st of previous row. Ch 1, * insert hook into upper loop of first st, pull yarn up about 3 inches with index finger of left hand, catch all 4 strands with hook and pull through, then pull yarn through two loops (6 strands on hook). Slip loop from finger. * Repeat from * to * across. Break off at end.

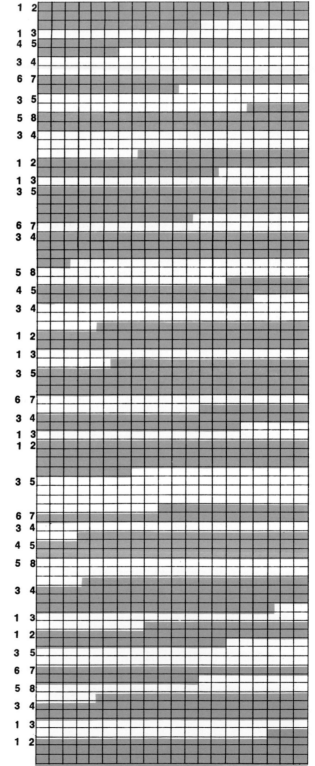

149

Basic Crochet Stitches

Start by making a slip knot on crochet hook about 6 inches from end of yarn. Pull one end of yarn to tighten knot.

Hold the hook between right index finger and thumb, as you would a pencil. Wrap yarn over ring finger, under middle finger and over index finger, holding short end between thumb and index finger. If you need more tension, wrap yarn around little finger. Insert hook under and over strand of yarn.

Make the foundation chain by catching strand with hook and drawing it through loop. Make the chain as long as pattern calls for.

Single crochet: Insert the hook into the second chain from the hook, under two upper strands of yarn.

Draw up a loop.

Draw yarn over hook.

Pull yarn through the two loops, completing single crochet stitch. Insert hook into next stitch, and repeat from steps.

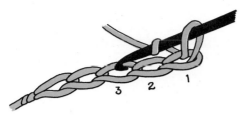

Half double crochet: With yarn over hook, insert hook into third chain, under the two upper strands of yarn.

Draw up a loop.

Draw yarn over hook.

Pull through the 3 loops, completing the half double crochet.

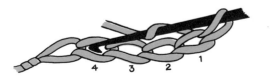

Double crochet: Holding yarn over hook, insert hook into fourth chain, under the two upper strands of yarn.

Draw up a loop.

Wrap yarn over hook.

Draw yarn through two loops.

Yarn over again and through last two loops on hook. This completes double crochet.

Slip stitch: After you've made the foundation chain, insert the crochet hook under the top strand of the second chain from the hook, and yarn over. With a single motion, pull the yarn through the stitch and loop on the hook. Insert the hook under the top strand of the next chain, then yarn over and draw the yarn through the stitch and the loop on the hook. Repeat this procedure to the end of the chain.

Hooking and Weaving

This chapter salutes the ancient arts of hooking and weaving with a parade of projects using materials, techniques, and designs right in step with today. You'll find traditional and contemporary ways of rug making, new approaches to weaving off the loom, on a box, or on furniture, and a new version of perhaps the oldest weaving technique, warp wrapping.

Hooked Wool Rug

Make your mark with a manhole cover by turning a rubbing into a rug. Here's a cover that moved into the house from the highway. Duplicate this design or get yourself a crayon and set out to find and copy one of your own. Either way, the results will be impressive.

Materials
- 3-, 4-, or 5-mesh-to-the-inch penelope rug canvas in sufficient quantity to make a 68-inch circle
- Olive green rug yarn (for quantities of yarn, see the directions below)
- Gold rug yarn
- Rust rug yarn
- Brown rug yarn
- White rug yarn
- Latch hook
- Waterproof felt-tip pens
- Heavy paper or brown wrapping paper
- Carpet thread or dental floss
- Rug binding (optional)

Directions
If a single piece of rug canvas large enough for a 68-inch circle is not available, join smaller sections together with carpet thread or dental floss. Make sure the warp and weft threads of the pieces run the same direction. (The warp threads are those parallel to the selvage.) Cut off the selvages, overlap the pieces an inch or two, and whip stitch them together. Cover the raw edges of the canvas with masking tape.

Following the directions on page 31, enlarge the central rug motif on heavy paper. Add a band 10 inches wide, 2 bands each 1½ inches wide, and a final band 3 inches wide to get a full-size pattern. (You may find it helpful to color the central motif and keep the pattern near you as you work.)

Lay the pattern on the floor with the canvas over it so the design is visible through the holes. Tape both pattern and canvas securely, and copy the design onto the canvas with waterproof pens. (Using different colored pens for different parts of the design will make working the rug easier.)

(continued)

1 Square = 2 Inches

Color Key
A. White   C. Rust
B. Gold   D. Green
            E. Brown

Latch the central motif first, working from left to right (for right-handers) and row by row, changing colors where indicated. Then, work the 10-inch band in brown, the first narrow band in rust, and the second in gold. Work the outermost band in green.

To hem, turn under the remaining canvas and sew it to the back of the rug with carpet thread or dental floss. Add rug binding, if you like. Coat the underside of the rug with liquid latex to make it skidproof.

You can also make this rug with a punch needle and a heavy burlap or Monk's cloth backing. Mark a 64-inch circle on a 68-inch square of backing, but don't cut it out. Stay stitch the edges of the fabric. Transfer the design to the backing with dressmaker's carbon and then draw over the outlines with waterproof pens. Stretch the canvas on a frame, making sure grain lines are straight.

Thread the needle and practice making loops in the margin until you find a satisfactory loop size and density. Then, work from the top to the bottom, rolling the finished portion out of the way as you progress. When hooking the center, outline the small shapes first, fill them, and then hook the background.

Either leave the yarn loops uncut or cut and trim them. (The central motif would look nice beveled slightly at the edges.) After hooking and hemming, you must coat the back of the rug with latex to keep the yarn from pulling out and to make the rug skidproof.

How to Buy Rug Yarn

• To work a square inch of canvas with precut yarn (2½ inches long), you'll need 9 pieces of yarn for 3-mesh-to-the-inch canvas, 16 pieces for 4-mesh-to-the-inch canvas, and 25 pieces for 5-mesh-to-the-inch canvas.

• Salespeople in rug supply shops usually know the yardage in skeins of rug yarn and can help you estimate how much yarn you'll need.

• Buy yarns in the same dye lots to avoid unsightly color variations.

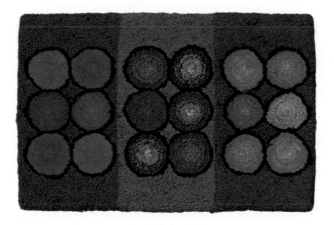

Hooked Rag Rug

This accent rug, even though its design is contemporary, lends itself to the old-fashioned technique of hooking rugs. This method, handed down from generation to generation, involves using old garments and blankets cut into narrow strips rather than yarn. Instead of an automatic hook, use a crochet-type hook with a wooden handle.

Rugs hooked from recycled fabrics were extremely popular in early America. The colonists' ingenuity in the face of scarcity resulted in folk art creations with lasting appeal. Colonial hooked rugs often had floral or pictorial designs and plain, scalloped, or scrolled borders. Your rugs can have any of these designs or some of your own creation.

Materials
- 36x54-inch piece of heavy burlap
- Rug hook
- Rug frame
- Carpet thread or thumbtacks (for attaching burlap to frame)
- Wool fabric or old garments or blankets to cut into strips for hooking
- Rug binding
- Rug sizing to coat back of rug
- Felt-tip marking pens

Directions

Lay burlap on a smooth work surface and, with felt-tip marking pen and yardstick, draw 30x48-inch outline for rug. Sew rug binding along outline, then cut burlap flush with outer edge of binding.

Next, draw three lines on the 48-inch length 16 inches apart. Divide each 16x30-inch segment in half lengthwise and crosswise. Using the intersection of these two lines as a guide, draw six 6-inch diameter circles (this leaves a 2-inch space at the sides of each segment and a 6-inch space at top and bottom.

Attach burlap to frame with thumbtacks or by lacing with carpet thread. Use a standing rug frame or improvise one with 1x3-inch boards held at right angles with C clamps.

Before cutting, wash all fabric (even wool), to clean and shrink it. Bleach or dye any pieces that need it, being sure to consider original color of fabric when overdyeing.

Cut fabric along grain into strips between ¼ and ½ inch wide. Width depends on weight and texture of fabric; generally, the more loosely woven the fabric, the wider the strips.

For hooking, use a large-tipped, crochet-like hook with a wooden handle. Begin by holding hook in your palm and your fingers on the shank, much as you'd hold a fork when cutting. With other hand, hold a fabric strip under frame. Insert hook from front, through space between threads in burlap. Catch strip with hook and pull end of it to face of rug. Move hook two to four spaces away and reinsert it. Catch strip with end of hook and pull up a loop. Continue, using your left hand to guide strip beneath frame.

Practice making loops to find right height and density before starting rug. Generally, loops should be about as high as they are wide (a ¼-inch-high loop for a ¼-inch-wide strip). Pack loops closely enough so that burlap is not visible between the loops.

Outline each circle with one row of black, then fill in the circles with shades of red, blue, green, and orange. Work all of the circular motifs first, then fill in the background, using a single shade of brown or rust in each of the three areas.

Remove the rug from the frame, fold under the rug binding and overcast, and coat the back of the rug with sizing.

156

Rya Rug of String and Twine

If you're hooked on rugs, latch onto some line and do your thing with string. The rug opposite shows that even the simple string can be beautiful when hooked into a deep-pile rya rug. This swirling design combines a variety of string, jute, sisal, and twine in pleasing natural colors. The strands range from plump to slender. The effect is stunning and the feel surprisingly soft.

As you hook this contemporary design, you will be continuing the centuries-old tradition of creating fine handmade rugs. In Scandinavia, the rya rug has been a popular art form since Viking days. There, craftsmen weave rugs on handlooms instead of hooking them, but the results are much the same.

String code
1. #12 natural jute
2. #28 dark brown jute
3. White polished cotton
4. Fine sisal
5. Medium brown warp or package string
6. White cable cord or seine twine
7. White nylon seine twine

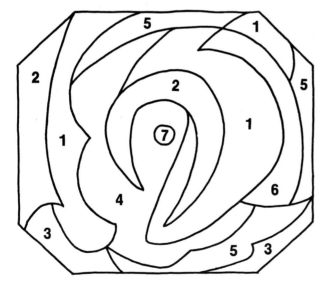

Materials
- 33x36 inches 4-mesh-to-the-inch rug canvas
- 6½ balls #12 natural jute
- 5 balls #28 dark brown jute
- 1½ balls white polished cotton
- 2 balls fine sisal
- 1 lb. medium brown warp or dyed cotton package string
- 2 lbs. #15 white cable cord or seine twine
- ¼ lb. #21 or #24 white nylon seine twine
- Heavy paper
- Carpet thread or dental floss
- Waterproof felt-tip pens
- 4 yards rug binding

Directions
Fold back the corners of the rug canvas to make an octagon, as in the diagram. Trim the corners and catch stitch a 1½-inch hem on all sides, using the carpet thread or floss.

Following the directions on page 31, enlarge the pattern to fit the canvas. Lay the pattern on the floor with the rug canvas over it. Tape both in place. (The lines of the design should show through the holes in the canvas.) Transfer the design to the canvas with waterproof pens. Use different colored pens for the different sections of the design to make hooking easier.

Cut all the string into 8-inch lengths by wrapping it around a 4-inch piece of cardboard and then cutting along one side. (Keep the different strings separate by cutting each kind directly into paper bags. Mark the bags with the code numbers on the diagram.)

Working from the center of the rug outward, attach the string to the canvas with the latch hook. Double the thin string whenever necessary to keep the rug from looking skimpy.

When the rug is finished, sew heavy rug binding around the edges on the back, mitering the corners. Coat the back of the rug with liquid latex to make skidproof.

Take care to clean the rug properly. Do not wash it. Vacuum it regularly and have it professionally cleaned.

Tapestry-Woven Pillow Collection

Watch out for the weavers! They're a joyful and exuberant bunch whose passion for their craft is contagious. And no wonder, for weaving today is exciting, innovative, and provocative. Tapestry weaving in particular, is increasingly popular with home weavers.

Even if you've never woven before, you can create beautiful fabrics such as those in the pillows shown opposite. The diamond-design pillow is explained in detail here. After you've tried it, you can go on to free-form or striped designs, such as those at the top and bottom of the photo, or to the more exacting patterns in the center.

Materials

- 1 pair 19-inch artists' stretcher bars
- 1 pair 22-inch artists' stretcher bars
- 4 metal braces or corrugated fasteners
- 47 yards cotton or linen carpet warp
- 59 yards thick, nubby brown wool yarn
- 23 yards thick, nubby beige wool yarn
- 13 yards thick, nubby gold wool yarn
- Large-toothed comb
- Large-eyed needle
- Waterproof pens
- ½ yard beige linen
- 1 yard muslin
- Polyester stuffing

Directions

Note: Quantities of materials above are for a pillow front only. To estimate amounts needed for both a front and back, see page 179. Also, the quantities given are only approximate; the actual amounts used will vary with the weight and texture of yarn.

For a pillow front only: Make the loom by assembling the stretchers into a 19x22-inch frame. Stabilize the corners with metal braces or corrugated fasteners.

Warp the loom in a figure eight. Starting 2 inches inside the upper left corner of the frame, carry the warp thread from the upper front of the loom, across the center (the open part), and under and around the lower edge. Go over the lower edge, back across the center, and under and over the top. Tie the cord at the top. Bring the warp across the center again, and under and around the lower edge ¼ inch from the first warp. Go over the lower edge, back across the center, and under and over the top, ¼ inch from the first thread at the top. Continue, spacing the warps ¼ inch apart, to within 2 inches of the

(continued)

A Weaving Primer

- The *warp* consists of the vertical threads that support the fabric. Warp thread or yarn can be any color or texture but generally should not have much stretch. Firm cotton and linen carpet warp are ideal.
- The *weft* is the yarn, thread, or other material used to weave across the warp. Experienced weavers prefer natural fibers to synthetic ones.
- The *web* is the woven cloth.
- The *loom* is the frame on which fabric is made. For off-loom weaving, use cardboard, plastic meat trays, old picture frames, artists' stretcher bars, or wooden or heavy cardboard boxes.
- The *cartoon* is the drawing (on paper the size of the warp) of the design to be
- The *needle* should have a large eye and a blunt tip. A curved carpet needle with the point filed down is ideal. You can make a needle from a long, thin piece of brass by drilling an eye, rounding the tip, and bending it slightly.
- The *beater* is used to push the weft against the warp. Use your fingers, a large-toothed comb, or a fork.

Woven Slat Window Shade

Don't be blind to the weaving possibilities in the common, garden-variety slat window shade made from slim strips of bamboo or plastic. Rather than discard your old shades, why not recycle them with a little weaving for a few more years of usefulness.

Shade weaving also has advantages for the first-time weaver. It makes good use of scraps of yarn leftover from other projects. And the vertical cords in the shade are a ready-made warp. So half the work's done before you even start on your project!

Materials

- Slat window shade made from thin strips of bamboo, plastic, or other material
- Heavy rug yarn, lightweight cord, or twine in colors to match your room decor (the quantities depend on the amount of weaving you want to do)
- Large-eyed tapestry needle
- Waterproof marking pens
- Large-toothed comb
- Graph paper

Directions:

Note: The vertical cords in the shade must be in good condition. Replace weak sections by cutting them out and knotting in new cord. If you plan the weaving along the areas where the knots are, the yarn will cover the knots when it is beaten down firmly.

Work out a design for the tapestry on graph paper. (Window shades lend themselves to designs of wide and narrow stripes in a variety of colors. Refer to the photograph for design suggestions.)

Draw a rectangle scaled to represent the shade. Mark damaged areas on the sketch. (These are the slats you'll want to remove and replace with weaving.) Work up your design around these damaged areas. Also, mark the sections of undamaged slats you want to remove and reweave.

With waterproof pens, lightly indicate the areas on the shade you will reweave.

Spread the shade full length across the top of a table or over the back of a chair. Sit facing the shade, holding the bottom in your lap. (The weight of the shade will hold the slats and warp threads taut as you work.)

Beginning at the bottom of the shade and working toward the middle, remove slats one at a time from the first section you intend to weave. As you remove each slat, weave in a row of yarn or twine in plain weave (see diagram 5 on page 160). Depending on the width of the slats and the weight of the yarn, you may have to weave two or three rows of yarn in place of each slat. In that case, use the comb to beat down each row of weaving against the previous row. (Don't pull the weft too tightly through the warp threads, or the warp will buckle.)

Use yarn lengths that are only about 1½ times the width of the shade. Longer lengths not only are unmanageable, they tend to look unsightly, too. To start new lengths of yarn in the middle of a row of weaving (see diagram 4 on page 160), overlap the tail end of one length and the beginning of the next.

When you finish each section, reweave the beginning and ending pieces of yarn back into the body of the shade (this makes the shade as attractive from the back as from the front).

When you reach the middle of the shade, reverse it and work from the top back toward the middle, rolling the finished section of the shade up in your lap as you progress.

If the shade is too long for the window, make a valance for the top of the window, as in the photograph. Weave in a few rows of yarn and then staple the top of the valance to a wooden frame that fits the window.

Before hanging the shade, coat all the woven areas with a soil-resistant finish to help keep them clean and bright.

Woven Aztec Wall Hanging

This woven hanging has real contemporary pizzazz. Its Aztec-inspired design, shape, and interesting textures make it an exciting point of interest in any setting.

You can't duplicate this design on a traditional floor loom. Instead, make a round cardboard loom, then suspend the circular weaving inside a Hula-Hoop.

Here, traditional weaving is combined with a collection of off-loom techniques. You'll get a chance to try tapestry knotting and warp wrapping as well as plain weaving. If you like variety, this one is for you.

Materials
- 1 Hula-Hoop
- 16-inch corrugated cardboard circle
- Large tapestry needle
- 100-yard ball light orange macrame jute
- 100-yard ball dark orange macrame jute
- 100-yard ball black macrame jute
- 8 ozs. natural white Greek 2-ply handspun goat's hair (or a ball of jute twine)
- 3¼ oz.-skein charcoal gray Rygja yarn (or other sports-weight yarn with little or no stretch)
- Scraps of white knitting yarn
- Mat knife

Directions
Note: If you are not able to find orange jute in two colors, use two balls of the same color. In the instructions OR means orange jute (either shade), WH represents white yarn, and GR signifies gray.

Make the loom by numbering 97 marks, ½ inch apart, around the edge of the cardboard circle. Notch the marks ¼ inch deep (see the diagram) with a mat knife.

Note: There are three separate warping operations in this weaving. First, you need to warp the cardboard loom through about ⅓ of the notches so you can weave the center without too much bulk. A second warping — and more weaving — is necessary on the loom to fill in all the notched spaces. The purpose of the third and final warping is to connect the finished circular weaving to the Hula Hoop. As you warp, pull the warp yarns as tightly as you can without buckling the loom.

Warp the loom the first time with a full ball of GR. Slide the yarn end through notch 1 (see diagram), and tape it to the numbered side of the loom (this will be the back). Draw the yarn across the face of the loom and through notch 48. Bring the yarn along the back to notch 45, go through it, and draw the yarn across the loom face again and through notch 93. Draw it along the back to notch 91 and go through. Then, draw it across the face and through notch 43. Continue warping the loom in this way, going through the rest of the notches in this sequence: 39 to 86, 84 to 37, 31 to 79, 74 to 26, 23 to 71, 69 to 21, 18 to 66, 59 to 12, 9 to 56, 54 to 6. Draw the yarn

(continued)

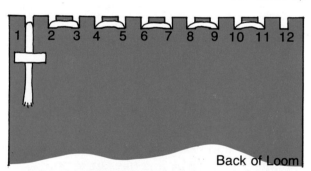

Back of Loom

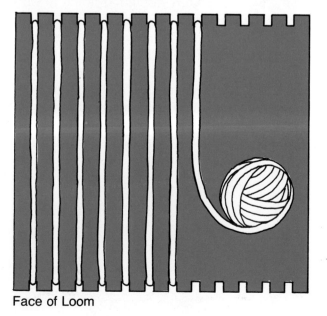

Face of Loom

through notch 2. Break it off, leaving a 2-yard length.

Thread the needle onto the leftover 2 yards of GR. Draw from notch 2 to the center of the circle to form the final warp. Tie this last warp securely to one of the warp yarns at the center of the loom. Then, using the rest of the yarn as a weft yarn, weave in plain weave (see diagram 5 on page 160) around the center of the circle, pulling this first round of weft as tightly as possible to avoid a hole in the center of the weaving. Continue working plain weave in circles, beating the weft down against each previous row, until you have a 1-inch-diameter circle. Break off GR, leaving a 3-inch end to tie off later.

Cut several 3-inch lengths of WH, OR, and GR. Mentally divide the woven GR circle into thirds, and work six rows of WH Ghiordes knots (see diagram 8 on page 160) around ⅔ of the circle. Work six rows of OR Ghiordes knots around the remaining ⅓. Next, work 2 rows of GR Ghiordes knots around the entire circle.

Thread the needle with 2 yards of OR and work plain weave around the GR Ghiordes knots until you run out of yarn (2 or 3 rounds). Beat the OR rounds down firmly to hold the Ghiordes knots. (Because of the difference in weight between warp and weft, you won't be able to fully cover the warp.)

Next, warp the loom the second time. Add OR, WH, and GR warp at this point to form a foundation for weaving the Aztec motifs. To warp, bring the yarn through a notch toward the center of the loom, then under the outside row of OR weft and back up to the next empty notch at the loom edge.

For example, for the first section of WH warp, thread the needle with a length of WH, then tape the end to the back of the loom at notch 27. Bring WH warp through notch 28, along the back of the loom to notch 29, through notch 29, down under the OR weft and up through notch 30. Notch 31 already holds a GR warp, so bring WH warp along the back to notch 32, through 32, and down under the OR weft. Continue until you reach notch 36.

Bring the yarn through 36 and down to the OR weft. Tie the WH warp to the OR weft and cut it off, leaving a 3-inch end to tie off later. (When warping ends at the edge instead of the center, cut the warp and tape the 3-inch end to the back of the loom.)

Use this technique to fill out the warp as follows: Fill empty notches from 91 to 94 with WH. Fill empty notches from 47 to 75 with OR. Fill other empty notches with GR.

Next, at the outside edge of the loom, work two rows of GR chain stitch (see diagram 6 on page 160), then 2 rows of alternating Ghiordes knots with 3-inch lengths of WH. Work 2 rows of OR chain stitch, beating the stitches down firmly against the WH Ghiordes knots to anchor them.

Now, return to the center of the loom, and work two or three rows of WH plain weave over and under both old and new warp yarns.

Work the Aztec motifs in plain weave and the wrapping technique in the space left between the inner circle and the outer woven edge. Pull the weft tightly so that warp yarns bunch together and emphasize the tapestry-slit spaces between the woven patterns (see diagram 3 on page 160). (Where the warp yarns show on a diagram, they should show on the finished piece. The diagrams are meant only as a guide for weaving. Pack weft yarns much more densely than shown in the illustrations on page 167. You may want to vary the proportions shown.)

For example, return to the first WH warp section, from notches 27 to 36. The weaving diagram looks like Motif A. Starting at the inner edge of the circle with a length of white knitting yarn (not the goat's hair) in your needle, work plain weave across all 10 warp yarns, beating each weft row back against the previous one. Do this until the weaving is about halfway to the outside circle of OR chain stitches. Then, work plain weave across only the inner six warps. When the weaving is about ¾ of the distance to the OR chain stitch, work plain weave across only the center two warps until you reach the OR chain stitch and can't squeeze in any more weft rows. Cut off the white yarn and leave a 3-inch end to weave into the back of the piece later when the weaving is finished.

Work from the center to the outside edge when weaving all the motifs.

Following the diagrams, weave the remaining motifs as follows: With GR, work two of Motif B, across warps 17 to 26 and 37 to 46. Work two of Motif C in GR, across warps 76 to 90 and 95 to 12. Wrap one strand of GR around warps 56 and 57 to cover them completely.

With OR, work two of Motif D, across warps 47 to 55 and 67 to 75. Turn the diagram upside down and work this reversed Motif D in OR, across warps 58 to 66.

Wrap warps 13 to 16 into a single strand with OR, working from the center to the OR chain stitch. Stop wrapping just before you reach the chain stitch row, letting the warps show a little at the edge.

With WH, wrap warps 91 to 94 as a single strand from the inner edge halfway to the outer edge, then continue to wrap only the center two warps the rest of the way.

Next, warp the finished circle weaving to the Hula-Hoop. Wrap the ball of black jute around the hoop, just as if the hoop were a warp yarn being wrapped. When the entire hoop is covered, cut off the excess jute, leaving 12 inches or so. Thread the needle onto the end and secure it by pushing the needle through the last four or five rounds of wrapping. Cut off the ends.

For the final warping operation, work on a large, flat surface—a table or a floor.

Place the finished weaving (still on the loom) inside the hoop, and move it around until you like the way it looks. Decide where you want the OR warp yarns to connect the weaving to the hoop by studying the photograph or by extending paper strips in various widths from the inner to the outer circle. When you have decided where you want the OR warps to go, thread a needle with a long piece of OR. Bend the needle a bit with pliers to aid in going through the hoop wrapping. Tie the thread end to one of the little loops of warp that show on the loom back. Work the warp back and forth between the hoop and the weaving, making sure that every warp loop on the weaving holds at least one new OR warp yarn. Catch two or three wrapping rounds on the hoop at each stitch—but

don't try to fill every wrapped round on the hoop.

When you run across a taped warp-end on the loom, tie it with a square knot either to another taped warp-end or to one of the loops to form a new loop.

As you finish each section of OR warp, pull the jute off the needle and leave a 12-inch end at the cardboard loom side—but don't tie off the end yet.

When you've added all the OR warps you want, tighten the warp so the inner weaving will hang firmly inside the hoop.

Go back to the first section of OR warp. Pull the loops off the cardboard loom. Starting where you knotted the OR warp to the loom, tighten the warp by pulling it. At the end of the first warp section, when all these warps are tight and tension is even, tie the end securely to a warp loop on the circular weaving, leaving a 3-inch end.

Remove the loops from the loom on the next warping section and tighten it in the same way. Continue tightening warps until all the sections are finished.

Throw the cardboard loom away, and turn the weaving over. Either weave in or tie off (or both) all the loose ends, and hang!

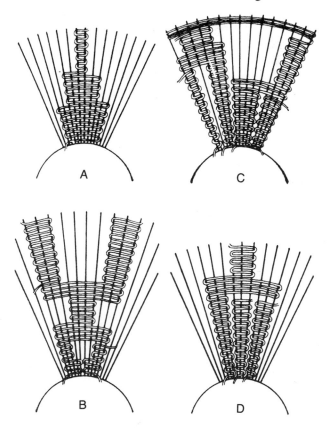

Woven Fabric-Strip Rug

When the weather outside is cold or dreary, round up the kids for a romp on a rainbow. This cheerful rug, woven with bright felt strips, will take the bite out of any dark day. Soft, yet firm enough not to upset your children's building blocks or model racing cars, it's also a fun project that the entire family can enjoy crafting together.

Materials
- ⅔ yard 72-inch-wide yellow felt
- ⅔ yard 72-inch-wide green felt
- ⅔ yard 72-inch-wide orange felt
- ⅔ yard 72-inch-wide magenta felt
- ⅔ yard 72-inch-wide hot pink felt

- ¾ yard 72-inch-wide navy blue felt
- 3 162-foot balls strong, non-stretchy cotton string
- 16½ feet 2x2 pine (for the frame)
- 6d box nails

Directions

Build a frame of 2x2 lumber (see the diagram) to serve as a loom. Butt the corners. (The inside dimensions are 35x60 inches.) Drive 6d box nails at ½-inch intervals down the two long sides of the frame.

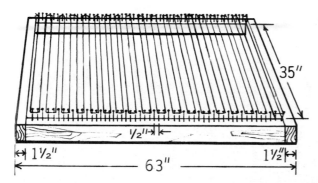

Warp the loom with cotton string. First, tie string securely to the first nail on one side. Then, take the warp across the loom to the opposite nail and go around two nails. Go back across the loom, skip one nail, and go around two nails. Pull the warp tightly, but not so tightly that you bend the nails. Continue in this way until the entire loom is warped. Knot the ends of the warp string together when necessary (the weft will cover the knots). Double warp by following the same pattern in reverse.

Cut all the felt into 3x72-inch strips. Fold the strips in half lengthwise and press. Next, fold the side edges to the center to make strips that are ¾-inch wide. Press again.

Begin the weaving with a blue strip. Weave over and under warp threads, treating double-warp threads as one. On the next row of weft, weave under those warps you went over and over those you went under on the previous row. Remember to weave strips into warp in an arc so you don't pull the sides of the warp out of shape. As you work, use your fingers to beat down each row of weft firmly against the row beneath it.

Leave six inches of felt free at each end of the weaving for the fringe. Weave the colored

trips in this sequence: blue, yellow, hot pink, magenta, orange, and green.

When you've completed the weaving and before you remove the rug from the frame, cut a length of cord 3½ times the length of the loom. Use this cord to tie single half-hitches along the edges of the loom, as shown in the diagram.

Remove the woven rug from the loom. Finally, baste the strips of fringe into a neat row, and machine-stitch along the inside edge to stabilize them. Remove the basting stitches, and the rug is ready for the floor.

More Weaving Tips For Beginners

- Many ready-made boxes make excellent looms. Try cardboard packing boxes cut down to a comfortable size. Use sturdy game boxes for smaller projects. Or, weave on wooden flats that fruits and vegetables are shipped in.
- Try weaving with all sorts of wefts other than yarn: paper, ribbons, old ties, nylon stockings, and strips of fabric, leather, or fur.
- Natural materials are fun for weaving and often beautiful. Try looms of driftwood or branches. Use wefts of straw, leaves, grasses, reeds, bark, raffia, moss, or bamboo.
- Work sample weavings into a collage for a lasting record of color combinations, techniques, and textures.

Punjabi Deck Chair

This classy, sassy chair was once ready for the trash, but a few fancy rope tricks saved it. And while the rope tricks do look fancy, you'll find that the weaving techniques are not difficult — they're basically a combination of weaving and crochet. So, rather than tossing your old chairs, stools, and camp cots, recycle them with practical, easy, and colorful Indian bed weaving.

Punjabi — Indian bed weaving — is traditionally left in the bed frame when the weaving is finished. That's what was done here — but instead of a bed frame, a furniture frame was used as the loom. Some bright macrame cord, a fork, and two crochet hooks are the only other materials you'll need.

Materials

- Metal lawn chair
- 165 yards purple 3-ply jute
- 165 yards pink 3-ply jute
- 1 pint red exterior enamel
- 2 metal crochet hooks, size H, I, or J
- Protective fabric coating
- Fork

Directions

Use large balls of cord so there will be fewer knots in the work. Tie in a new ball of cord with a loose overhand knot, which can easily be untied later. Leave the ends long enough to weave in after the weaving is finished.

Before you begin, remove the old chair webbing. Clean the frame, roughen it with steel wool, and paint it.

If the chair has a brace across the back of the seat, warp both the back and the seat simultaneously by wrapping the cord around the brace. Or, leave the brace exposed by running the cord from the front of the seat, under the brace, and to the top of the frame.

Start with the frame and the ball of purple cord in front of you. Tie the cord securely to the back left corner of the seat frame (or brace), leaving a tail on the knot. You now have one strand running across the frame, with the ball of cord in front of you.

Take the cord under the front of the frame and bring up a loop to the left of the strand on top. Put the crochet hook through the loop to hold it (diagram A).

Bring the cord back under and then over the frame. Carry a double strand to the back of the seat (where the brace is). The ball remains in front of you.

Wrap the brace by putting the cord over and under it, and bring up a loop *between* the double strand. Carry the double strand to the frame at the top of the chair back, going over and under it. Next, bring up a loop to the left of the cord. Secure it with a second crochet hook (diagram B). Wrapping the cord the opposite way around the brace (under, over, and through) makes the brace visible from the front of the chair.

As you crochet the warp in place, you'll find that one side of the loop holding the hook is tight because it is secured on the opposite

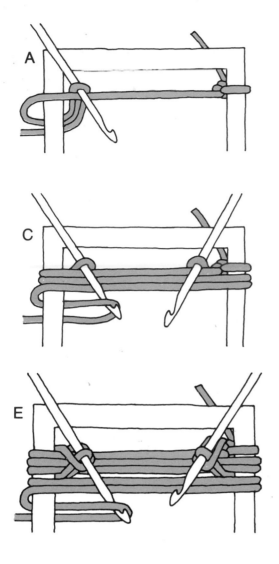

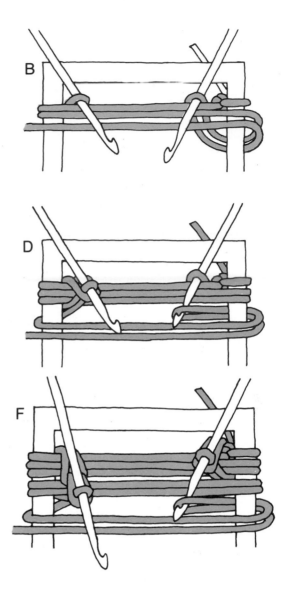

side of the frame, while the side coming from the ball is loose. Pull the left strand from the top to tighten it as you make a loop. Pull the right strand (running from the ball) tight when you crochet on the seat front. Cords must always be firm and even in the frame.

Bring the loose cord back over and under the front of the frame (diagram C). Catch a loop of cord with the crochet hook and bring it across the three strands of cord and through the loop already on the hook. Leave the hook in the loop.

Next, bring the cord back over the top of the frame. Take a double strand across the seat again, wrap the brace as before, and carry the double strand up the back and over and under the frame. Pull up another loop, bring it across three strands and through the

loop on the hook. Pull the strands taut. Leave the hook in the loop (diagram D).

Continue, bringing a loop across two strands each time, until the frame is filled with cords (diagrams E, F, and G).

Make sure the cords lie flat over the frame and don't twist across one another. Fasten the back corner by pulling the cord through the loop and cutting it, leaving a tail. Leave the hook in the lower right loop.

Select one of the patterns on page 173. (The wave pattern on the chair is in the upper left corner.) Tie the pink jute to the left front of the frame, with the ball of cord to the left. With your fingers separating the cords, work a *double* strand over and under the number of cords that correspond to the pattern.

For the wave pattern, weave a double strand over then under eight cords, across the first row. On the second row, go over six cords

(continued)

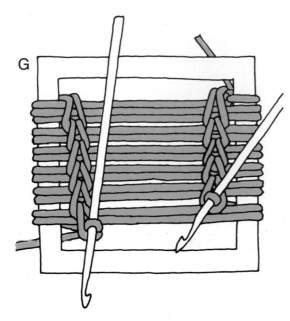

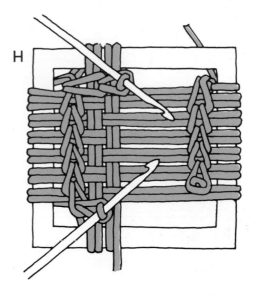

before beginning the eight-cord sequence. On the third row, go over four cords and begin the sequence. On the fourth row, go over two cords and begin the sequence. On the fifth row, begin the pattern again at the edge of the frame.

When you have woven the first double strand across the frame, fold the cord into a loop and pull it through the purple loop already on the hook. Then, work a crochet hook into the first loop of the purple jute on the left and pull through a loop of pink.

Continue weaving the pattern with the pink jute, looping the cord over and under the frame and crocheting the cord in place (diagram H). Keep the strands tight and the crochet loops loose enough to get through easily. (This is especially important on contoured frames such as the metal lawn chair.)

Save wear and tear on your fingers by using a fork to push the cords in place against one another. Pack the cords tightly or loosely to get the pattern to fit the frame.

If you discover a mistake, you can correct it without taking out a complete row. Simply unfasten the loop side of the crochet (opposite the ball), pull out the row or rows back to the mistake, and reweave them correctly.

When only a few inches of weaving are left, separating the cords with your fingers is diffi-

cult. Borrow a crochet hook from one of the loops to get the cords through, or use a hairpin as a needle.

Fasten off one corner by pulling the cord through the loop and cutting it, leaving a tail. Pull the tail of the last pink loop through the other loop to fasten it. Next, work all the tails into the weaving with a crochet hook, making sure they don't show on the right side. Finish the chair and strengthen it by undoing any knots and weaving in the ends on the underside of the chair.

Cover the finished weaving with a heavy coat of silicone fabric protector.

Note: When designing your own pattern for Punjabi weaving, arrange cords in multiples of two. Remember that in a two-color pattern on a rectangular frame, the color wrapped along the long side will be predominant.

If your project is different from the chair, estimate how much cord you need by figuring out how many cords laid side-by-side are in an inch. Next, measure the frame both ways, allowing for a loop under the frame. Multiply this second number by the number of cords per inch, then divide by 36 for yardage. Buy colorfast, tightly wrapped cords.

If you begin weaving the weft and find there is an extra cord in the first (warp) color, work a group of three warps at the edge. Also, if the pattern must be centered, count strands to locate the middle.

Pattern Alternatives

BACK   METAL LAWN CHAIR

SEAT

I LINE = 2 CORDS

1 LINE = 2 CORDS

I LINE = 2 CORDS

I LINE = 2 CORDS

I LINE = 2 CORDS

I LINE = 2 CORDS

Cane Chair Seat

As professional cane weavers become harder to find, more and more amateurs are taking up chair caning. This isn't a difficult kind of weaving (although fast work takes practice), and the results are always lovely.

Materials
- Chair
- Paint
- Ruler
- Electric drill with ³⁄₁₆-inch bit
- Fine or fine-fine cane in sufficient quantity for the chair seat
- Pieces of ¼-inch dowel that have been sharpened on one end
- Binder cane for trim
- Caning needle

Directions

Repair and paint the chair. Then, draw ruled pencil lines around the inner edge of the seat, ½ inch from the edge. Mark off lines in ½-inch segments, starting at the corners. With a ³⁄₁₆-inch bit, drill holes through the chair at the marks.

Wind each strip of cane around your hand to form a small looped bundle. Tie string around it. Keep bundles of cane soaking in water so it is pliable while you are caning. *Note:* Obtain the cane at a hobby shop or upholstery supply store.

Start caning at point 1 (diagram A). Fasten a strand of cane in the hole with a piece of dowel. Take the strand across to 2, underneath and up through 3, then across to 4, underneath and up through 5, and so on. Keep the strand fairly taut, and use dowels to hold it in place.

Add a second layer of cane at right angles to the first, in the same way (diagram B).

Remove the dowels from the chair and fasten the loose strands beneath the chair in knots around the strands that run from hole to hole. Run the next layer of strands parallel to the first, over the first and second layers, in the same way (diagram C).

Start weaving, using a caning needle to speed up the process. Each time you pull the strand through the hole, thread it into the needle and weave it across to the other side (diagram D). Arrange the woven strands in pairs, forcing them close together in straight, parallel lines. (Good work here is essential to the remainder of the caning.)

To weave diagonally, follow diagram E, running two strands into each corner hole, with one hand above and one beneath the chair.

Weave the remaining diagonal strands from the opposite direction (diagram F). As in the previous step, run two diagonals into each of the four corner holes. When weaving the edges, be sure the weaving is run over and under the right strands. Completed caning should look like diagram G.

Using binder cane, frame the edges of the woven cane (diagram H). Lay the binder over the holes and loop the fine cane through each hole or alternate ones, catching in the binder. Pull the cane tightly so the binder fits snugly. To finish, lap the binder cane over two or three holes, fastening down these ends together. After the last loop, fasten the end of the strand by plugging the hole from beneath or by tying it.

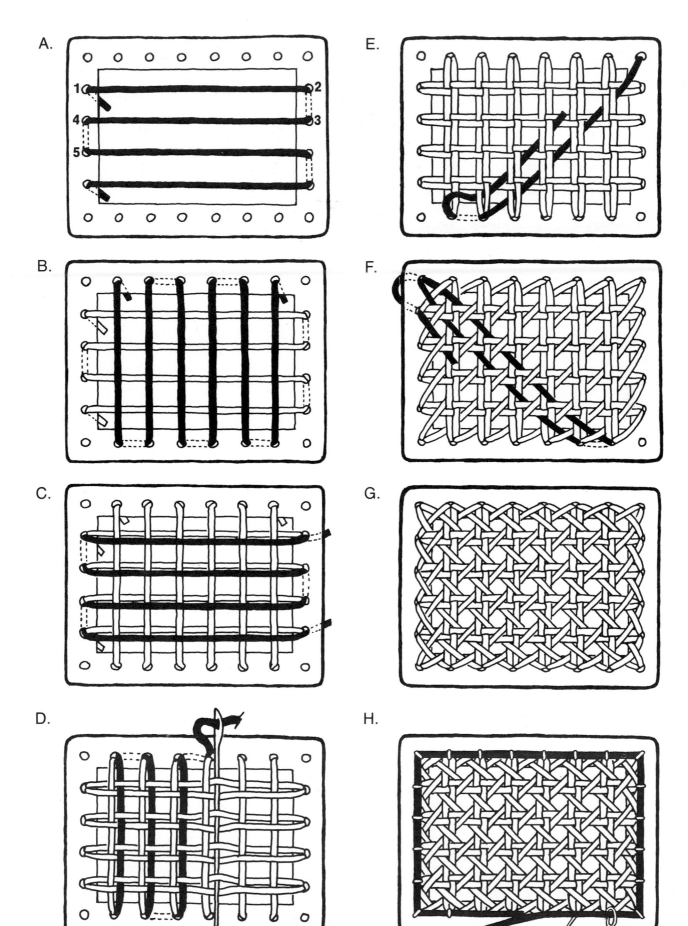

A.

B.

C.

D.

E.

F.

G.

H.

Warp-Wrap Indian Baskets

The origins of the ancient art of weaving are lost in the mists of man's pre-history. But warp wrapping is thought by many to be one of the earliest forms of weaving. Our distant forebears, thousands upon thousands of years ago, gathered wild reeds, willows, and grasses to twist them into a core around which they wrapped leaves, broad-leaf grasses, and other lightweight fibers. The wrapped core was then bound and shaped into mats and baskets that, for all their pedestrian practicality, were skillfully and durably crafted.

The updated version of this ancient basketry technique presented here is easy enough for an all-thumbs beginner, and fast enough for a jet-setter. It's a simple matter of wrapping yarn around a core of jute, rope, or even clothesline. Following, you will find the pattern and instructions for the tall basket above, left. Once you've mastered that, you'll have a grand time making other baskets.

You can wrap flat place mats, too. Then, try broad, shallow containers, perhaps with a design worked into the base. Make gently curving covers for pots and bowls and spectacular large baskets for dried weeds, yarn, even umbrellas! Or turn a hand to an exquisite, small covered basket with a knob on the lid made from beads, feathers, or shells. Whatever you make, you'll have the satisfaction of crafting in a way that men and women have been crafting for millenia.

176

Materials

- 25 yards ½-inch-diameter cord
- 200 yards thick, nubby black yarn
- 24 yards thick, nubby brown yarn
- 25 yards thick, nubby purple yarn
- 2 yards thick, nubby red yarn
- 22 yards thick, nubby white yarn
- Tapestry needle
- 4-square-to-the-inch graph paper

Directions

Select a sturdy, but flexible cord such as jute, upholstery cord, sisal, or clothesline for the warp (the cord the yarn is wrapped around). Yardages given for yarn are approximate. You may use more or less yarn, depending on how tightly you wrap the cord and on how thick your yarn is.

Enlarge the design on page 179, according to the directions on page 31, on graph paper. (The pattern is for one side of the basket.)

Before beginning, study the drawings of the five steps for starting a coil on page 178.

1. Taper the end of the warp cord. Leave the cord in a coil or a heap on the floor beside you, pulling it out as you wrap. Cut a 30 to 36-inch piece of yarn and thread one end through a needle. Begin wrapping the *unthreaded* end around the warp cord 2 inches from the end, overlapping the first wind to anchor it. Wrap to within about ½ inch of the tapered end of the warp.

2. Bend the warp and pull the yarn through the center opening, using the needle. Hold the tapered end and begin forming a loop, wrapping tightly.

3. Wrap until the tapered end is securely anchored to the warp. Push the needle through the center of the loop.

4. Bend the cord to form a coil and, using the needle, push the yarn between the warp, wrapping from front to back.

5. Begin working the figure-eight stitch between the coils, as shown. Wrap the yarn around the warp several times, using the needle to push the yarn through the coil underneath and up and around to form a figure eight. Wrap tightly. (The more figure eights you make, the tighter and sturdier the basket will be.)

Space figure eights up to ½ inch apart. If gaps begin to show between coils, add more figure eights spaced closer together.

Add new yarn or change colors by wrapping until only a few inches of the original yarn remain. Lay this tail along the warp and hold it tightly. Cut another length of yarn, thread it, and lay the unthreaded end on the warp beside the tail. Hold both firmly in one hand and wrap with the other hand. Continue wrapping and making figure eights as usual. The wrapping will cover the tails.

For the base of the basket, wrap the cord in black and coil it into a flat circle 7 inches in diameter. Then, begin working the pattern and building the sides.

When working on a section such as the first coil above the base where colors intermingle or are only a short distance apart, carry both colors along the warp by holding the color not in use in one hand and wrapping the color in use over it. To change to the other color, reverse the process. When there are long intervals between colors, save yarn by clipping off the yarn of the color not in use and bringing it back in later as needed.

Work the design from the bottom up, following the graph-paper pattern. The first coil above the base, for example, has ½ inch of black followed by ¼ inch of brown completely around the coil. Bring in purple for the second and third rows. Then, switch to one row of black followed by black with white for one of the lower motifs on the fifth coil. Carry the white along the warp, covering it with black for several inches. Put in white for the other motif, then switch completely to black while wrapping around the sides and back until reaching the front on the sixth coil. Add more white. Continue wrapping, putting in the design on the front while working.

While wrapping the cord and putting in the design, shape the basket. Make sides that curve inward or outward by placing the top coil a little inside or outside of the previous coil. When starting the sides, keep the coiled

(continued)

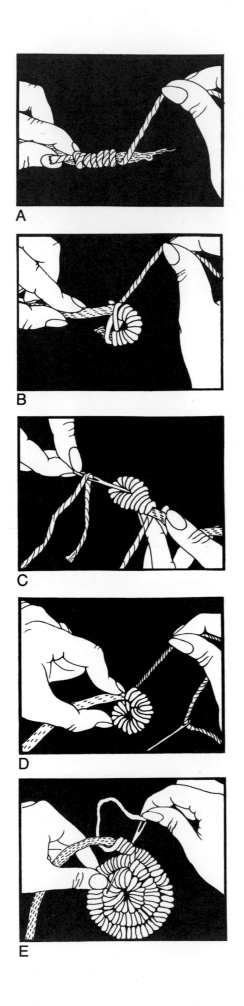

A

B

C

D

E

base facing away from you so you are working on the near outside of the form.

End the basket at the top by cutting the warp so it extends several inches beyond the wrapping. Taper the end of the warp so it gradually decreases in size and blends into the previous coil. Wrap the tapered end until it is completely covered. Then, make several extra winds around it and the previous coil with the needle to anchor the wrapping permanently.

Run the needle back through an inch or so of the wrapping, clip the excess yarn, and adjust the coil so the tail is covered.

If you run short of warp cord, splice 2 pieces of cord together. (They should be of the same thickness and texture.) To do this, first, taper the tail end of the existing warp. Also taper the end of the new warp. Fit these ends together until they are about the same size as the rest of the warp cord. Glue the ends together with a dab of white glue. When the ends are thoroughly dry, continue wrapping as usual.

When designing your own basket. begin by deciding what size and shape basket to make. Usually a low, round basket is about 4 inches across the base, 8 inches in the center at its widest point, and 4 inches high. Taller baskets are about 7 inches across the base, 12 inches at the widest point, and 12 or 13 inches high.

Make a pattern by marking off the dimensions of the basket on graph paper and drawing in the shape you want to approximate. Decide on a design and color combinations, and chart these on the basket outline. If the cord you plan to use is ¼ inch in diameter, one row of squares on the paper will represent one coil. If cord is ½ inch, one coil will equal two rows of squares.

After you've drawn the design, you can see how much of the design appears on each coil. This helps in centering the design and determining where to position each motif as you coil the basket.

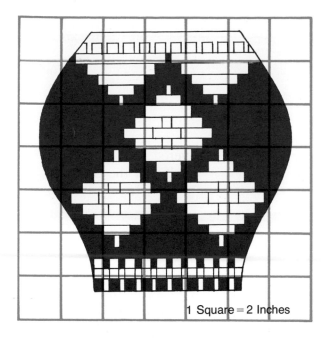

1 Square = 2 Inches

Color Key:
A. Brown
B. Purple
C. White
D. Red
E. Black

Begin wrapping and coiling the basket, spacing figure eights ⅛ to ¼ inch apart.

Start your design on any side of the basket (wherever you start becomes the front). If you plan to put a design on the back, start it directly opposite the design on the front, for evenly centered designs.

Weaving Free-form Designs

• Use scraps of yarn in related colors to weave free-form, wavy designs.

• Weave free-form designs without a cartoon, unless you think you need one.

• Strive for a fluid, rolling design, as in the top pillow in the photograph on page 158. Begin with a few rows of plain weave. Then, start shortening the rows until the woven area is wavy. To straighten the line, fill in vacant areas, lengthening the rows gradually.

• Lend textural interest to your design with an assortment of knotting stitches.

How to Estimate Quantities of Yarn in Plain and Fancy Weaving

To estimate for warp thread:
1. Count the no. of warps on the loom, or multiply the width of the weaving (the web) by the no. of warps per inch.
2. Add to no. 1 any extra threads for special purposes. For example, if double-warping the loom, then double the amount you have figured so far.
3. Multiply no. 2 by the length of the warp (from top to bottom).
4. Divide no. 3 by 36 for yardage.
5. Add about 10 percent for wastage to no. 4 to get the final amount needed.

To estimate weft thread for plain or tabby weave:
1. Measure the width of the web and add 25 percent to determine how long a weft you need for one row of weaving.
2. Estimate how many rows of weft make up 1 inch of weaving. Working a small sample helps here.
3. Multiply no. 1 by no. 2.
4. Multiply no. 3 by the length (in inches) of the web (from top to bottom).
5. Divide no. 4 by 36 for the approximate number of yards of weft you need.

To estimate weft thread needed for knots and warp wrapping:
1. Work a sample of knots or warp wrapping about 6x6 inches, keeping close track of the amount (in yards) of thread you use.
2. Estimate how many square inches of the web will be worked in knots and wrapping.
3. Divide no. 2 by 36 (square inches).
4. Multiply no. 3 by the number of yards used in the sample.
5. Add 10 percent for wastage.

Framing

The right frame enhances the beauty of paintings, etchings, prints, family portraits, and candid snapshots. You can buy the same materials professional framers use, and produce equally professional results. If you're a novice, start with a simple frame.
As you become more expert, advance to more complex designs.

Crown Molding Frame for Still Life

There are many molding patterns for your framing pleasure. Use them individually or, for interesting and unusual effects, combine two or three moldings in a single frame. Master the basic framing techniques on pages 181-182, and then move on to more creative designs.

Combine different sizes, media, types of frames, and subject matter in your picture groupings in your home.

The large oil painting on the opposite page has added impact because the width and depth of the frame are scaled to the size of the picture. To duplicate this frame, use two types of wood molding. Try a wide, gracefully curved crown molding, and a corner guard that hugs the canvas stretcher.

Choose a finish that is compatible with the colors in your painting and the subject matter. (See page 187 for information on frame finishes.)

Materials
• Wide-crown molding (3½ inches from outer corner to inner corner), amount to be determined by length of four sides of canvas stretcher frame, plus allowance for mitering corners
• ¾-inch corner guard, amount to include allowance for mitering corners
• Glue
• Small nails
• Miter box
• Corner clamps (one is essential, but four speeds up the work)
• Light hammer
• Small nail set
• Ruler
• Fine-toothed saw
• Corner fasteners
• Fine sandpaper

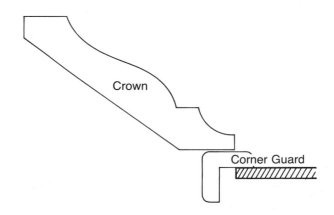

Crown

Corner Guard

(continued)

Directions

Select your wood moldings, and assemble the necessary tools. Choose a work area where you can leave partly constructed frames undisturbed during the glue drying step. Now, you are ready to start construction.

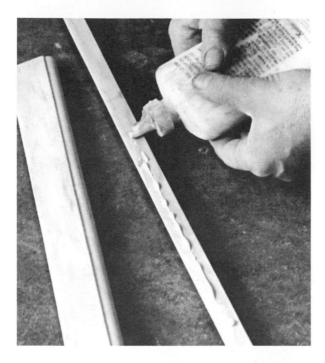

Glue the molding strips for the frame together, and clamp them or weight them until the glue has set.

Measure bottom edge of picture. Add ⅛ inch to this measurement, and transfer measurement to molding—starting from edge of miter where picture inserts into frame. Then, mark and cut a 45° miter at the opposite angle of the one just cut. Cut an identical piece for the top. Use the first piece as a guide in cutting the second one.

Measure the side of the picture, and cut two pieces of molding the same length—remember to add an extra ⅛ inch to this measurement. Measure the second side piece from first one. Now, start to assemble your frame.

When glue is dry, saw off the end of the molding at a 45° angle.

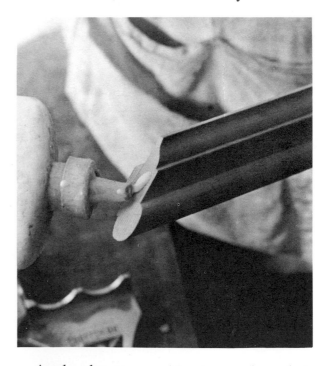

Apply glue to one side piece and one bottom piece, and place in corner clamp.

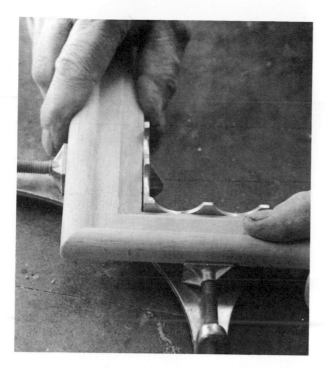

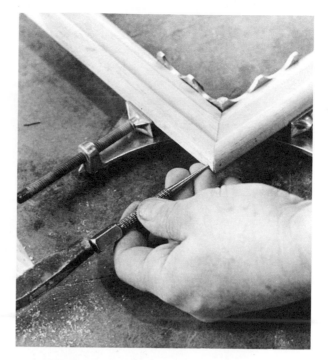

When the corner is aligned properly, tighten the clamp to hold the pieces securely while you are nailing the corner together. Wipe off any excess glue.

Finish driving brads with a small nail set so the heads of the brads are about $\frac{1}{16}$ inch below the surface of the frame.

Fill nail holes with a wood putty or fine sawdust mixed with a little glue. Let dry. Four clamps come in handy, if your frame is made of wide molding. Use a corner fastener to further strengthen joint. Follow same procedure on the other corners.

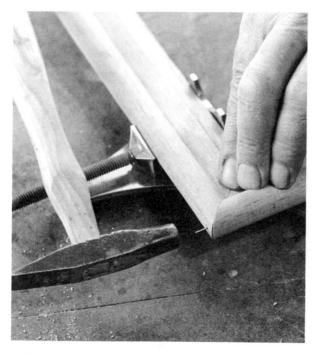

Drive two or more brads through the corner from each side allowing the brads to protrude slightly.

When your frame is completely dry, rub it lightly with fine sandpaper.

184

Gold Frame with Linen Liner

After you've mastered basic framing techniques, try your hand at a more complex framing project. Duplicate the one on the opposite page or let it inspire you to greater creativity. The oil painting is enhanced by the slender antique gold finish frame with its beaded design. Between the frame and the painting, there is a linen liner with a gold beveled edge.

Materials
- Narrow molding with a beaded design in antique gold finish (purchase at art supply store or frame shop)
- Wood molding for liner
- Linen to cover liner
- Glue
- Long brads
- Miter box
- Corner clamps
- Light hammer
- Small nail set
- Corner fasteners

Directions
Construct outer frame first, following steps on pages 182-183; add ⅛ inch to outside dimensions of liner for frame rabbet size. Liner dimensions should be slightly larger than canvas stretcher size, about ¼ inch larger than outside dimensions. Make liner next, following instructions at bottom of page. Place frame face down on floor, insert liner, also face down. If liner is a little loose, slide scraps of matboard between liner and rabbet.

Fasten liner to frame with long brads, angling brads so each one enters frame rabbet. Next, place canvas face down in liner. Attach with long brads, or with spring clips or mending plates.

Liners
A desirable combination frame combines molding with an inside liner. Actually, the liner is a smaller fabric-covered frame em-

ployed to provide a smooth transition from outer frame to picture.

Cut molding for liner as you would to make a basic frame. Join four strips in

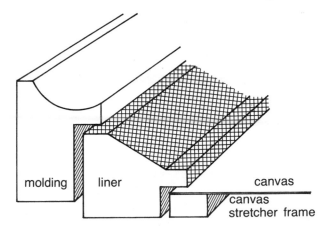

same manner, but it is not necessary to countersink nails, because all of liner except top is concealed by outer frame.

To cover liner, lay smooth fabric on a flat surface wrong side up. Apply fabric glue to right side of liner, and carefully position it on fabric. Press down firmly. When adhesive is dry, cut a 1½-inch margin of fabric around liner. Glue edges to wrong side. Cut around inside border of liner allowing 1 inch to fold under. At inside corners, cut 1 inch allowance at a 45-degree angle. Pull border fabric around to under side of liner and glue securely.

Matting
Pictures covered with glass require a mat. This prevents moisture from glass touching the subject. Mat also serves as a break between frame and surface of artwork. Use a sharp knife or a mat cutter, that cuts perfect bevelled edges at 45° and 90° angles, to cut matboard. Leave a slightly wider border at bottom than on top and sides.

Purchase pre-cut or sheet matboard at your art supply store. For special effects, cover with fabric or wallpaper. Tape picture to top of mat only. This keeps print from wrinkling if it should shrink. Use backing to hold print against mat, and small brads or glazier's points to hold picture in frame. Add hanging fixture.

Inexpensive Framing and Finishing

Framing needn't be expensive or difficult. The frames on the opposite page aren't. Each is made from standard builder's moldings, available at building supply or lumber dealers. With instructions for making the frames, there are also finishing techniques.

1. Glue together the back band and the crown moldings, and paint the back band blue. Paint the crown molding flat black, and rub it with coarse sandpaper to give it a textured effect. Simulate the "worm holes" by using a nail to make small indentations.

2. Combine a stop molding and an "L-" shaped corner bead to make this frame. Cut notches on the edge of the corner bead at intervals, and give it a coat of silver finish. Wipe ebony stain on the completed frame, just enough to give it a pewter-look.

3. Use two sizes of shingle molding for this frame. Give it a gold finish and wipe on a stain overglaze.

4. Combine a picture molding with a shoe molding. Stain them and finish them with a coat of clear varnish.

5. Use a parting strip between two sizes of cove molding. After staining and glazing the completed frame, drive upholstery nails, spaced evenly, in the depression.

6. Cut and glue lengths of ¼- and ½-round moldings to make this frame. Use corner of file to add bamboo-like effect. Paint frame red; wipe on stain, and let dry.

7. Glue two sizes of stop molding back-to-back and distress lightly with sandpaper and a nail to make slight indentations. Finish the frame with a coat of gold paint and wipe with a glazing stain.

8. Combine a cove molding with a glass stop. After cutting and gluing the frame, finish it with a coat of bright gold.

9. Use a glass stop with a door stop molding. After you have assembled it, apply a bright gold finish, then copper paint along the inside edge.

10. For this contemporary frame, combine a blind stop and a drip cap molding. Finish with shiny black enamel and aluminum paint.

Finishes for Frames
You have many options when it comes to selecting a finish for your frame—natural, stained, painted and textured, or gilded.

For a natural finish, sand lightly after each of two or three coats of white shellac, and buff with paste wax.

If you wish a stained finish, use the same shellac and wax treatment after stain dries.

For painting and texturing, the process is more time-consuming but you do have more freedom in matching the frame color to the tone and texture of the picture.

Start by brushing on a coat of warm or cool gray heavy-bodied paint (latex works well). Before the paint sets, texture the surfaces you wish to treat. For a stippled effect, use a cellulose sponge or line with a discarded comb. When dry, color the surface with thinned-out paint applied with a cloth. Apply and rub off colors until you achieve the right blend. When finished, dry and buff on a coat of wax.

Gilding frames was once very costly and difficult, and better left to a professional. Now gilding can be accomplished in several different ways. There are sheets of metal leafing which come in gold (actually bronze) and silver (actually aluminum). There are also numerous metallic finishes that you can apply by brushing, spraying, or rubbing. To tone down brightness, apply thinned-out paint or antiquing glaze with a cloth, until you achieve desired color.

Patchwork Covered Picture Frame

Don't discard old patchwork quilts. When they've outlived their usefulness in the bedroom, use the best portions in other ways. Add a feeling of nostalgia by making a patchwork wall hanging or table cover, or by combining it with an inexpensive, ready-made picture frame, as shown above.

Because it adds a touch of sentimentality, this type of frame lends itself especially well to family photos.

Materials
- 8x10-inch wooden picture frame with beveled edge
- 5x40-inch strip of patchwork fabric
- 5x30-inch strip of patchwork fabric
- White glue
- Pushpins
- Soil-resistant coating

188

Directions

Remove the backing, mat, and glass from the picture frame. Spread white glue along the rabbeted edge of the frame (the edge the glass rests on).

Lay the 40-inch patchwork strip right side down on a flat surface and fold over one end to form a 90-degree angle.

Place the frame (with its back facing you) over the edges of the strip of fabric, as shown in the sketch below. Then turn the inner edge of the strip along the rabbeted edge and press to glue. Do the same with the top edge of the patchwork strip, gluing it to the beveled edge. Hold the fabric in place with pushpins until the glue has had ample opportunity to dry.

Continue folding and gluing the strip, mitering the corners by folding fabric over itself at right angles.

When you have covered all four sides of the frame, turn it right side up. At the last mitered corner, trim the fabric and turn under the raw edge and glue down, making absolutely sure that you overlap the fabric slightly at the starting point.

Cover the picture mat in the same manner you did the picture frame, using the 5x30-inch patchwork strip.

Use a soil-resistant coating on both frame and mat. Finally, replace glass and mat, insert picture, and attach cardboard backing. Glue heavy wrapping paper, cut to size, over the entire back so it conceals the raw edges of the patchwork strip.

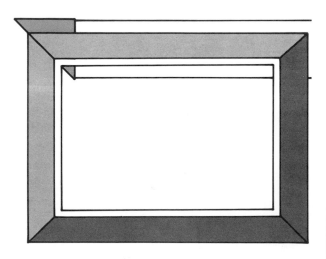

Scalloped Mirror Frame

There are many trims you can use to frame mirrors, and the one pictured here is concocted of cord, stiffened with glue, applied in a deep scalloped design, and painted your favorite color. This technique is especially suitable for a bedroom or powder room.

Material
- Rectangular mirror
- ¼-inch diameter cord
- White glue
- Paint
- Masking tape
- Pushpins

Directions

Immerse cord in a solution of half glue and half water. Lay the mirror on a cardboard surface, and pin the cord in scallops around the rectangular shape. With undiluted glue, secure the areas where cord touches mirror.

Use masking tape to protect the mirror while you paint the cord to match your decor.

Denim Frame and Desk Accessories

Use your sewing, cutting, and gluing skills to make this denim-covered easel-type picture frame and the matching desk accessories.

Buy inexpensive desk accessories at a stationery, department, or variety store. Cover the items with lightweight denim from your favorite fabric shop. Or use denim pieces cut from old, faded jeans.

Materials
- One yard lightweight blue denim
- 2 buckles to fit 1-inch wide belts
- Pencil holder
- Penholder
- 8x10-inch picture frame (with easel)
- Letter opener
- White thread
- White glue

Directions
General: To make the belt loops that trim each item, cut a strip of denim fabric 1x24 inches. Fold into thirds lengthwise, and press. If any edge shows below fold line, trim it. Topstitch strip with white thread about ⅛ inch from folded edges. Cut strip into nine 1¾-inch lengths. Fold under ¼ inch at ends of each piece and press.

To make the belts for the pencil holder and the penholder, determine belt length by measuring the area where the belt will be positioned. Add 1 inch extra at the end where the buckle will be attached. Also, allow about 1¼ inches overlap to buckle the belt. Cut 2½-inch wide denim strip; fold it lengthwise, and make a ¼-inch seam. Turn strip to the right side, and press. Cut strip in proper lengths. Attach buckle to one end of belt. Make a hole at other end. Wrap belt around accessory to check correct hole placement. When hole is punched, hand-bind with white thread in overcast stitch. Topstitch edge of belt, using white thread.

Picture frame: Remove cardboard backing and glass. Place frame, front side down, on cardboard removed from frame. Trace outline of inside of frame onto the cardboard.

Measure a 5x7-inch rectangle in the center of this piece of cardboard and cut it out. Now, you have the mat to cover with fabric.

Trace the cardboard mat onto fabric with chalk. Sew a row of white stitching ¼ inch from the traced lines. Sew stitching along both outside edge and inside edge (hole where picture will fit). Cut the fabric about an inch from the traced lines.

Glue fabric onto the cardboard mat, holding up to the light to see if the stitching is centered. (Stitching should be about ⅛ inch from edges of cardboard.) Clip corners; glue excess of fabric to back of mat.

Attach the belt loops. Fold them over the edges and glue them onto the back of the mat, rather than sewing them on the front.

Cover the outside edge of the frame with denim by brushing on glue and attaching fabric to completely cover the frame. Let glue dry. Replace the glass in the frame, then glue the fabric-covered mat directly onto the outside of the glass. Place a 5x7-inch photo under the glass, and replace the backing with the built-in easel.

Pencil holder: Measure height and circumference of container. Cut a piece of fabric to cover the container, allowing ¼ inch extra at the top and the bottom, and 1 inch overlap at the side seam. Turn under allowance at the top and bottom and press. Turn under ½ inch at one side, press and topstitch a row of white stitching ¼ inch from the edge at both top and bottom. Glue the fabric cover to the container.

Make belt to fit circumference of container and three belt loops. Attach belt loops with glue. Thread belt into loops; buckle.

Penholder: Glue fabric to both side ends of penholder, allowing ¼ inch extra all the way around. Clip the corners diagonally, and glue excess fabric to top, bottom, front, and back edges.

Measure width of base from side to side. Measure around base, starting at front edge, over the top and across the bottom to the starting point. Cut the fabric the base width plus ½ inch by the measurement obtained from going around the base plus 1 inch. Fold under ¼ inch on three sides and press. Topstitch these three sides with white stitching. Wrap this piece around the penholder so that the stitched end falls at the front edge. Mark the spot where you will make the hole to slip over the pen, then unwrap the piece. Cut the hole, just large enough to slide over the pen, and overcast with white thread around the hole.

Now, slip the hole over the pen, and glue the cover to the base with the stitched end lapped over the raw edge at the front edge.

Make two belt loops and glue in place. Make the belt long enough to completely wrap around the base. Thread the belt through the loops and buckle.

Letter opener: To cover a large-handled letter opener with fabric, follow the instructions for covering the penholder base. Make a seam in the center of one wide side.

Cut a piece of belt looping for each wide side, ½ inch longer than the side. Fold under ¼ inch at top and bottom. Press and whip together with overcast stitches on sides. Glue loops to letter opener, covering the seam with one of the loops.

Art-Deco Circular Mirror Frame

This ingenious mirror frame is one that doesn't require a knowledge of mitering corners and other basic framing techniques. The geometric design stems from an unlikely source—an old floor register. Use the design reproduced here, or create your own. The method of reproducing the design shown here is simple—it's called rubbing.

For your first attempt at rubbing, try a manhole cover, an old-fashioned register, the cornerstone of a building, or a plaque on a wall. Almost any surface that is raised or in bas-relief lends itself to rubbing. To take a rubbing, you need a roll of shelf paper, masking tape, and a wax crayon, available at art supply stores.

Tape the shelf paper securely over the item selected. Rub the crayon over the paper from the center out to the edges, and watch your design appear. Continue until all of the elements are sharp and clear.

Materials
- 36-inch circle of ¼-inch plywood
- 1¼ yards of dark brown wool or other even weave fabric (suitable for crewel embroidery)
- 8 skeins (40 yards each) of white 3-ply Persian wool yarn
- Polyester batting

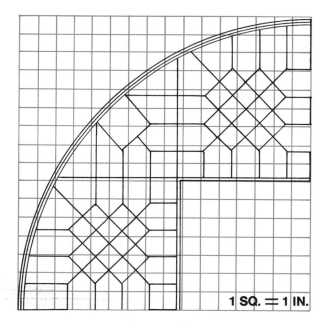

1 SQ. = 1 IN.

- 12x12-inch mirror tile
- Mirror mounts
- Staple gun or small tacks
- Large-eyed crewel embroidery needle
- Dressmaker's carbon
- Tracing wheel
- Embroidery hoop or artist's stretcher
- 36-inch square piece of paper

Directions
Draw a 32-inch diameter circle on the paper, and fold the circle into quarters. Enlarge the design in the drawing to full size and transfer the design to all four segments of the paper circle. Use dressmaker's carbon and a tracing wheel to transfer the design to the dark brown fabric.

Fasten the fabric to an embroidery hoop or artist's stretcher to keep the material taut while you are embroidering it. Cut the yarn into 36-inch lengths and use a double thread (actually six strands of yarn) to give it a heavy, raised effect. Work the entire design in stem stitch (see pages 28-29). When the embroidery is finished, turn the piece to the wrong side, lay a damp cloth on top of it, and press lightly with a warm iron. Cut the embroidered fabric to fit the plywood frame, allowing one inch to fold around the back of the frame.

Cut an 11-inch square out of the center of the plywood circle. Cover the plywood with one or two layers of polyester batting. Top with the embroidered fabric, and staple or tack the excess fabric to the back of the plywood frame. Cut away the fabric and batting inside the square in the center of the frame, leaving a 1-inch margin to tack or staple onto the back of the plywood (cut slashes in each of the four corners so the fabric and batting will fold back smoothly). Attach the mirror tile to the back of the frame with mirror mounts.

Framing Kits

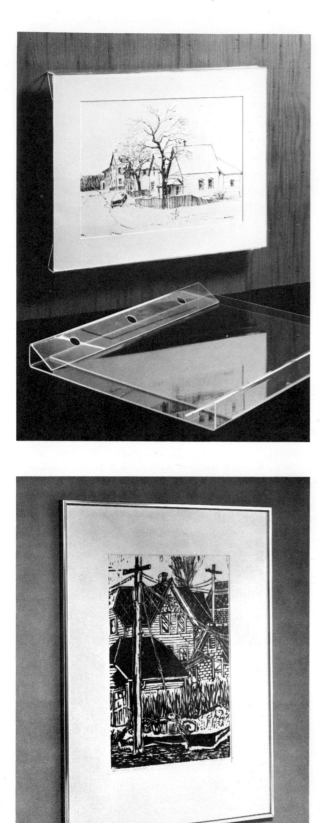

Do-it-yourself framing is easier for everyone because of the great variety of framing kits available.

You can assemble frames of plastic, wood, metal, and metal-wood combinations. The materials come in different sizes and shapes, and some require no construction. Simply use spring fasteners or corner locks to hold the moldings together. These pre-mitered moldings come in lengths of 4 inches to 30 inches, and are sold in art supply and department stores. Each package contains two sides and the joining pins. Buy two packages — one for the sides and one for the top and bottom — to make one frame.

Whether your tastes run toward modern or traditional framing, you will find kits suitable for your pictures.

Stores also have a wide selection of ready-made frames both unfinished and prefinished. Some have extra deep rabbets so you can frame thick items such as needlepoint or crewel wall hangings.

The ink drawing country winter scene at the upper left of this page is shown in a wraparound clear acrylic frame that hangs horizontally. You simply slip it apart to insert the picture and mat, and it is ready to hang without any mounts.

Use this frame for graphics when you wish to emphasize the art, not the frame.

The wood cut engraving at the lower left is framed with slim aluminum moldings that come in an easy-to-assemble kit. Combine two pairs of sections, whatever two lengths you need to fit your work of art. Each package of two strips has the length of the inside measurement printed on it. This is the length of the frame edge which will be next to the mat or picture. Assemble the frame according to the directions on the package.

Cut glass, mat, and backing cardboard to fit the inside of the frame. Hold them in place with spring clips to bridge the corners. Special clips to hold the hanging wire also are included in framing kits.

The large poster at the right also has a narrow metal pre-packaged frame, colored black to add the perfect contrast. When a poster has a wide border, such as this one, it is not necessary to add a mat. Select two packages of moldings in lengths to fit the size of your poster. Assemble the frame, following the directions on the package.

These easy-to-assemble aluminum framing kits are available in both shiny and brushed metal finishes, in black and white, and in a variety of popular decorator colors. If you can't find the exact color you desire, you can paint the frame yourself to harmonize with your art work and your decorating scheme.

Three other framing choices are pictured at the lower right. For art that requires two-sided visibility, use the clear acrylic frame that can be made to stand either horizontally or vertically. Cut a piece of mat board the size of the frame and mount a picture on both the back and front. Slide the piece of mat board between the two acrylic frame sections and slip on the plastic edging strips. This stand-up is ideal for a desk or a table, where the picture is viewed from more than one angle.

The striking photograph hanging on the wall in the background is part of a series of pictures that comes mounted on heavy illustration board, with a hanging device fastened on the back. No framing is needed because the illustration board has a border around the edge and a mar-proof coating.

On the right, resting on the table, is a see-through box with clear plastic front and sides. This type of framing kit is ideal for prints and etchings. It is available in several sizes. You can hang it on the wall, stand it on edge, or lay it flat.

Choosing the Right Frame

Like selecting a work of art, choosing the right frame is primarily a matter of personal preference and depends upon the impression one wants to create in a room.

• *Decide the visual effect* you wish to create. A small picture or a miniature takes on a traditional or sentimental look in a shadow box frame. The frame becomes more exciting with an exaggerated liner and a stylized border. Add elegance to your picture by using a narrow liner and an ornate gold frame.

• *Increase the size of a picture* by placing it under a large mat enclosed in a narrow frame. As a general rule, mats should be larger at the bottom because an optical illusion causes a picture matted equally on all four sides to appear to have less area at the bottom.

• *Width, wood tone, and degree of ornamentation* are important when choosing a frame.

• *Size, texture, and color of liner or mat* are equally important in frame selection.

Guidelines to Effective Framing

Let the technique of the wall hanging point the way to the most suitable frame.

• *Oil paintings:* As a general rule, use a frame about 4 inches wide to complement oil paintings from 10x12 inches to 30x40 inches. With larger size oils, you can use a 6-inch or even an 8-inch molding. Due to their heavier texture, never use a glass over oil paintings. Instead, use wide, ornate frames. The cost of such wide frames is high, but you can achieve an equally attractive effect with a wide liner, or an insert within a 4-inch-wide frame. Use frames that are not less than 1½ inches in depth, 2 to 3 inches being recommended for oil paintings.

• *Watercolors and graphics:* Even though they are adaptable to almost any type of frame because they are more delicate, take care not to overpower such works with too heavy or dark a frame.

Mat them and cover them with glass for practical purposes. The thickness of the mat keeps the paper surface from coming into contact with the glass, preventing condensation from forming under the glass, spoiling the picture or causing it to wrinkle.

The glass, of course, protects the delicate paper from dust and careless handling.

Use glare-proof glass if you wish to eliminate annoying light reflections. Be sure to place it directly against the picture, since distortion and color variation can occur when there is space between glareproof glass and the artwork.

Regardless of the size of the watercolor or graphic, allow at least 2½ inches at the top side of the mat and at least 3 inches at the bottom. You may increase these dimensions proportionately, depending on the effect desired. Never glue the picture to the mat, as this will eventually destroy the quality of the paper.

• *Black and white etchings:* Set these off effectively by double matting, which provides a narrow strip of color in the border.

• *Subject matter:* Let the subject matter be an important guide to choosing the frame. Use ornate or simple frames for landscapes and still lifes, depending on the medium. Bold abstractions only require minimal frames.

• *Interior design:* Consider your decor in choosing frames. Choose them to contrast a furnishing scheme, in which case the frame attracts maximum attention to the picture, or select an unobtrusive frame that blends into the setting. If you are keeping pace with the current popularity of glass and chrome in home furnishings, use stainless steel, brushed chrome, or aluminum frames for watercolors and graphics; they can even be effective with some oil abstractions.

Again, let the visual impact desired be your guide. In a highly contemporary room, you may want to mat an abstract in a vivid shade, and frame it with simple, narrow strips for a striking effect that will blend into the total room design. If you plan that same painting as the *piece de resistance,* use a subtle shaping or coloring in the molding in contrast to the severity of the art to achieve a stunning effect.

Use more elaborate frames in a traditional room. Narrow gold frames with wide mats are perfect for a fresh, contemporary touch.

Let the family room take on a more informal and personal quality. Display family photos, collections, needlework, and children's art in narrow, flat frames without mats and under glare-proof glass. You can also find frames that provide multiple views to fit all sizes of snapshots, arrange these in an interesting grouping.

Novel Art Displays

Remember that all your artwork does not have to end up decorating walls. Here are some ideas that will stir your imagination.
• *Easel frames:* Use these for little pictures, graphics, or snapshots on tables.
• *Favorite posters or prints:* Place under glass, then back with a sturdy piece of plywood, and produce a unique serving tray.
• *Tabletop display:* Cover a table with a sheet of glass and display such novelties as picture post cards from faraway places, reproductions of old masters, menu covers, theater programs, etc.
• *Room dividers:* Use pictures as room dividers by suspending two or three from the ceiling on wire or chain to meet a credenza or buffet, artfully separating the dining area from the living room or kitchen.
• *Collage:* Create a collage on an ordinary folding screen. If you're handy with tools, cut a groove in the bottom of one bookcase shelf about ½ inch from the front edge of another shelf as far down as your picture is long. Affix a picture to a piece of plywood and insert in the grooves—presto, a decorative sliding door.
• *Place mats:* Heat-seal attractive prints, both traditional and abstract, between two sheets of plastic and make them into delightful, conversation-piece place mats.

Glossary

Framers, like other professionals, have a terminology that you should be familiar with.
• *Baroque, rococo, or Barbizon:* Styles of frames which are more or less interchangeable and characterized by elaborate carving, utilizing scroll work to form shapes of rocks, shells, or foliage.
• *Louis XIV frame:* Flowers carved on corners and often in center of frame.
• *Driftwood frame.* Gives effect of worn, weather-beaten wood.
• *Railroad frame:* Variation of the flat panel with smaller raised edge on each side.
• *Scoop frame:* Flat frame which slopes at an angle toward the painting.
• *Shadow box:* Glassed-in scoop frame.
• *Reverse level frame:* Sides slope at an angle toward the wall.
• *Platform frame:* Top molding containing picture is mounted on flat back panel.
• *Molding:* Material from which picture frames are made of.
• *Composition ornament:* Decoration made of putty, plaster of paris, or other materials, cast in a mold and used chiefly with gold leaf to give the effect of carving.
• *Mat:* Paper board, smooth or pebbled, often covered in fabric, and placed around edge of picture. Width of mat should be determined both by size of picture and style and size of frame. Mats are most effective when they contrast with width of frame.
• *French mat:* Series of tinted lines surround opening. When strips of antiqued gold, silver, or foil are mounted between lines, mat is called an *Empire* design.
• *Insert or liner:* Narrow strip of molding, placed inside picture frame to provide "breathing space" between picture and frame. It can be used to accent color or add depth or width to frame.
• *Frame close:* No separation between picture and frame. Oil paintings and reproductions of oils are usually framed in this fashion.
• *Flush mounted:* Picture placed in mat or liner with art surface even with surface of mat. This is used when an important segment of the picture is so near the edge even smallest overlap would detract from the effect.

Woodworking

Home building projects hold a fascination for people of all ages, especially if they have a well-lighted area with a workbench and an assortment of tools. In this chapter, you will find projects that add function and beauty to your home. In addition, there is a collection of handcrafted toys that will delight youngsters you love to surprise.

Mobile Butcher Block Server

Here's the perfect answer to the never-ending complaint of not having enough countertop space. This butcher block serving cart is exactly the height and width of the kitchen countertop and has a brake on each caster to hold the surface steady while you use the top for food preparation.

When it's time to serve, arrange food, beverages, and tableware on the shelves. Unlock the brakes on the casters, roll it into the dining area, place it where it is convenient for the person who is serving, and lock the brakes. This mobile server, with its glass shelves, is suitable for both casual and more formal entertaining.

The combination countertop and food server shown here has a top that measures 18x30 inches and is 35 inches high. Before you start this project, measure your kitchen cabinets and if the height and depth varies from these measurements, alter the dimensions to match your built-ins.

Materials
- Two 18x30-inch pieces of 2-inch-thick prefinished butcher block
- Two 18x30¼-inch pieces of 2-inch-thick prefinished butcher block
- Four 2½-inch ball-type locking casters
- Two 18x27-inch, ½-inch-thick panels of glass for shelves
- 12 1½-inch wood screws
- Wood filler
- Glue

Directions
On the inside of the 18x30¼ inch side pieces of the serving cart, cut out the slots for the glass shelves (see drawing on page 200) by first measuring 14 inches up and making a light pencil line across the side. Then, use a router with a straight bit or a band saw to cut the slot ⅝ inch wide and ⅝ inch deep. Repeat the same measuring and sawing procedure on the opposite side.

Measure the mark lightly with pencil 8 inches above the first slots, and cut another slot in the same manner across each side piece. **Note:** If you change the height of the shelves, always have the deepest space

(continued)

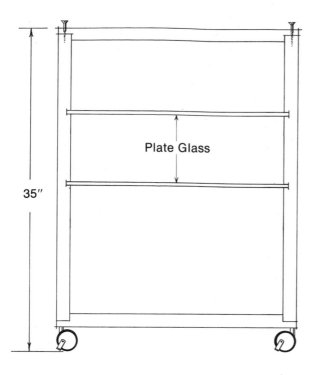

at the bottom of the cart, as this is where you are most likely to place the heaviest objects.

Next, cut rabbeted joints at both ends of the top and bottom pieces of butcher block (see sketch) by first measuring and marking with a pencil the width and depth of the joint— two inches for the width and one inch for the depth. Then, cut the rabbet with a back saw or a power saw with a dado attachment. (If you use a router, use a straight bit and adjust the cutting depth.) *Note:* Practice on a piece of scrap wood to make sure that your measurements are accurate. Before you attach the side pieces, check to be sure they fit the rabbet exactly. If you don't have a perfect fit, make additional passes with the saw until you do.

Next, glue the side pieces in place and use three wood screws on top and bottom of each end piece. Position the screws one inch from the end of the piece and equally spaced along the 18-inch width. Countersink the screws and use wood filler to conceal the holes.

Turn the serving cart upside down and attach the casters at the corners. Ball casters come with a plate-type mount or a socket-type mount. If you have the plate-type mount, attach each one with four screws. If you use those with a socket-type mount, drill a hole in each corner of the bottom large enough to accommodate the grip-neck mount. Then, slip the caster in place.

Turn the serving cart right side up, and insert the glass shelves in the slots.

Handy Tools for Handy People

Use this handy guide to help you select versatile hand tools in each category.

Hammers: For general carpentry and ripping out nails, use a curved claw hammer. Get a tack hammer for upholstery work, and a ball peen hammer for metalwork projects.

Hand saws: Use a crosscut saw for cutting against the grain and for cutting plywood, and a rip saw for sawing boards lengthwise. Use a coping saw for cutting curves and a hacksaw for cutting metal.

Screwdrivers: Start with two sizes each of standard and Phillips screwdrivers. Buy sizes that match screws you use most often. For very fine work, purchase a jeweler's screwdriver.

Pliers: Start out with the four most common types—slip-joint, long-nose, diagonal-cutting, and a combination plier-wrench.

Wrenches: Begin with an adjustable wrench, then add double-end, open-end and box wrenches, a socket wrench, and a pipe wrench.

Nail sets: Always keep a nail set handy to countersink nails.

Awls or gimlets: Use an awl or gimlet to get a screw started, before you use the screwdriver.

Rulers and tape measures: Use a folding wood rule and a steel tape measure.

Hand drills: Purchase a brace with an assortment of sizes of bits or a hand drill with several sizes of twist drills.

Decorative Wood Scrap Headboard

The headboard shown above is an ingenious way to use up wood scraps left over from your building projects. Random sizes, shapes, and thicknesses give an overall sculptured effect. Mount the scraps on the plywood backing in a casual formation.

Materials
- Scraps from woodworking projects
- ¾-inch plywood
- 1x2s for frame
- Stain
- Black paint
- Nails
- Glue
- Clear polyurethane coating

Directions
Note: The amounts of ¾-inch plywood for the headboard and 1x2s for the frame will depend on the size headboard you make. A twin-size headboard is 39 inches wide, a full-size is 54 inches wide, a queen-size is 60 inches wide and a king-size is 76 inches wide. The one pictured is 40 inches high.

Begin the project by cutting the headboard the desired height and width from ¾-inch plywood. Cut 1x2s to frame the sides and top of the headboard, mitering the corners. Sand the corners of the 1x2s, and glue and nail them to plywood. Paint headboard and frame black.

Sand different sizes and shapes of wood scraps smooth, and stain them in various wood finishes. Arrange the pieces of wood on the headboard in an interesting fashion, and glue the blocks in place.

Apply a coat of clear polyurethane, and bolt it to the bed frame.

Trio of Art Deco Stand-Up Planters

Tubes and circular shapes set the mood for this grouping of floor planters. Easy and inexpensive to make, the planters of varying height provide an attractive way to display large-leafed plants such as the ones shown here. Six-inch pots fit nicely into these planters, and the ebony cat stands guard.

Materials
(for each planter)
• Eight 1-inch wood dowels (length depends on height of planter — 15, 20, or 25 inches)
• 40x40-inch piece of ½-inch plywood

- 20x40-inch piece of ⅜-inch plywood
- Corrugated paper
- Wood filler
- White glue
- Nails
- Tacks
- Paint
- Sandpaper
- Six-inch flowerpots

Directions

For each planter, cut five plywood circles. Make one of ½-inch plywood with radius of 5 inches for the planter base (this remains a solid piece). Now, cut rings (see diagram). Cut one of ½-inch plywood with an outside radius of 5 inches and an inside radius of 3 inches; two with an outside radius of 4½ inches and an inside radius of 3 inches from ⅜-inch plywood; and a top ring of ½-inch plywood with an outside radius of 5 inches and an inside radius of 3 inches.

Next, drill eight 1-inch holes in all five circle layers to accommodate dowels. Use a 45° triangle to determine spacing. The center of each hole is 3¾ inches from the circle center (see drawing).

Next, place the plywood circles on the dowels and glue and nail in position, placing the solid ½-inch-thick plywood circle on the bottom. Arrange them in the following manner. For the 15-inch-high planter, position the second circle so its upper edge is 6 inches from the bottom. Place the two ⅜-inch rings 1 inch apart (the bottom ⅜-inch ring rests directly on the ½-inch-thick ring below it). Position top ring (½-inch-thick plywood) flush with top of dowels.

For the 20-inch-high planter, place the second ring with its upper edge 8 inches from the bottom and proceed the same as for the 15-inch planter. For the 25-inch-high planter, place this second ring with its upper edge 10 inches from the bottom. Assemble the same as for the 15-inch-high planter.

Cut corrugated paper to fit around the bottom of the planter on the lower two circles. Place it so the lines run vertically. Glue and tack the paper in place. (The corrugated paper sections are 6 inches, 8 inches, and 10 inches high respectively for the three planter heights.)

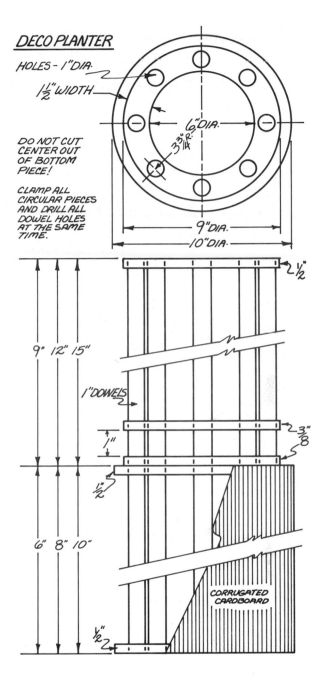

To finish, fill all the holes on the plywood edges with wood filler, then sand and paint the color of your choice.

Use pots that are 6 inches in diameter for these planters. To achieve the best decorative effect, use pots that are the same color as the planters and fit them into the stands with no more than 1 inch of the pot visible above the top ring. If necessary, place a small drip pan in bottom of stand.

Art Deco Tables Made of Dowels

The fluted or ribbed effect is a familiar Art Deco motif. Here, this well-known style of the 30s is translated into a design for a base for a glass-topped coffee table and an end table simply by using wooden dowels. You won't need as many dowels as the photo suggests because there's an interior plywood box. This makes it easy to arrange the dowels in the pattern shown and glue in place.

Materials

(for each table)
- 45 one-inch dowels 48 inches long
- 12x48-inch piece of ½-inch plywood for glass-topped table

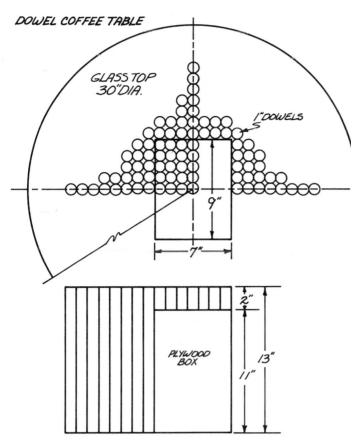

DOWEL COFFEE TABLE

GLASS TOP 30" DIA.

1" DOWELS

9"

7"

PLYWOOD BOX

2"

13"

11"

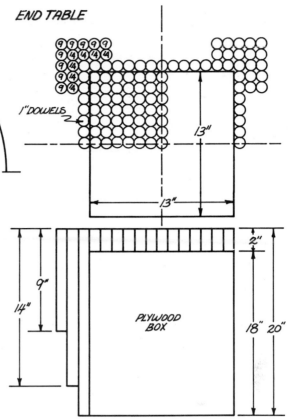

END TABLE

1" DOWELS

13"

13"

2"

9"

14"

PLYWOOD BOX

18" 20"

- 30x48-inch piece of ½-inch plywood for end table
- 30-inch-diameter circle of ½-inch-thick glass
- Plastic resin glue
- Clear protective coating
- Fourpenny nails
- Sandpaper
- Wood blocks
- Boards

Directions

Study the diagrams for the two tables to determine the pattern and placement of the dowels and the measurements of the components.

Next, build plywood box and nail it together, following illustration as a guide. (Make sure box will not be visible in your finished table.) If sides of table are not square, as in glass-top model, be sure box is back at least two inches from all edges. On square designs, such as the end table, the plywood box needs to be only 1 inch from each edge.

Note: The box is designed to be two inches shorter than desired height of finished table.

Next, nail a temporary framework around the outer top edge of the plywood box. Line 2-inch-long dowels within this framework and glue the dowels in place. Remove the frame when the glue is dry.

Cut the remaining dowels to the desired size, using the diagram as a guide, and glue them together in strips before you attach them to the table. You can do this most effectively by using clamps. Support two bar clamps on blocks of wood and fill them crosswise with dowels. To keep the dowels from buckling, place two boards top and bottom, and clamp them together with C-clamps. Glue the joints securely. Glue only one side of dowels that will be visible from one direction.

Attach the dowel strips to the plywood box with glue and secure with wood strips and clamps until dry. Then, apply next row. On projecting pieces, reinforce dowels with nails.

To finish, sand the top until the dowels are smooth and level. Apply a coat of clear, protective finish. Place the glass top on top of the coffee table.

Fold-down Workbench

This compact workbench is a happy solution for those who have space limitations. Besides serving as a base of operations for woodworking projects, it's a natural for crafts and sewing, flower arranging and re-potting plants, or even a mini version of a home office.

Use the back of a closet door, and build the bench top that folds down for work, then folds up into a self-storing unit between times. Cover the back of the door with a sheet of perforated hardboard, and arrange your tools so they are readily accessible.

Materials
- 1x8-inch boards
- Perforated hardboard
- ¾-inch plywood
- Three pieces of 1x3
- 1x2s
- Screws
- Nails
- Glue
- Molly bolts (for hollow door)
- Two piano hinges
- Two mending plates
- Screen door hook and screw eye
- Primer
- Enamel
- Saw (optional)
- Sandpaper

Directions

Construct the frame for the tool board and shelves from 1x8-inch boards. (Make the frame narrow enough to clear the doorknob and cut it shorter than the door height by a couple of inches, too, so it won't rub against the carpet when you open and close the door.)

Measure carefully for all the pieces, according to the height and width of your door. Cut them with a saw or have them pre-cut at the building supply dealer. Then, all you have to do is nail them together. Use a little more glue for extra strength. Nail in a couple more 1x8s for shelves, and make a frame for the perforated hardboard tool organizer from 1x2s. Use some pieces of 1x2 for the retaining strips on the shelves and for the little shelf on the tool board.

Fasten the entire unit to the back of the closet door with some screws through the 1x2s at the top and at the bottom of the frame. (If you have a hollow core door with nothing to screw into except ¼-inch plywood, use molly bolts.)

Make the bench top from a piece of ¾-inch plywood. Fasten it to the frame shelf with a piano hinge. Design your unit so the bench top ends up being about 36 inches high.

Build the fold-down leg for the top from three pieces of 1x3, screwed together. Fasten the leg joints with long screws and glue, plus a couple of metal mending plates screwed on for extra strength. Fasten the leg under

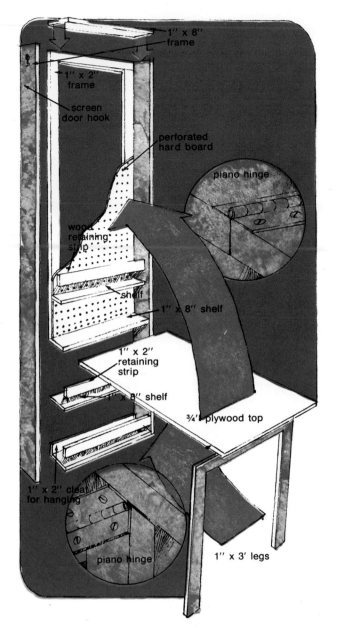

1" x 8" frame

1" x 2" frame

screen door hook

perforated hard board

piano hinge

wood retaining strip

shelf

1" x 8" shelf

1" x 2" retaining strip

1" x 8" shelf

¾" plywood top

1" x 2" cleat for hanging

piano hinge

1" x 3' legs

the bench top with another piano hinge. Put a screw eye in the edge of the bench top and a screen door hook on the frame to keep the top up when the unit is closed.

Sand the legs and the edges of the plywood top, and apply a coat of primer. Finish with two coats of enamel, sanding between coats. Now, you're ready to organize your tools and start a woodworking project.

Power Tools to Speed Up Production

The more home building projects you attempt, the more you will want to speed up and improve the various steps by using power tools. Before you make any large investment, rent one or more power tools when you are working on a woodworking project. This will give you an opportunity to test their usefulness and the ease with which you can handle them. Then you will be in a better position to evaluate what your needs are and what tools work best for you.

Drills: For most people, the power drill is the first investment in portable power tools. Besides a set of regular twist drill bits for use with wood and metal, you may want to also get several sizes of carbide drill bits for use on brick and masonry work.

Power saws: There are many types and sizes of electric saws. They are expensive to buy, so make a study of them, watch demonstrations of different types and brands, and try them out yourself before you decide which saw best suits your particular needs.

Sanders: Power sanders save many hours of tedious hand sanding. Also, they are relatively inexpensive compared to other power tools. There are many different types, sizes, and models. Some are equipped with polishing attachments.

Electric screwdrivers: If you tackle many home building projects, you'll find that an electric screwdriver provides invaluable assistance. It allows you to insert or remove screws rapidly with just a gentle push.

Remember that proper care and maintenance is vital to good performance and long life of power tools. Study the manual that accompanies each one, and check the warranty. Follow the manufacturer's instructions for use and care.

Kitchen Organizer

This well-turned kitchen grabber, with pegs to hold your most often used utensils, will make culinary life easier. Positioned between wall cabinet and countertop, it's within arm's reach of range and food preparation area.

Materials
- 24-inch stock turned leg
- ¼-inch dowels
- One screw
- Stain or paint

Directions
First, measure the distance between bottom of wall cabinet and top of base cabinet and cut the 24-inch stock turned leg to this length. Drill ¼-inch holes at random in the leg and insert ¼-inch dowels, allowing them to protrude about 1 inch. Stain or paint leg.

To fasten the leg to the countertop, drill a hole in the counter of the base cabinet and insert a piece of dowel (it should protrude about ¼ inch above the countertop). Slip the leg down over the dowel. Then, drive a screw down through the bottom of the wall cabinet into the top of the leg.

Countertop Spice Rack

Food preparation is always much easier when you have condiments within easy reach rather than having to poke around your cupboard to find the herb or spice you need. So make things easier and quicker for yourself. Build this nifty countertop spice rack and stock it with your favorites.

Materials
- Tall glass jars (olive jars were used here)
- 24x36-inch piece of ⅜-inch hardboard
- 8 feet of ¼x¼-inch screen molding
- White glue
- Nails
- Stain or paint
- Labels

Directions
Make a paper pattern of end pieces first, using photo as a guide (this one is about 9 inches deep and 12 inches tall). Trace pattern onto hardboard and cut out two end pieces. Cut three shelves and a back piece to fit inside end pieces (length depends on number of jars you place on shelves) and nail and glue together. Cut five strips of screen molding, two for each of two top shelves and one for bottom shelf. Glue to end pieces to hold jars upright. Stain or paint.

Building Blocks

Wood blocks always rate high on children's preferred toy lists, and this set of hand-crafted building blocks has an intriguing bonus—the blocks are parts of a puzzle.

To store blocks neatly, a youngster must complete the puzzle, carefully fitting each piece in its appointed place so the grain on alternating blocks runs at right angles.

Materials
- 3-foot length of 2x4 fir
- 4-foot length of 1x2 pine
- 15-inch length of 1x12-inch pine shelving
- 10-inch length of 1-inch dowel
- White glue
- Finishing nails
- Wood filler
- Clear, matte, or polyurethane varnish
- Sandpaper

Directions
Cut each of the 11 blocks from the fir 2x4, following the designs in the illustration at the top of the next column. Cut three

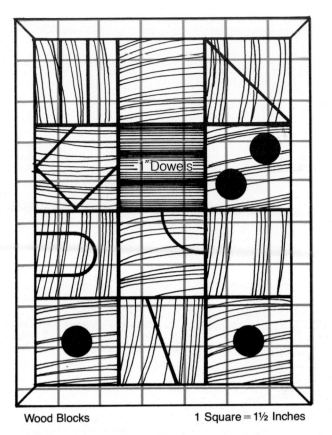

Wood Blocks   1 Square = 1½ Inches

3-inch lengths of 1-inch dowel to fit in the remaining section of the tray. Sand all of the edges smooth. *Note:* Sand the corners of each block until they are slightly rounded so there is no danger of small children hurting themselves on sharp corners.

Drill the holes (as shown in the illustration) through the blocks, large enough to insert the 3-inch lengths of the 1-inch dowels. Sand the edges of the holes smooth.

To build the tray that contains the blocks, cut the bottom piece from 1x12-inch pine shelving. Make the bottom piece 9½x12½ inches (slightly larger than the assembled blocks) so that the blocks will be easy to remove and replace in the tray.

Cut the four sides of the tray from the 1x2-inch pine strip (two 9½-inch and two 12½-inch lengths), mitering the corners. Attach the sides of the tray to the bottom with glue and finishing nails. Countersink the nails, and fill the holes with wood filler. When filler dries, sand smooth.

Finish all of the blocks and the tray with a coat of clear, matte, or polyurethane varnish (your choice will depend on the degree of gloss you prefer).

Toddlers' Woolly Ride-On Lamb

Here's a toy that will impress the nursery school set, and will also be fun for the weekend hobbyist to make. The soft, shaggy coat makes the lamb comfortable to sit on, and the wheels provide mobility.

Materials
- 24x36-inch piece of ¾-inch plywood
- One 20x30-inch shag carpet remnant
- Scraps of red, green, and black felt

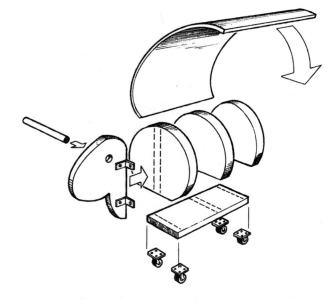

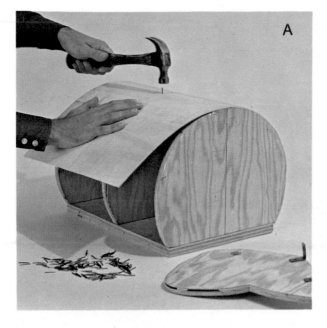

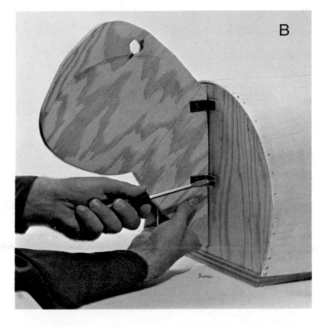

- Four plate casters
- 10-inch length of 1-inch dowel
- 14x28-inch piece of ⅛-inch template board
- ½-inch wood screws
- Nails
- Four small angle brackets
- White glue
- White paint

Directions

Cut out one 10x14-inch piece of ¾-inch plywood for the base, three 10x12-inch elongated circular pieces to support the body, and the 9½x13-inch head piece (see drawing at bottom of opposite page). Nail the three circular pieces to the base (one at each end and one in the center).

Carefully wrap the 14x28-inch piece of template board around the curve of the support circles (see photo A). Nail the template board to the three support sections, checking the alignment as you go.

Drill a 1-inch hole through the head, as shown in the drawing, and insert the dowel in the headpiece. Glue the dowel in place.

Center the head at one end of the body and attach it to the body with small angle brackets (see photo B).

Paint the lamb white. After the paint is thoroughly dry, cut and glue a 14x30-inch piece of shag carpet to the rounded back, two 4x6-inch pieces to the ears, and a 5x6-inch piece to the tail. Cut the facial features out of felt scraps in appropriate colors and glue in place.

Screw on the four casters, one at each corner of the base (see drawing).

Metric Equivalency Chart

Following are the standard equivalents for converting inches to millimeters and centimeters (with figures rounded off):

Inches	MM	CM	Inches	MM	CM
⅛	3		5	125	12.5
¼	6		6	150	15
⅜	10	1	7	180	18
½	13	1.3	8	205	20.5
⅝	15	1.5	9	230	23
¾	20	2	10	255	25.5
⅞	22	2.2	11	280	28
1	25	2.5	12	305	30.5
1¼	32	3.2	20	510	51
1¾	45	4.5	24	610	61
2	50	5	30	760	76
2½	65	6.5	36	915	91.5
3	75	7.5	40	1015	101.5
4	100	10	48	1220	122

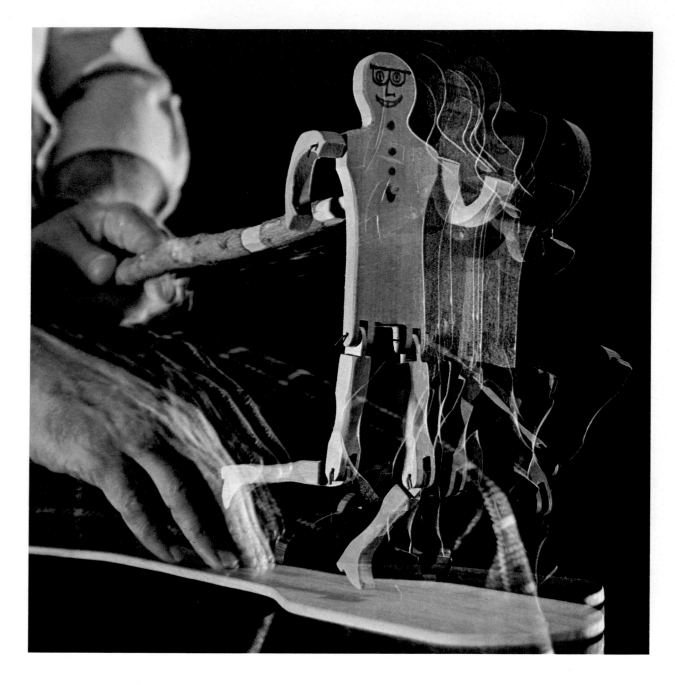

Limber Jack—The Dancing Man

This wooden doll, dancing so energetically on a tapping board, is known as a Limber Jack (some people call it a Stomper Doll). An authentic American folk toy, it will be a favorite of hobbyists—and of children:

Materials
- 6x30-inch piece of ¼-inch mahogany or other suitable semi-hardwood
- 6x18-inch piece of ⅜-inch lumber
- Wire
- Dowel or twig
- Tracing paper
- Carbon paper
- Sandpaper
- Art knife
- Felt-tip markers
- Clear mat or gloss varnish
- Jigsaw

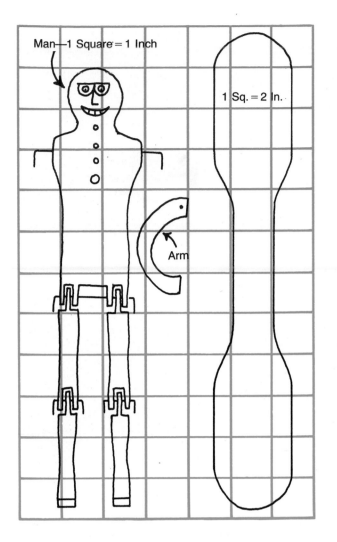

Man—1 Square = 1 Inch

1 Sq. = 2 In.

Arm

Drill a hole in the dancing man's back and insert a dowel or twig for a handle. Draw the facial features and buttons with felt-tip marking pens. Finish with a coat of clear varnish in a mat or gloss finish.

To manipulate the dancing man, sit down on one end of the paddle and hold the man by the handle with his feet slightly above the protruding end of the paddle. Strum rhythmically on extended end of paddle with your fingers to make the man dance.

How to Enlarge Patterns

In case you're not familiar with the grid system, its purpose is to enable the craftsman to duplicate a design drawn exactly to scale. There are two parts to the system—the first is the combination of parallel horizontal and vertical lines that form a graph, and the second is the line drawing superimposed on top of the lines.

Look for the scale given with the grid that accompanies the project—one square equals one inch, one square equals two inches, etc. The number listed means that each square of the grid will measure exactly those dimensions after it has been enlarged.

Select paper large enough to accommodate the finished design (brown wrapping paper works well). Draw horizontal and vertical lines as far apart as scale indicates. Next, transfer your pattern onto it. Then, reenact the paths of the lines as they move from square to square, using the illustration as a guide.

Use this method, regardless of whether you wish to make a pattern larger or smaller. Simply vary the size of the grids according to the scale to alter the size of the design.

Directions

Enlarge the pattern pieces (see illustration on the opposite page) on the grid and trace them onto tracing paper. Then, using carbon paper, transfer the pattern of the paddle to the ¼-inch mahogany board. Cut out the paddle with a jigsaw and sand all surfaces smooth. (This paddle becomes the platform that activates the dancing doll.)

Next, transfer the pattern for the dancing man onto the ⅜-inch-thick lumber. Cut out the pieces, using a jigsaw. Sand the edges and corners smooth, and use an art knife to whittle some roundness on leg and arm pieces.

Drill holes in leg and shoulder joints slightly larger than thickness of wire. Insert a short length of wire in each arm and leg joint and bend it at right angles to hold pieces together securely. *Note:* If you have small children, for their safety twist wire ends into loops and cut off any protruding sharp ends with a pair of pliers.

Menagerie Full of Surprises

These whimsical wood toys have lots of play value. The Trojan horse opens to reveal tiny clothespin soldiers and tortoise has a secret compartment. The others have nothing to hide — they're just themselves. The jolly-stack-toy farmer presides over all.

Materials
- 4x4-foot sheet of ¼-inch plywood
- 4x4-foot sheet of ⅜-inch plywood
- ¾x6-inch-thick pine board 24 inches long
- Wooden clothespins
- Dowel
- Hinges
- Two knobs
- Yarn
- Undercoat
- Enamel
- White glue
- Small brads
- Sandpaper
- Tracing paper
- Carbon paper

Directions
Note: Enlarge patterns according to the grid on page 216, and trace onto tracing paper.

Trojan horse: Transfer the pattern (sketch 2) twice to ⅜-inch plywood (for each side of horse). Cut two more of the head and body portions (above legs, see dotted lines) from ¾-inch pine. Drill a starting hole and saw out the inside of the two pine body parts, about ½ inch from top and bottom edge (see dotted line on sketch). Tack the four pieces together, with the complete horses of plywood on the outside and the head and body pieces sandwiched in between. Sand the outer edges.

Take the pieces apart and cut a door in one of the horse's sides. Tack and glue the two inner hollow body pieces together. Sand the hollow surface and inside the body area. Undercoat and paint these inner compartment surfaces. When the compartment is finished, attach the body to the outside of the horse, using nails and glue.

Fit the hinges and the doorknob. Remove them while you paint the horse. Undercoat the remaining parts of the horse and door, and sand when dry. Drill a ¼-inch hole for the tail. Paint the horse and door, and re-assemble when paint dries. Make a yarn tail, wrapping the top 1½ inches and tying it together. Glue tail in place.

To make the soldiers, cut off the ends of wooden clothespins to the proportions of a man. Drill a ¼-inch hole through the top and glue in dowels for arms. Apply undercoat, then paint soldiers, using the photo as a guide for color selection. For a smooth finish, apply several coats of paint, sanding between each coat.

Turtle box: Transfer the pattern pieces (sketch 4 on page 216) to ¼-inch plywood and ¾-inch pine, as indicated on the illustration. For all A and B sections, cut at one time from a sandwich of plywood-pine-plywood, nailed together. The head and tail are part of the pine body section; the feet belong to the plywood outer body. Four pieces of plywood plus pine are needed for the over-shell.

After cutting the shell liner off the top and making the box lid, separate the other pieces, then trace the legs, head, and tail. Cut the legs off the B body piece; cut out the inside for the box container. Put two A pieces together and cut off the head and tail sections. Glue and nail (use small brads) the three lid sections with pine between plywood. Assemble all pieces in same manner.

Glue and nail the three shell liner sections together, matching shapes. Heavily sand the outside edges of A pieces, allowing over-shell to fit after painting. Undercoat all pieces, allow to dry, and sand lightly. Paint the insides of C sections, inside curve of shell liner, section B of inside of turtle, and insides

(continued)

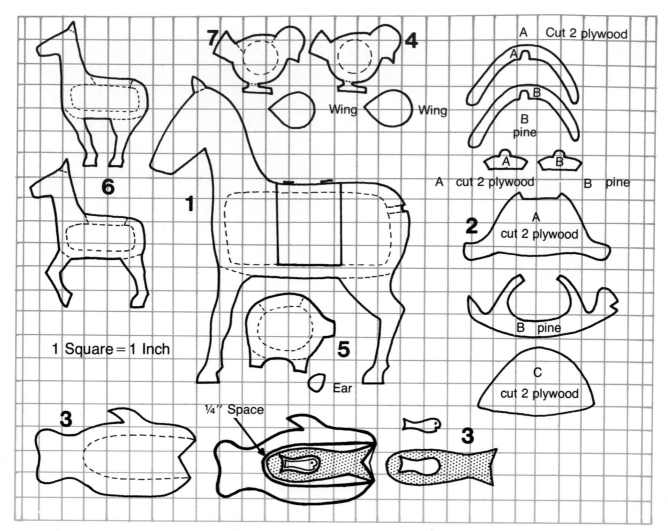

1 Square = 1 Inch

(wrong side) of A (leg) pieces with three thin coats of enamel. Decorate the turtle before final assembly. Also do the underside of the lid at this time.

When paint dries, glue and nail A pieces of turtle body on each side of B section. Glue and nail C pieces of turtle shell to shell liner. Sand exposed areas. Paint and decorate remaining exposed wood areas.

Food-chain fish: Using the pattern for the pieces in sketch 3, make a wood sandwich (plywood-pine-plywood) for the large fish. Cut the medium-size fish of ¾-inch pine, leaving ½-inch border around all sides except the mouth opening. (Tail shape of medium fish should be the same dimensions as mouth of the larger fish.)

Drill a starting hole in the medium-size ¾-inch pine fish, and cut out a fish-shaped hole. From ¼-inch plywood, cut three identical small fish to fit the hole.

Assemble the largest fish with glue and small brads, matching the edges carefully. Undercoat all surfaces except the largest fish opening. When dry, sand lightly. Finish with three coats of enamel and add decorations, using photo on page 214 as a guide.

Bird with egg: Using the pattern for the pieces in sketch 6, cut out two bird pieces and two wings from ¼-inch plywood. Cut the body and head (no legs) of ¾-inch pine. Assemble the body, except for the wings, using glue and nails.

Drill a pilot hole in the center of the bird, and saw out a circle 1¼ to 1½ inches in diameter (make sure the wing will cover the hole when the bird is assembled). Sand and undercoat all surfaces, including body cavity and wings. When undercoat is dry, sand smooth, then paint bird and wings. Nail and glue one wing in place; fasten the other wing with one nail only so it will swing open to reveal the egg.

Use an acorn, bead, ball, or small oval nut for the egg. Hold the object on a pin, and paint the egg to match the breed of the bird you've created.

Stack toy: Cut six 4-inch squares from ¾-inch pine. Cut a dowel several inches longer than the stack of squares. Drill a 1-inch hole through the center of each except the bottom square, which is drilled halfway through. Sand all surfaces, rounding the blocks' vertical edges. Undercoat and paint all surfaces of blocks, but not the center hole. Paint the blocks in a variety of colors, as shown. Sand the dowel so it will pass through the blocks easily, and glue to bottom block.

Stack the blocks on the dowel, and trace around paper pattern of a figure tall enough so that each square has some portion of the figure on it. If you wish, you can paint figures on all sides.

Animal boxes: Using the pattern for the pieces in sketch 5, cut out two pig pieces and two ears from ¼-inch plywood. Cut the head and body (no legs) from ¾-inch pine. Drill a pilot hole in the ¾-inch pine piece, then saw out the inside of it, leaving ½ inch all around. Saw top off for lid (see sketch). Sand all pieces, then assemble, glue, and nail. Apply undercoat. After it dries, paint and decorate, using sketch as your guide. Attach a knob to lid.

Using the pattern for the pieces in sketch 1, cut out one horse of each from ¼-inch plywood; cut out the head and body section (no legs) from ¾-inch pine. Saw out the inside and the lid of the center section, as explained above. Assemble and finish the same as you did the other animals.

Using the patterns for the pieces in sketch 7, cut out two bird pieces of ¼-inch plywood and one without legs of ¾-inch pine. Saw out the inside and the lid of the center section, as explained above. Assemble and finish the same as you did the others.

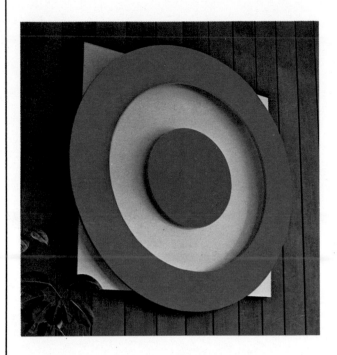

Target Wall Hanging

This attention-getting, three-dimensional plywood wall hanging adds color and flair to a plain wall. And just as importantly, it's easy and inexpensive to make.

Materials
- 4x4-foot sheet of ½-inch plywood
- Two colors of paint
- Glue

Directions
First, cut an 18x18-inch square of plywood for the background board. Then, using a string compass, scribe a 24-inch-diameter circle in the remaining wood and cut out. *Note:* To make a string compass, tie a nail to one end of string and a pencil to other end. Length of string is radius (for 24-inch circle, you'll need 12 inches of string). Hold nail upright in the center of plywood piece, and swing pencil completely around to mark circle.

Next, scribe an 18-inch circle (9-inch radius) inside the 24-inch circle with string compass and cut out the center. Cut out a 12-inch plywood circle for the bull's eye. Paint the background piece one color and the ring and circle a contrasting color. Glue the circular pieces in place.

217

Nature Crafts

*Explore the absorbing hobby of working with natural materials and
discover a fascinating world for creating artistic crafts.
Collect flowers, leaves, shells, rocks, feathers, seeds, pods, twigs,
branches, weeds, grasses, driftwood, and cornhusks. Blend
upbeat ideas with down-to-earth materials for fun crafts from nature.*

Family of Rock Characters

Start with rocks of different sizes, shapes,
and textures, and decorate them so that each
one has a personality of its own.

Materials
- Rocks of various sizes and shapes
- Shells
- Walnut scraps for bases
- 2 feet of bronze tubing
- 2 silver-plated forks
- Metal washer
- Acrylic polymer paints
- Flat black paint
- High-gloss 2-solution plastic coating
- Clear plastic coating
- Epoxy cement
- Soldering iron and silver solder

Directions
General: Be sure rocks are free from dirt.
Use acrylic polymer paints for features on
all of the characters.

Owl (far left): Choose an egg-shaped rock.
Paint features; finish with high-gloss two-
solution plastic. Attach metal washer at bottom with epoxy cement to act as a base.

Owl (in metal base): Pick an elongated rock.
Paint features; add coat of clear plastic. Bend
strip of bronze tubing around rock and solder
ends together. Bend another strip under
bottom of rock and solder to horizontal band.
Bend forks to resemble legs and claws; solder
to back of horizontal band.

Owl (center): Paint a large, oval rock flat
black. Add features, and seal with a coat
of clear plastic. Make a 1½-inch thick
square walnut base. Taper sides so bottom
is slightly larger than top. Coat with clear
plastic, and sand lightly. Attach with epoxy
cement.

Frog: Use an oval-shaped flat rock and paint
features with acrylic polymer paints. Add
a coating of 2-solution clear plastic for high-
gloss finish. Cut a 1½-inch thick rectangular
walnut base slightly larger than the rock.
Taper the sides as you did for the owl. Coat
base with clear plastic; let dry, and sand
lightly. Glue on base with epoxy cement.

Mouse: Pick a round rock, and grind the
bottom to give a flat base. Paint mouse features, and glue on clam shells for ears with
epoxy cement. Coat figure with clear plastic.

220

Drying Flowers Naturally

Decorate your home with winter bouquets of wild and cultivated flowers. Gather and dry your selections during the growing season.

The photo on the opposite page illustrates the method used by early-day settlers to dry flowers and weeds. They suspended them upside down from the rafters in dry, dark areas such as barns or attics. The dried flowers were then arranged in vases, bowls, or baskets partly filled with sand to keep the stems from shifting.

You can dry flowers the same way—a a dark closet works as well as a barn or attic. Expensive materials aren't necessary. Just pick your flowers and collect some cord.

Materials
- Baby's Breath
- Scarlet and blue salvia
- Butterfly weed
- Goldenrod
- Clover
- Cockscomb
- Common Thistle
- Hydrangea
- Statice
- Strawflower
- Sage
- Bachelor's Button
- Heather
- Milkweed
- Larkspur
  Columbine
- Chinese Lantern
- Stock
- Snapdragons
- Cord to hang flowers

Directions
As a general rule, pick flowers when they reach maturity—right after they bloom. One exception is strawflowers. Pick them before they are fully open to avoid browning in their centers.

Pick outdoor blooms when they're dry, not when the petals or leaves are wilting. Noon on a hot, clear day is the best time. Never pick them following a rain, and do not set them in water as you would fresh flowers.

Select light-colored blossoms for drying because they hold their true color. If you are using flowers that change color as they mature, pick them at the desired color stage and they will retain that color after drying. For example, hydrangea can be picked when it is green, white, pastel pink, or deep pink and keep the same tint after drying.

To prevent flowers from mildewing, tie those with small stalks, 10 in a bunch; tie those with large stalks individually. Hang them in a dark, dry location such as in a closet or in an attic. Usually, you can use the flowers in arrangements in seven to 10 days. (They are ready when the petals are slightly brittle to the touch.)

Fill tall vases halfway with sand to give them weight. Shallow bowls need sand and a flower holder to support the stalks. Insert the tallest stalks first, and add the shorter lengths until your arrangement has the proportions you desire.

Flowers with thick petals need to be dried with chemicals. The chemicals remove the petal moisture better then the hanging method. Instructions for chemical drying are given on the next two pages.

Tip Box

- Pick flowers when they're in their prime, and select perfect blossoms.
- Never pick them just after a rain, and do not immerse them in water as you would with flowers you plan to use while they are fresh.
- Pick flowers around noon on a hot, clear day.
- Pastel blooms retain color best.

Drying Flowers

Dry your own garden flowers during the growing season. Arrange them just as you would freshly cut flowers and you'll maintain a breath of spring no matter how dreary the weather is outside.

This method of drying flowers with chemicals is an outgrowth of the hanging method described on the previous pages. This process allows you to preserve flowers so they retain their original form and color.

Materials
- Assortment of flowers in bud stages to mature bloom stages
- Silica gel (found in garden and hobby shops)
- Containers with tight-fitting lids (such as covered cake carriers). Be sure containers are deep enough to cover entire head of flower
- Medium-weight florist wire
- Green florist's tape
- Masking tape

Directions
Be selective when you pick your flowers for drying. Choose perfectly shaped blooms and buds that are white or have pastel colors. Colors intensify during the drying process (pink turns to deep red), so avoid selecting blooms with vivid colors, unless you want dark shades. Pick flowers on a warm, sunny day, and start the drying process as soon as possible to preserve the original colors.

Sift a layer of silica gel crystals in the containers you are using. Lay the flowers in rows with stems buried by a half inch. (See the photo below.) Gently add more silica gel, until the whole head of the flower is covered. Place the lid on the container. Use masking tape to seal the lid of the container so it is airtight.

Inspect the blooms after 10 days. They are ready when the petals are dry—but not brittle. Remove the flowers from the containers; shake off the silica gel crystals, fasten on additional stem lengths of florist's wire, and arrange the flowers. Save the silica gel as you can use it over and over to dry other flowers.

Arrange them in the bouquet of your choice just as you would freshly picked flowers; intersperse heather with the dried blooms.

Preserving Evergreens

Concoct a tabletop garden from a collection of evergreens, bittersweet, and gourds.

Dry the evergreens as below, and coat the gourds with clear lacquer. The bittersweet dries naturally.

Materials
- Evergreen branches
- Micronized iron plant food
- Light corn syrup
- Chlorinated household bleach

Directions
To a gallon of hot water, add and mix four tablespoons of micronized iron plant food, two cups of light corn syrup, and four teaspoons of chlorinated household bleach.

Pound the bottom two inches of the evergreen stems and immerse in this mixture. Add more formula daily as the level evaporates, and your evergreen arrangements will remain fresh.

Preserving Foliage

Make a vibrant centerpiece of autumn leaves, eucalyptus, cattails, and zinnias to create a lasting reflection of Indian summer. Preserve the foliage and combine the branches with other long lasting materials in floral displays to decorate your home.

Materials
- Glycerin
- Quart jar
- Fall foliage such as fall leaves, eucalyptus, cattails, and zinnias

Directions
In a quart jar, combine one-fourth to one-third glycerin with two-thirds to three-fourths warm water.

Remove two inches of bark from each stalk of foliage and cut slits in stems. Insert foliage in an upright position in glycerin solution and leave it for one to two weeks.

At least once a day, rub a glycerin-saturated cloth over both sides of leaves. When liquid level finally stops decreasing, branches are ready to mix with other materials in long lasting arrangements.

Leaf Art Greeting Cards

Start your children on a project that will nurture their interest in nature. Here is their opportunity to make their own greeting cards decorated with dried leaves.

Collecting leaves is an adventure in itself, so do this on a nice day, when the sun is shining and it's fun to be outdoors. Next, comes the drying and that can be done anytime. Keep a supply of dried leaves available so you can indulge in leaf art whenever the mood strikes you.

This is especially a good rainy day project. Along with the dried leaves, all you need are a pair of scissors, glue, cardboard, and lots of imagination. Once you've started, you'll find there are endless designs for decorating greeting cards.

Materials
- Construction paper, Bristol board, or lightweight cardboard
- Scissors
- Leaves
- Glue
- Clear, adhesive-backed plastic
- Envelopes
- Newspapers or blotting paper

Directions
When searching for leaves, try to find perfect specimens. Examine them closely, and discard them if they have such defects as insect holes.

After collecting a variety of shapes and sizes, press them between layers of news-

paper or blotting paper, and weight them down. Exchange the damp pages for dry ones every 10 to 12 hours, until the leaves are smooth and dry.

Note: Avoid using colored newsprint or textured paper towels. The color from the newsprint might bleed onto the leaves, and the textured paper towels will leave an imprint. Do not use coated magazine pages because the surface does not absorb moisture. During the period when you are pressing the leaves, keep the project in a warm, dry place to hasten dehydration.

Before starting the greeting cards, find out what sizes of envelopes are available to fit your finished cards. Always make the cards slightly smaller than the envelopes so they will slide in and out easily.

If you plan to include a personal message, fold the construction paper, Bristol board, or lightweight cardboard in half by first scoring very lightly with a ruler and a razor blade or sharp knife. Write or print an appropriate message inside.

If you prefer smaller size cards, use 3x5-inch white index cards, and decrease the size of the design accordingly.

Use the designs in the photo as a guide, or work out your own designs. Place the designs at the angle you think looks best before you glue them in place, overlapping the leaves occasionally to give your collage added dimension. Use glue sparingly—this will shorten the drying period.

Coat the finished cards with a layer of clear, adhesive-backed plastic. Cut the plastic to overlap ½ inch on all sides. Peel off the backing, and press the plastic, with the sticky side down, over your leaf art. Trim the plastic coating neatly at the edges, or fold it over to the underside.

Use this same technique to make wall hangings, bookmarks, place mats, folders, and album covers.

Summer Treasure Box

Display shells, rocks, feathers, starfish, and driftwood in a shadow box for happy vacation reminders all year.

The shadow box shown here is made of weathered wood lath, and it is easy to make. Alter the dimensions to suit your collection of natural materials.

Materials
- Weathered wood (Use 5½ feet of ¼x3-inch lath for a 12x16-inch box)
- 6 feet of 1x1-inch plant stakes
- Slats from an old crate
- Contact glue
- Varnish
- Brads and finishing nails
- Shells
- Stones
- Star fish
- Driftwood
- Feathers

Directions

Spread out your collected treasures on a large sheet of wrapping paper, and arrange them in a variety of groupings that appeal to you. When you are satisfied that the composition is pleasing and well balanced, sketch in the placement of the divider shelves, and then sketch the outer dimensions so you will know what size shadow box to build. Now move your vacation treasures to another surface, keeping them in the same groupings as nearly as possible.

Use a ruler to straighten the lines of your rough, hand-drawn sketches, and record the measurements for use in constructing the shadow box.

Use 1x1-inch plant stakes to build the four-sided frame for the treasure box (see drawing A). Fit slats of weathered wood to the frame, and nail them in place at the top, bottom, and sides, keeping all edges even with the frame.

Frame the back panel (see drawing B) by cutting the slats the length of the sides and ends. Lap the ends over the side pieces and nail them to the base frame of 1x1-inch plant stakes. After attaching the frame, stain what is constructed thus far.

Measure and mark the divisions for the shelves on the back of the box (see drawing C). Next, cut a second set of slats which will fit inside the first set. (The second set will rest on the back of the box.) Nail and glue them in place.

Make dividers by cutting slats the lengths of marks made on the back of the box. Place dividers inside inner frame (see drawing D) and nail through sides of box to hold them securely. Then turn the box upside down and nail from the back, securing the longer dividers first.

To preserve the wood, finish with a coat of flat or low luster varnish. Arrange your collected items the way you wish to display them, and glue them in place.

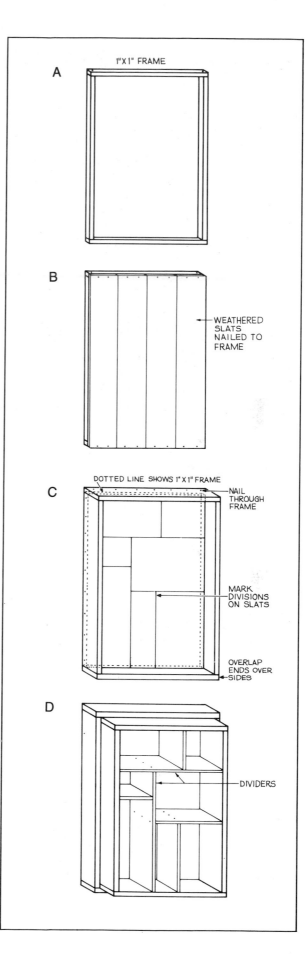

A — 1"X1" FRAME

B — WEATHERED SLATS NAILED TO FRAME

C — DOTTED LINE SHOWS 1"X1" FRAME — NAIL THROUGH FRAME — MARK DIVISIONS ON SLATS — OVERLAP ENDS OVER SIDES

D — DIVIDERS

Decorative Accessories from Shells

Get out those shells you've been collecting at the shore, and transform them into a variety of imaginative figures. If you don't have shells, purchase them from a hobby or craft shop or order them by mail from shell shops in coastal areas.

The grouping shown here includes flowers, dolls, whimsical animals, and birds. Follow the instructions for these designs, or create your own designs. The shape and size of the shell will dictate the figure you design. It is easier for beginners to work with larger shells on their first projects.

Materials
- Shells
- Silicone adhesive or epoxy cement
- Wire for stems
- Green floral tape
- White plastic tubing or white drinking straws for white stems
- Green felt scraps
- Yarn for hair
- Felt-tip pens
- Poster paint
- Chenille stems
- Masking tape
- Bleach
- Tweezers

Directions
To clean your shells, place them in a solution of two ounces of bleach in one quart water. Remove them from the solution when the blemishes are gone. Rinse in fresh water, and dry in the sun or on paper towels.

Group the shells according to shape and size. Use the small sizes for feet, ears, or eyes (or purchase movable eyes). Save the larger ones for bodies, heads, and bases.

Attach the shells with a silicone adhesive or epoxy cement. Glue the larger or heavier shells together first, holding them in position with masking tape. Let the glue dry completely and remove the masking tape before adding smaller varieties, such as tiny whelk shells. Handle the small shells with tweezers, if necessary.

Shell Creatures: Youngsters will be enchanted with the amusing characters shown in the lower portion of the photo. The shape of your shells will determine your choice of animated creatures. The smaller shells make great wings, tails, and facial features.

Shell Flowers: Glue two shells together in the center, and hold the shells together with masking tape while the glue sets. Then individually add the shell petals until the flower is the desired size and shape. Cover the wire stems with green floral tape, making sure the wire is sturdy enough to support the weight of the flower. If you prefer white stems, insert the wire through white plastic tubing or plastic drinking straws cut to the desired length.

Attach the stems with epoxy cement. Cut a tiny hole in the center of a green felt disk, a little smaller than the base of the flowers. Slip the disk over the stem, and glue it to the bottom of the flower for added support. Glue tiny shells to the wire stems to simulate leaves.

Dolls: Glue two small scallop or pecten shells together at the top; then overlap two more shells and glue them over the first, forming the skirt. Glue two smaller sizes together with concave sides facing each other for the blouse. Glue a small shell inside a larger scallop-shaped shell for the head and bonnet. Add yarn hair or paint hair and features with felt-tip pens. Attach arms or muff that you shape from lengths of chenille stems. Paint the doll's skirt, blouse, and bonnet, in pastel tints, or leave them in their natural state.

Feather Finery In Glowing Tones

Use pheasant plumage to create these glowing feather projects. Mandalas, like those on the opposite page, make lovely wall decorations and butterflies on page 232 can be framed or used as fashion accessories.

The multi-shaded colors of feathers automatically lend themselves to artistic designs. Create a collection of feather finery to display or to wear. You need very few materials, and even beginners will find feathercraft easy.

Materials

- Feathers—ring necked, Amherst, and golden pheasant; and bantam cock
- Contact cement or quick-dry epoxy

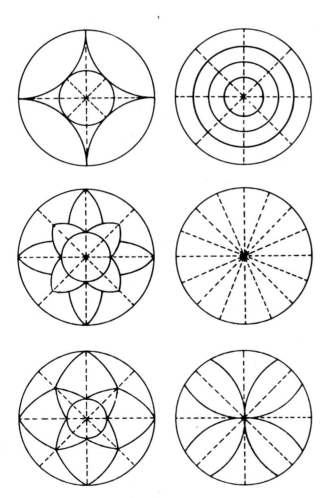

Note: Never use rubber cement to glue feathers.
- Leather
- ¼-inch thick plywood or heavy cardboard
- Fabric
- Pin-backs for barrette backs (if used as jewelry)
- Small scissors
- Tweezers
- Compass
- Straightedge

Directions

Mandalas: The sizes for the mandalas shown here range from 9 to 12 inches in diameter. To create the patterns for these feather mandalas, use a compass and straightedge. Draw the geometric designs on circles of leather, using the lines in the sketches at the left as guides.

Select feathers of similar design for each project, and use small scissors to trim them. Cut off the lower downy portion, and shape the tips of the feathers. (See drawing on page 232.)

To attach the feathers, first position them in a kaleidoscope of colors—reminiscent of a mosaic motif. Next, apply a small daub of glue to the leather backing. Using a pair of tweezers to hold each feather in place, press with your fingers to secure the glue to the leather backing. Make sure the glue doesn't come through the part of the feather that will be exposed.

Start gluing the feathers from the outer edges of the backing, and work toward the center of the mandala. Apply the final feather by allowing glue to become tacky; then apply center feather with extra care because you won't be lapping another one over it.

If you wish more of a three-dimensional effect, make mandalas of several layers. Cut out the different layers of leather, and glue feathers on the outer edges of all but the inner circle. Make sure feathers cover the outlines you've drawn. When feathering smaller, inner pieces, make sure feathers overlap the edge so no leather is exposed.

(continued)

After gluing the feathers on all the layers, carefully glue the pieces together using contact cement.

To mount the finished mandala, cut a piece of ¼-inch plywood or heavy cardboard to the size you plan for your finished wall hanging. The plywood must be larger than the measurement of the leather piece covered with feathers. Using either glue or staples, cover the board with fabric, bringing it around the edges and to the back. Mark the center of the board and cut a circle out of the fabric, using a craft knife. Cut out the circle slightly smaller than the size of the mandala. Glue the mandala directly to the board, using contact cement.

Frame the finished mandala mounted on the fabric-covered backing in a shadow box frame to give it added dimension or in a conventional picture frame.

Butterflies: The butterflies shown here range in sizes from 5- to 8-inch wingspans. Enlarge the pattern of the wings below to the size of the butterflies you wish to make. Transfer the pattern to a piece of leather. Cut out the pieces—each wing has a separate upper and lower portion, and the body is a separate piece. Draw the wings and the body on the leather backing before applying the feathers.

Prepare the feathers as shown in the drawings at the bottom of the page. Experiment with positioning the feathers, until you are satisfied with the combination of colors, markings, and sizes. Start gluing down the feathers at the tips of the bottom wings; point these feathers down. Next, cover the top wings, Here, point the feathers up and out. Let the top wings slightly overlap the bottom wings. Use hairy or narrow feathers for the body of the butterfly; glue the body on top of the wings. Always use crown feathers for the butterfly antennae.

When the butterflies have dried thoroughly, mount and frame them to use for wall hangings or back them with pin-backs or French-style barrettes if you plan to wear them as fashion accessories. Use quick-drying epoxy glue to attach the pins and barrettes to the leather backing.

Preparing a Feather

cut   trim   glue

one square = 1½ "

Seed Centerpiece

Concoct this spectacular centerpiece from a variety of different colored seeds and beans. Look in your kitchen cabinets to see what materials they yield. You may find you have enough foodstuffs on hand for the project. Use several pyramid-shaped plastic foam bases and plastic foam balls.

Making these seed-encrusted table decorations takes time and patience, but it is an easy craft project. When you're looking for a rainy-day project to keep the children busy, let them work on these seed and bean projects. You'll be surprised at how adept they are at artistically arranging the seeds and beans in contemporary designs. Display them on a tabletop or a mantel.

Materials
- 16-inch tall plastic foam obelisk
- 3-inch plastic foam balls
- Assorted seeds (pumpkin, sunflower, kidney beans, white navy beans, black-eyed peas, lentil beans, watermelon, cantaloupe, split peas, coffee beans, and sunflower shells.)
- Small star-shaped pasta
- White glue
- Hairpins

Directions

Note: Spread layers of newspapers on a table, assemble the plastic foam forms, seeds, and glue.

Obelisk: Use a nozzle-type applicator for the glue and cover only a small area at a time. Starting at the base of the plastic foam obelisk, glue on a single seed or bean. From this start, work rows on the diagonal, horizontal, or vertical. Follow the pattern in the photo at the left for inventive ideas on arranging the rows to form geometric designs in pleasing color combinations.

Make a row using one kind of seed or bean, then use another variety for the next row. Alternate the rows with large, small, round and oval seeds and beans, and different colors. Measure frequently to be sure the rows are straight.

Continue working toward the tip of the obelisk, with the rows spaced so closely together that none of the plastic foam form shows through the seeds.

Ornaments: Use a nozzle-type applicator for the glue and cover only a small area at a time, as you did with the obelisk.

Starting at any given point on the plastic foam ball, glue on a single, round seed such as a lentil bean. From this starting point, use another variety of seeds or beans to make a row around the starting bean. Continue in this manner, making row after row until you have completely covered the ball.

Insert a hairpin in the top of the ball for a hanger, and secure it with glue. If you're going to use the balls as table decorations rather than tree ornaments, omit the hairpin ornament hangers.

Cornhusk Butterflies

Decorate your evergreen tree at holiday time with butterflies made from dyed cornhusks and whittled balsa wood.

Most people are familiar with cornhusk dolls—usually turn-of-the-century models with long, flowing dresses that were fashionable at the time. Before the colonists made toys for their children from cornhusks, they used them to weave chair seats.

Now you can enjoy a different version of this homespun craft. These cornhusk butterflies are an up-to-the-minute design of a craft that dates back to early colonial days. The whole family will enjoy taking part in this inexpensive craft project.

Materials
- Cornhusks
- ¼-inch thick balsa wood
- Food coloring or fabric dye
- Felt-tip marking pens in a variety of colors
- Nylon fish line
- Mat knife or craft knife
- Sandpaper

Directions
Make a paper pattern of the basic wing shapes by tracing the butterfly at the bottom of the page. Use the narrow ends of the husks to make the wings because the vein pattern at the narrow ends strongly resembles real butterfly wings.

Dye the husks by simmering them in a pan of water containing food coloring or fabric dye and one teaspoon of vinegar. When they reach the desired shade, remove them to dry on a paper towel. Cut the wing shapes while the husks are damp. Then, press the wings flat by placing them between sheets of absorbent paper and then inside an old book.

Be sure to let the husks get completely dry, then use felt-tip marking pens to draw the butterfly markings. Draw the designs on the smooth side of the husk because the ink runs on the rough side.

Cut the insect's body from balsa wood in proportion to the size of the wings. Whittle and sand it to shape. Cut very thin slits in each side of the body. Press the wings into the slit, with the back wing underlapping the front wing. Glue in place.

Make a pinhole through the body of the butterfly at the balance point. Tie a knot in the end of nylon fish line; trim the end, and force it through the pinhole and put a dot of glue on top. This hanging thread allows you to suspend the butterfly.

Cornhusk Birds

Add a touch of your own craftsmanship to your Christmas tree with these graceful cornhusk birds, or hang them from a mobile to enjoy year long.

The only materials you need to fabricate these fragile-appearing birds are cornhusks and balsa wood. Besides being attractive, they're lightweight and break-resistant.

Materials
- Cornhusks
- ¼-inch thick balsa wood
- Felt-tip marking pens in a variety of colors
- Nylon fish line
- White glue
- Mat knife or craft knife
- Coping saw or saber saw
- Sandpaper
- Hinged clothespins

Directions

Trace the pattern for the bird at the bottom of the page and draw it on cardboard. Cut out cardboard for patterns, and trace around them on balsa. Have the beak and bird lengthwise on the wood grain so the beak won't break. Cut the bird shape with a coping or saber saw. Sand the wood, tapering the edges and refining the shape. Cut vertical slits through the body — ¹⁄₁₆ x ½-inch slits for the wings, and a notch at the back for the tail (see drawing for wing slits).

Mark the bird with the felt-tip marking pens, being careful not to let the bird get wet, as the colors will run. Insert the wings and the tail and fasten with glue.

Pleat a piece of damp cornhusk for wings — about five folds on each side. Then, cut to size. Pinch in the center with a clothespin until the wings are dry. Pleat another husk for the tail to the same width, and cut to size. Hold the end with a clothespin until the husk is dry.

Pierce a pinhole into the body above the wings. Tie a knot in the end of the nylon fish line, trim the end, and force it into the pinhole. Dot glue on top.

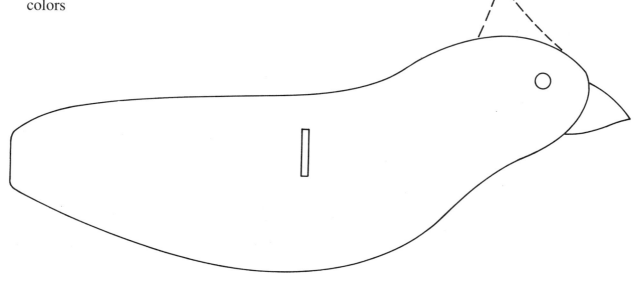

236

Cornhusk Christmas Angels

These cornhusk angels were inspired by the cornhusk dolls that flourished during colonial days, when there was a vast supply of husks and few toys. (Maize, or corn as we call it, was a principal crop for the colonists.)

Now, with the revival of colonial crafts, these cornhusk angels are bound to steal the show wherever they are displayed.

Materials
- Cornhusks
- Small amount of raffia
- Tiny strawflowers
- 12-inch length of ½-inch dowel
- Wire
- Cotton stuffing
- Food coloring or dye
- White glue

Directions
Note: If using fresh green husks, first dry them outdoors until they are the natural color. If they are stained, bleach them. Always dampen the husks when working with them so they will be more pliable.

For each dress simmer cornhusks in a pan of water with food coloring or dye and one teaspoon of vinegar. When the desired shade is achieved, remove the husks and blot on a paper towel. For each color of hair, use three cornhusks and a strand of raffia and dye them in the same manner.

Choose a smooth, strong husk for the face. Wrap cotton around one end of a six-inch dowel, forming an oval about two inches long. Then, roll the dowel in the husk, with the widest part covering the cotton. Using three husks for the hair, place the narrow ends in front of the face and let the wide ends stand straight. Tie the hair to the husk of head with raffia. Pull down the tail part of the head; tie at the neck. Shred the hair with a pin and tie around head to hold the bangs.

To make the arms, wrap each half of an 11-inch length of wire with a damp husk. Fold the excess husk back over the wire and tie to form the wrists and hands.

For the upper torso, split the husk which remains under the head at the shoulders. Pad the dowel to the waist with cotton. Place the arm wire inside the back, and wrap a one-inch wide damp husk over each shoulder and around the body. Using raffia ends from the neck, cross the chest, and tie raffia around waist tightly.

For the dress, overlap three damp, natural color husks around the waist; gather slightly, overlap with two dyed husks, and tie tightly with raffia. Place the doll over a jar to dry. Cut the sleeves of dyed husks, wrap them around the arms; tie above the elbows. Cross two 1¼-inch wide damp husks over the shoulders for the bodice. Tie at the waist with raffia, then with the dyed husk. Glue the sleeve seams together. Trim the bottom of dress evenly.

Cut wings from a large, thick husk. Place between two glasses (see drawing) to form bows of wings and secure with rubber band until dry. Pin and glue wings to back between shoulders. Cut a halo from a ⅛-inch wide strip of husk—long enough to sit on top of the head when it is joined, glue on tiny strawflowers. Glue the ends together.

More Craft Techniques

The previous chapters in Creative Crafts and Stitchery were each devoted to a single technique or to an area of interest. In this final chapter there are a variety of equally exciting craft projects—old trunk restoration, metalwork, rosemaling, stenciling and painting, decoupage, macralap, planters, art from the oven, and sculpting.

Decorating and Restoring Old Trunks

Restoring an old trunk, such as the one shown here, is painstaking, but gratifying. Use the round top or the barrel-top trunks for storage, and the flat top trunks for end tables, coffee tables, and night stands. A restored and decorated trunk adds a special personal touch to any house, as it is both attractive and functional to use for storage.

Materials
- 1 quart pecan semigloss paint
- ½ pint each of orange, brown, pale blue, gold, and ivory semigloss paint
- 1 pint American walnut oil stain
- Gold paste wax
- Burnt umber antiquing liquid
- Clear varnish
- Aluminum putty and wood putty
- Paint stripper and turpentine
- Rustproof undercoating
- No. 320 sandpaper
- Lint-free wiping cloths
- Lining fabric (amount determined by size of trunk)
- Cotton upholstery batting
- Large cardboard sheets (thickness of shirt cardboard)
- Gold filigree buttons for tufting
- Decorative braid (to finish off edges of lining)
- White glue
- Staples

Directions
Take a quick inventory of your trunk to see what repairs are necessary.

If the leather handles are missing or worn, remove hardware that holds handles. Get new handles at a luggage or shoe repair shop, and attach them in the same position.

Apply paint stripper to staves, following manufacturer's instructions. Then, sand with No. 320 sandpaper until smooth.

If your trunk is metal, fill nail holes and torn places with aluminum putty. Tack down jagged or loose metal and smooth over with aluminum putty. Sand putty when dry. If your trunk is wooden, fill nail holes and scars with wood putty, then sand entire trunk. Most old trunks have loose hinges; be sure to tighten them. Turn trunk over and check the bottom.

(continued)

Many of them have bottom slats with casters attached for easy rolling. If they are missing or in poor condition, replace them with ball bearing casters.

Remove all loose paper on inside of trunk, including paper around inside lip of trunk. (Later you will undercoat and paint the inside lip the same as the outside.) After repairs are made, wipe down entire trunk with turpentine or paint thinner.

Color staves with American walnut oil stain; let stain set up 10 minutes, then wipe off excess. Add light coat of clear varnish.

This seals staves so stray paint can be removed easily with a turpentine-dampened cloth.

Next, use the turpentine-dampened cloth to wipe trunk, eliminating all lint and dust particles. Let dry overnight. Paint trunk with pecan semigloss. Use two coats; let each coat of paint dry 24 hours.

You are now ready to antique the trunk. Use burnt umber antiquing liquid over pecan color of trunk. Do one complete panel at a time, starting on back side of trunk. Do top back lid, brushing all the way across until you have applied antiquing glaze over entire section. Glazing liquid starts to set up 15 to 20 minutes after application. With lint-free cloth, starting from one side, wipe excess glazing off in one direction. Wipe center a little cleaner than sides. After removing most of the glaze, change to a clean cloth or steel wool for final glazing or blending. Do bottom of back next, then sides, front, and top.

Note: If you're not satisfied with your glazing, wet a cloth with paint thinner, wipe the glaze off and start over. Important: Once antiquing glaze has set, don't patch up a spot. You will smear the glaze and make a more obvious spot.

Rub gold paste wax over all decorative hardware. Antique hardware with burnt umber antiquing glaze. When it starts to set up, remove the desired amount of glaze. Use orange, brown, pale blue, gold, and ivory semigloss paints for designs on trunk. Use velvet lining fabric as a guide in reproducing identical designs on the outside. If freehand painting is not one of your skills, trace designs from fabric, then transfer them to exterior of trunk.

Next, line the trunk. For a good fit, put lining in by sections, using material over a cardboard backing with cotton upholstery batting sandwiched between to pad lining. Use only half thicknesses of batting in all sections except top. In the top, use full thickness. Cut cardboard about ¼ inch smaller than actual measurements to allow for thickness of material and padding. (Example: If your measurement is 24x36 inches cut cardboard 23¾x35¾.)

Label cardboard as you cut it—side, back, front, etc. Try each cardboard in trunk to fit; each should move back and forth easily.

If your trunk has a tray or till, cut end cardboard in two sections, one for above the runner (wooden piece the till sits on) and one below. Glue a piece of lining fabric directly over runner, then glue top end section and bottom end section in place over runner and under runner.

When you measure your cardboard both top sides are alike; but when you cut the sides out, the right side section has a semi-circular cut to allow for arm to close. (Arm is metal piece that supports top when lid is open, as shown on opposite page.)

To measure inside top and sides in a rounded trunk top, make a paper pattern first; then transfer pattern to cardboard and cut out. When all cardboard pieces are cut out and marked, lay each one on cotton batting and cut batting to fit. Next, cut lining. Fabric used in this trunk is velveteen, so place all cardboard pieces in a straight line on material to make sure nap is going in one direction. Cut fabric 1 to 1½ inches larger than cardboard on every side.

Lay material right side down; place layer of cotton batting on top of it; and then place a piece of cardboard on batting. Fold fabric allowances over edges of cardboard and paste, mitering corners to ensure a good fit (use white glue).

After you cover each cardboard, place them inside trunk to ensure proper fit. If the fit is too tight, undo one side of material, trim back batting and cardboard, and reglue. When all sections fit, glue them in trunk. Start first with bottom section of trunk, then sides, front, back, and bottom. Use this procedure in lining top of trunk, making sure you line inside of cover last. For tufted effect in top, mark a diamond pattern on back of cardboard. Use heavy-duty thread and a long needle. Bring thread from back of cardboard through layers of batting and fabric, attach filigree button, then stitch through all layers to back of cardboard. Draw up thread and fasten securely. Do this in each tufted area.

If your trunk has a barrel top such as the one pictured, add extra padding in curved part of top to keep lining from bowing. This gives a better fit.

To make sure lining fits securely around bottom edges of trunk top and top edges of trunk bottom, use staples in addition to glue. Glue on a row of decorative braid to cover staples and give a neat, finished look.

Metal-Tooled Wall Cabinet

This hand-tooled cabinet design and motif are reproductions of a colonial tin cabinet found in Mexico. Sheets of tooling aluminum were substituted for the tin because it is softer to work with and allows more freedom in design choice. It is also readily available.

The curlicues, scallops, helixes, and undulating borders are highly reminiscent of the baroque style that was introduced in Mexico by the Spaniards many years ago.

Materials
- 4¾x7¾x24½ inches of pine for sides, top, and bottom
- 1¾x6¾x23 inches for shelf
- 2¾x11¼x24⅜ inches for doors
- 1¾x10½x30 inches for decorative top
- 1 24½x26-inch piece of ¼-inch plywood or hardboard for back
- 4 10x27-inch pieces of 36-gauge tooling aluminum for sides, top, and bottom
- 2 12x25-inch pieces of 36-gauge tooling aluminum for doors
- 1 12x33-inch piece of 36-gauge tooling aluminum for decorative top
- 4 1x12-inch pieces of 36-gauge tooling aluminum for top and bottom door edges
- 4 1x25-inch pieces of 36-gauge tooling aluminum for side door edges
- 2 1x25-inch pieces of 36-gauge tooling aluminum for decorative top edges
- White glue
- 1-inch and 1¾-inch finishing nails
- 2 pairs of ¾x1½-inch butt hinges
- Black flat enamel
- Contact cement
- Sculptamold
- 2 corner braces with 1½-inch legs for attaching decorative top
- 2 sets of magnetic door catches
- 2 small wooden knobs
- 2 screw eyes
- Wire for hanging
- Black spray paint for metal
- Kitchen appliance wax
- Medium and fine grades of sandpaper
- Paintbrush
- Small, flat stick for spreading cement
- Soft cloth
- Wooden modeling tools
- Brown wrapping paper
- Masking tape
- Carbon paper
- Tracing wheel, leather tool, stylus, or any other tool suitable to stipple background

Directions
On brown wrapping paper, enlarge pattern for decorative piece A (see drawing on page 245). Tape pattern to ¾x10½x30-inch piece of pine; trace around pattern and saw top piece.

Next, assemble cabinet. Following assembly diagram (see drawing on page 244), butt top and bottom to sides; attach with white glue and 1¾-inch finishing nails. Attach back to cabinet frame with 1-inch finishing nails. Nail and glue in shelf, flush with back, 13 inches from bottom.

Inset hinges on doors and cabinet so that they are flush. Try doors for fit, then remove them. With medium and then fine sandpaper, sand inside of cabinet and doors, paint inside with black flat enamel.

Starting with top, bottom, and sides and working on one piece at a time, use a small, flat stick to spread contact cement over aluminum sheets; line up edges of sheets with back edge of cabinet. Smooth down aluminum with your hands and a soft cloth. Fold over front edge and cement it in place. Mark corners for mitering, cut miters, and trim off any excess aluminum overhanging front edge with a single-edged razor blade. Rub down edges well with a modeling tool to ensure good bond.

Tape a pad of newspapers to a drawing board or tabletop. On brown wrapping paper, draw a 1-inch grid and enlarge design patterns (see drawing on page 245); cut out paper patterns. Place one aluminum panel on newspaper-covered surface; center matching pat-

(continued)

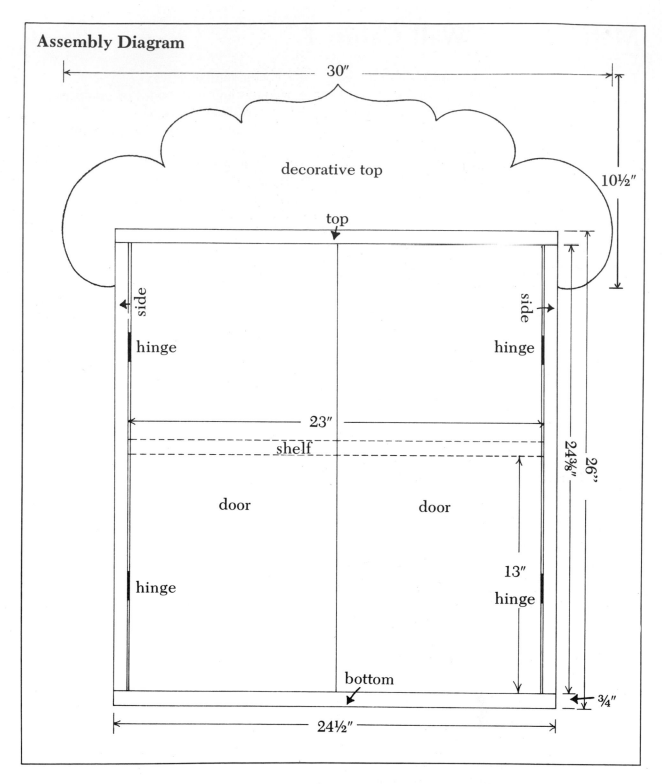

Assembly Diagram

decorative top

30"

10½"

top

side

hinge

side

hinge

23"

shelf

door

door

24⅜"

26"

13"

hinge

hinge

bottom

¾"

24½"

tern over it and tape down two edges. Slide carbon paper, face up, between metal and pattern (to make a reverse pattern on back of paper for other door panel) and tape down two remaining edges of pattern. Trace over design lines with a soft, blunt pencil. Turn metal over to make sure that all details have been marked. Remove pattern and carbon.

Note: Practice tooling on a piece of scrap metal first to master the technique.

With a modeling tool, begin modeling on back side. Following photograph, push out areas to be raised. Occasionally, turn work face up on a smooth, hard surface and, working around outside of outline, flatten background areas. Remember, aluminum is soft enough to push sharp edges through, and it does scratch easily. Handle it with care.

When the entire pattern has been completed, work background. Turn work right side up on a hard smooth surface and stipple all background areas, using a tracing wheel, leather tool, or stylus.

Turn the tooled aluminum face down. Mix Sculptamold according to the manufacturer's directions. Pour it into all depressions and smooth off with a straightedge so it is flush with background. Let dry.

Cement panel to door. Bend excess metal over edges. Cut out spaces for hinges with a razor blade, and cement metal to sides. Pinch corners together and cut off excess. Cement on strips to cover door edges. Burnish all edges with wooden modeling tools to ensure a good glue bond.

Repeat this same procedure for second door, reversing pattern so the two birds will face each other. To do this, turn pattern over and work from back side. Follow same procedure for decorative top piece.

Screw corner braces to back of decorative top; slide decorative top onto cabinet flush with the front. Screw braces to top of cabinet.

Using screws, hinge doors to the cabinet. Position magnetic catches under the shelf and inside doors in appropriate position. Attach knobs to doors. Attach screw eyes and wire to cabinet back, for hanging.

If you wish an antique finish, spray the door panels with fast-drying black paint, wipe off the high spots, and let dry. Polish with a soft dry cloth. For an even higher shine, apply kitchen appliance wax.

Square = 1 inch

A

B

C

245

Metalwork Jewelry from Tubing and Wire

Some very old metal jewelry was made with cutting, hammering, and shaping techniques similar to those described and illustrated here. Coiled wire designs that date back to early Roman times were made in this simple way, and they still have an attractive contemporary look that makes them especially flattering to today's casual wearing apparel.

To get started on this fascinating project, you need some simple, inexpensive tools from the hardware store. You don't need welding or soldering equipment, and dexterity is more important than strength in making jewelry.

When you're looking for specific materials to work with, check first at the hardware, building supply, and welding shops. But as you shop, keep your eyes open—you may find many other materials in unlikely places that will adapt well to handcrafted metal jewelry.

Materials
- Brass rods
- ¼ inch copper tubing
- Copper wire
- Nail or other hard instrument
- Tube cutter
- Hammer

Directions
The necklace, pendant, and bracelet shown here are only intended as examples of the ways you can combine brass rods and copper tubing to make jewelry. Use these same techniques to create your own designs, depending on your individual taste and the material you find available in your locality.

Use a tube cutter to cut the copper tubing. You can make a neat cut simply by twisting the tool (see drawing A). Copper wire and tubing come in many sizes. It can be cut, twisted, etched, hammered, and polished. With brass wire, you must heat it before you hammer it into the desired shape.

If your design calls for a flat strip of tubing, hammer it on a smooth, hard surface such as metal or concrete (see drawing B).

To add decoration to a flat piece of metal, use a nail set or some other hard instrument (see drawing C) to make the indentations.

To shape strips of thin metal, hammer them around a solid object (see drawing D) or bend them with a pair of needlenose pliers.

As you work with metal, experiment with various weights of wire, tubing, and embellishments. Adorn your handcrafted copper and brass metal jewelry with beads, macrame knots, leather strips, pebbles, antique finishes, and enameled motifs.

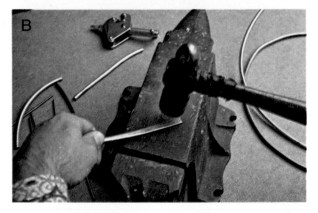

Rosemaling – Decorative Painting from Norway

Rosemaling, a Norwegian work whose literal translation is "rose painting," is a style of decorative craft that developed in the rural areas of Norway during the late 18th century and continued until 1870.

This style of folk art has two distinct categories, Hallingdal and Telemark – the most prolific painters came from these two areas. Hallingdal style shows a more imaginative use of forms, treatments, and colors. Telemark work is more controlled, and is recognized by its disciplined brush strokes and organic design.

But these were not done by commissioned artists, but by country people who have been accomplished wood carvers for some time. Now, they turned their attention to adding painted decorations to their home furnishings. The country people embellished their walls, and ceilings, hand-crafted furniture, trunks, and ale bowls, with these painted decorations which were usually closely related to the home and family who occupied it. Often these were quotations and verses, birthdates, names, and historical facts—in addition to the flowers and leaves created with the four simple brush strokes.

Materials
- Wooden plates, bowls, trays, breadboards, trunks, kegs, furniture
- Semigloss paint (for background)
- Artists' oil paints
- Brushes for each color of paint
- Satin finish varnish
- Wide soft-haired brush for varnish
- Sealer
- Primer
- Wood filler
- Medium (four parts linseed oil to one part turpentine)
- Foil-covered palette
- Palette knife
- Sandpaper
- Tack cloth
- Pumice
- Graphite paper
- Plain wrapping paper

Directions
General instructions: Rosemaling designs are composed of four variations of a few simple brush strokes. They include the "C" and reverse "C" or parentheses stroke; the "S" curve stroke; the "O" or circle; the straight line; and the dot. These four simple brush strokes lend themselves to unlimited design combinations. Practice these four strokes until you can manipulate the brush skillfully, then you're ready to start a rosemaling project. Don't expect to reproduce identical brush strokes. When decorations are painted freehand, it is expected that there will be slight variations and that no two designs will be identical. These slight variations add to the charm of hand painted rosemaling designs.

Rosemaling Tips
- Rosemaling is most effective on wood objects, but repair, sand, and seal the objects before painting.
- Use this type of folk art painting on old articles, but not on antiques. Valuable antiques should be restored to their natural wood finish, not painted and decorated.
- Buy only good quality artists' oil paints.
- Mix paint colors on a palette with a palette knife, using enough medium to form a creamy consistency.
- Never start in the middle of a stroke. If you run out of paint in the middle of a stroke and must stop to refill your brush, start again at the beginning position. You can divide a scroll into lengthwise brush strokes, but never divide it into crosswise strokes.
- Never let paint dry in the brushes. Wash the brushes in turpentine, and work in a little vaseline to keep the bristles supple. Shape the round brushes to a point, and the flat brushes flat. Brushes used for background painting should be cleaned with turpentine or paint thinner, and washed with liquid detergent.
- Do not stir high-gloss varnish, as it causes bubbles. Flat or satin varnish must be at room temperature and it must be mixed before use.
- Make a collection of photos, drawings, illustrations, and other information to help you in your selection of designs and your rosemaling technique.

In selecting paint colors, remember that virtually every shade of every color was used in some area of Norway. For the most part, dull blues and blue-greens, dull red, and red-oranges were used for the background colors. Moderate greens, reds, whites, yellows, and some shades of blue formed the basic designs. Yellow ocher was always more popular than pure yellow and was often used for lining.

(continued)

For your first project, choose a small item such as a plate, bowl, or breadboard. Fill holes, scratches, or nicks in the wooden article with wood filler. Sand well, and apply a coat of sealer. Next, apply a coat of primer. Then, apply a coat of semigloss paint in the background color of your choice. Sketch the design you wish to use on wrapping paper. Transfer this pattern to the wood article using graphite paper. Trace only the main areas of the design (see drawing A on page 250). Use these lines as a guide as you add the painted decorations.

Do not fill in the sketched areas on the plate with paint, but use the brush-stroke technique outlined in the general instructions. If you wish to duplicate the colors here (see drawing B) use the following for the underlay or first coat of the design: olive green (mix green with a bit of red);

muted red (mix red with a bit of green); gold (mix wood with yellow); muted white (mix white with wood). Use one brush for each color. If you are a novice, work with only two or three colors on a single project, and proceed to more colors as you gain expertise. One color should be the dominant force in a single project.

Mix the paint colors on a foil-covered palette (see drawing C), using enough medium to form a creamy consistency. (For medium, mix together four parts linseed oil with one part turpentine). Use a small container for medium, one for turpentine to keep brushes clean, and a tack cloth to wipe each brush.

Combine green and white for a light accent, and mix red and yellow to outline the flower and to add accent near the top of the plate. Start the border, using "C" strokes to encircle the flange. Steady the plate with your free hand while you are painting with the other.

After completing the design and allowing the paint to dry thoroughly, wipe off any smudges, finger marks, or tracing lines, and then apply varnish. The type of varnish you use depends on the amount of wear the item will receive. For normal wear, one coat of satin varnish is all that is necessary. If the article will receive hard usage, use a high-gloss varnish which is the most durable. Follow with a coat of satin or flat varnish to eliminate the shine. The gloss can also be rubbed down with pumice and water, but this is tedious. Apply the varnish at room temperature with a wide, soft-haired brush (see drawing D). Use a minimum of strokes to get an even coat.

Stenciled Wood Floor

The stenciled floor in the studio above is a happy choice for the artist in residence. The geometric design is contemporary, and the restful colors are conducive to a good work atmosphere. Large, bare windows permit good lighting, and provide a scenic view.

Materials
- Light blue semigloss paint for background color
- Primer (if the flooring is new)
- Slate blue semigloss paint
- Beige semigloss paint
- Off-white semigloss paint
- Rust semigloss paint

252

- Stencil board
- Polyurethane coating
- Paintbrushes
- Sandpaper
- Paint thinner
- Tracing paper
- Graph paper
- Carbon paper

Directions

Sand the floor (apply a coat of primer if the flooring is new and unfinished). Next, paint the entire floor light blue.

Enlarge the design below to measure 18 inches square, using graph paper. Transfer the design to tracing paper, then to stencil board, using carbon paper. Draw the design on four separate stencil boards. Cut out the blue area on one, the beige area on the next one, the off-white on the third one, and the rust area on the fourth stencil.

Position the designs and colors as shown in the photo at the left. Paint all one color; let them dry; then paint the second color. Continue in this manner until you have painted all the designs. Finish with two coats of polyurethane to add durability.

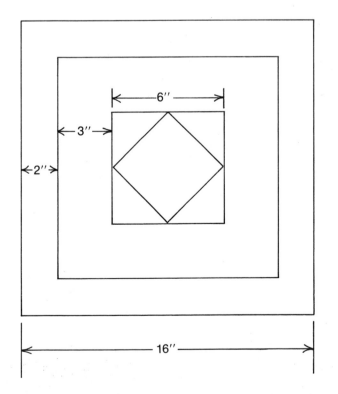

Stenciling Tips

- Use architect's linen, a fine cloth treated so it resembles stiff paper, for making stencils. Or, use stencil paper for fabric stenciling. For walls and floors, use stencil board.
- When you trace a design, use masking tape to hold tracing paper in position and use a technical fountain pen and India ink to trace the design.
- For cutting stencils, use an X-ACTO knife, a single-edge razor blade, or a surgical knife. Be sure the blades are sharp. If you use scissors, they must have very fine and pointed blades, such as surgical scissors, decoupage scissors, or embroidery scissors.
- Use a dental or paper punch, rather than a knife or scissors, to make an easy opening slash in the stencil paper. Also use the punch for a design with small dots, as these are difficult to cut with a knife or scissors.
- When stenciling on metal surfaces, check for rust. If there is rust, remove with rust remover.
- Stencil brushes have round bristles that are flat on top. Always hold the brush in an upright position so the entire flat top hits the surface of the cutout area you are painting.
- If your knife or scissors slips while cutting a stencil, and cuts the wrong area, fasten a small piece of Scotch tape on both sides of the stencil over the cut and recut the area covered by the tape.
- Always store stencils flat to keep them from curling. Keep them between the pages of a scrapbook or in large manila envelopes sandwiched between sheets of cardboard.
- Although you can use almost any design that appeals to you, the traditional garlands, baskets of fruits and flowers, and landscapes are still the most popular.

Stenciled Three-panel Folding Screen

Folding screens are invaluable when you need something that is lightweight and movable to conceal a particular view. In the photo to the left, it's the kitchen that the occupant wishes to conceal in an attractive manner. You can do the same to cut off a sleeping area in an efficiency apartment or to separate two areas in an apartment or home.

So, use the decorative folding screen in your home not only to hide a view you wish to ignore, but to divide space. Just purchase an inexpensive wood folding screen; paint it to harmonize with the background color in your room, and then stencil the three panels with designs and colors that complement your decor. This stenciling is as much fun to make as it is to view the results.

Materials
- 15-inch square of stencil paper
- Three-section wood paneled screen
- Red spray paint
- Blue spray paint
- Yellow spray paint
- 1 quart of primer
- 1 quart white enamel
- Masking tape
- Spray adhesive
- Turpentine
- Wrapping paper or old newspapers to use for masking off areas

Directions
Cover the three-section, wood paneled screen with a coat of primer. Let dry thoroughly, then paint with white enamel.

Make a grid of three-inch squares on the 15-inch square of stencil paper and draw the geometric patterns shown on the illustration below. Cut on lines to make two stencils, A and B. Use masking tape to cover the screen edges and hinges.

Note: If paint leaks through to the back of the stencil while you are painting, clean the back of the stencil with turpentine before repositioning it. If the edges of the stencil become curled or bent, cut new stencils and continue with your project. After you have completed this, clean both sides of the stencils with turpentine and store them flat in a large manila envelope.

Spray the back of stencil A with adhesive, and position it at the top of the first screen panel just below the edging. Mask out the area just below the stencil with wrapping or newspaper and spray the exposed areas with blue paint. Let dry.

Remove the wrapping or newspaper that masks out the area below the design. Spray stencil B with adhesive and position it, allowing six inches between the design repeat. Mask off the area above and below the stencil and spray the exposed area with yellow paint. Carefully lift off the stencils and let paint dry.

Continue in this manner, following the placement of colors in the photo until you have stenciled the designs on all three panels of the folding screen.

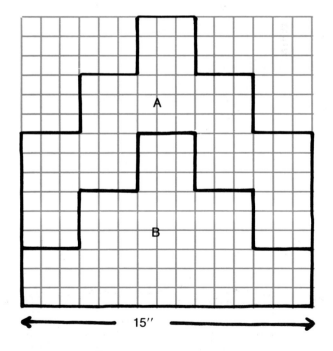

15″

255

256

Stenciling Motifs on Window Shades

In the room shown here, the large stenciled motif on the window shade was taken from the crewel embroidered fabric on the large wing chair. One bloom was traced and enlarged to decorate the Bristol blue window shade. The grosgrain band on the shade hem and the wool tassel pull add another touch of individuality to the unique customized window treatment.

To integrate window shades with a particular pattern in your room, stenciling is the answer. It helps match, blend, or accent patterns and colors. If you wish to stencil something other than a single large motif as shown, try applying a border design that complements your color scheme to the shade hem and the cornice topper.

Materials
- Window shade(s)
- Textile paints
- Textile paint extender
- Textile paintbrush cleaner
- Stencil paper
- Stencil knife
- Stencil brush
- Blue grosgrain for shade hem
- Wool tassel for shade pull
- Masking tape
- Tracing paper

Directions
Enlarge the pattern at the right on tracing paper. Then, trace the design onto the stencil paper, leaving at least a two-inch margin. Make a separate stencil for each color. Cut out the designs with a sharp stencil knife. Place the stencil in position on the window shade and hold it in place with masking tape.

Mix colors of textile paints on an old plate to create the desired shade; add an equal amount of extender and re-mix. Gently dip the stencil brush in color and wipe most of the paint on a piece of paper towel.

Note: Brush must not be too wet for this technique. Hold the brush in a vertical position and work the color onto the surface in a circular motion, starting at the edge of the cutout area and moving slowly to the center. Carefully lift off the stencil and wait for the first color to dry before placing the second color over it or next to it. Clean the brush thoroughly in textile brush cleaner before reusing.

Leave the stencils to dry for one hour. Then wet a clean cloth with textile paintbrush cleaner. Gently wipe off the paint from the stencil edge toward the center of the cutout shapes.

After the stenciling is completed, let the finished design dry for 24 hours. Then "set" the color permanently with a warm iron (set iron at low temperature). Press each section of the design six minutes, using a dry pressing cloth between the iron and the window shade.

Glue the blue grosgrain onto the window shade hem, and fasten the wool tassel to the center of the shade bottom.

Place Mats and Napkins With Folk Art Stencils

Use this amplified version of the Quakertown dinnerware pattern to stencil on place mats and napkins. Or adapt the design on your dinnerware pattern to a stencil and follow the same instructions for applying it.

Materials
- 2 yards 36-inch wide linen or linen-like fabric (makes 4 mats, 4 napkins)
- Yellow, blue, green, red, and white acrylic paint
- Stencil paper
- Stencil knife
- Stencil brush
- Masking tape
- 16x20-inch hardboard
- Mylar to protect work surface
- X-ACTO knife
- Paper towels

Directions
Wash, dry, and press fabric to remove sizing so paint will adhere properly to fabric (do not use fabric softener).

Cut four 14x18-inch place mats and four

258

or hand stitch a ½-inch hem around place mats and napkins.

Enlarge the design shown to measure about 12 inches long; trace it onto tracing paper. Use carbon paper and transfer pattern onto stencil paper. Then reverse the design and cut another stencil so that each design will face the other at either side of place mat. While cutting stencils, lay the stencil paper on a piece of hardboard or a sheet of glass to provide a firm backing. Fasten stencil paper with masking tape, and use an X-ACTO knife to cut out the design. Cut stencil edges sharply so design will be clearly defined. When several colors are used in an overlapping manner, such as in the flowers, cut additional stencils for each color.

Cover the sheet of hardboard with Mylar, fastening it with masking tape across the corners. The Mylar prevents workboard from absorbing excess paint that could penetrate through fabric.

Place a napkin or place mat on workboard; use masking tape to hold it securely. Determine pattern placement and mark it lightly with a pencil. Tape the stencil in place. *Note:* For napkins, use only a portion of total design. On place mats, use complete design.

Dip stiff stencil brush in paint; wipe excess paint against side of paint jar or on piece of paper towel until brush is almost dry. Then, apply paint from outer edge to center of cutout areas. Always hold brush in an upright position while stenciling. Work with a gentle pouncing motion, rather than a brushing motion as in freehand painting. *Note:* Do not stroke back against the edges of the stencil because this will cause a heavy buildup of color against the edge. Wipe excess paint from the stencil frequently with dampened paper towel.

Paint all of one color at same time, then go on to next color. Be careful not to remove stencil until paint is dry. Repeat placement and painting of stencils until all patterns are completed. After removing stencil, add the shading, dots, and other small designs freehand for a folk art effect.

1 Square = ½ Inch

Stenciled Coverlet with Swagged Border

This stenciled coverlet adds a warm touch of Americana to a bedroom furnished in antiques. Although the colorful design has a contemporary flavor, the stenciling technique itself remains traditional.

Materials
- Preshrunk unbleached muslin bedspread
- Textile paint and extender
- One stencil brush per color
- Masking tape
- Tracing paper
- Stencil or mat knife
- Turpentine
- 18x24-inch sheets of stencil board
- Carbon paper

1 Sq = 1½ In.

1 Sq. = 1½ In.

Directions

Enlarge grid drawings on tracing paper and label each colored area. Use this same drawing to trace onto all of the stencil boards, using carbon paper and making a different stencil for each color.

Position all designs the same way on all boards. Stack stencils, and hold up to the light to check design placement. Remove sections to be painted with stencil knife and cut a V (register mark) in upper right and lower left of each stencil so they match exactly.

On bedspread, lightly pencil placement of stencils at register marks. Motif on spread top is about 12x15 inches; border design is 14x18 inches. Put spread on flat work surface covered with newspapers.

Test washability of your paints and fabric by completing one design on a muslin scrap. Set colors as explained next, and wash the scrap separately in your machine.

Checking register marks, tape the first stencil in place. Put a small amount of paint in a saucer and mix to desired color. Use red, black, peacock blue, dark green, and light yellow. Mix yellow and red for orange, and green and yellow for chartreuse.

Hold brush vertically, dip in paint, and blot on paper to remove excess paint. To achieve a crisp outline, stamp the brush up and down over the cutout areas, moving from outer edges toward center. Avoid paint build-up on edges that might run under stencil; hold brush vertically.

Print repeats of first stencil in same manner. When first color dries, put on second stencil. Check register marks, tape down, and repeat second color with new brush. Repeat for rest of colors. After painting is done, add the fine details, such as the butterfly antennae, with a small paintbrush freehand.

Flip stencils over on the left side of spread top so the pattern will be a mirror image from center out. To flip stencils, clean off the paint with turpentine, allow to dry and continue stenciling. Register marks will now be in reversed position.

Stencils have holding strips to keep designs together. These do not print when you paint the stencil, but should be filled in with a stencil brush after you remove stencil. To set paints, turn your iron to a warm setting and iron each pattern for six minutes. After this treatment, the stenciled designs will retain their vibrant colors indefinitely.

Basketry-Patterned Canvas Mat

This canvas floor covering is great in leisure living areas such as a sunroom or porch, or a room where reed and rattan furnishings abound. The design was inspired by the weaving on an antique Indian basket. It also has an affinity for antiques.

Similar floor mats go back to the days when carpeting as we know it today was uncommon in homes. Families, especially those along the Eastern seaboard, fashioned their own floor coverings from sailcloth. They called them floor cloths; painted them, decorated them with lavish stenciled designs, and then toughened them with protective varnish so they would last for years.

Floor cloths require little care. To clean them, wash them right on the floor with a mild suds and rinse with clear water. One disadvantage is that the cloths do not lie flat unless the floor is smooth.

Make your floor mats whatever size and design you wish. To recapture the early American spirit, use a quilt-top motif. For a modern decor, select an abstract design and free-form shape.

Materials
- 54½x62-inch piece of artist's canvas
- Gesso
- Brown acrylic paint
- Beige acrylic paint
- Black acrylic paint
- Acrylic matte varnish (or gloss, if you prefer)
- Paintbrush
- Tracing paper

Directions

Coat the 54½x62-inch piece of artist's canvas with gesso. Then, enlarge the basketry pattern on the opposite page and trace it onto the canvas being sure to define the pattern with the triangular border along the edges of the 62-inch strip.

Use a brush to paint the pattern and use acrylic paints.

Note: Use the acrylic paints that come in jars because the paint is thinner, requiring no dilution such as is necessary with acrylic paints that come in tubes. Also, you achieve a smoother and more even effect by not diluting your colors. If it is necessary to mix colors to get the desired shade or tint, mix the entire amount needed at one time and store it in a tightly sealed container until you are ready to use it.

Reproduce this design as freely as you wish because this type of pattern does not call for the precise lines necessary in geometrics and striped designs. Paint all the areas of one color at the same time. Let each color dry thoroughly before going on to the next color.

After the design on your canvas floor covering is complete and is totally dry, apply a coat of acrylic matte varnish to the cloth for a flat finish. Or apply a coat of acrylic gloss if you prefer a shiny finish. When the first protective coat is dried completely, use a second coat of acrylic varnish to give your floor canvas greater durability and to ensure that it lies flat on the floor. Be sure the cloth is thoroughly dry before use.

Accent Rug Drawn With Pastels.

If you have a basement, porch, or patio with a concrete floor that needs a spark of individuality, draw an accent rug with pastels.

Use colors and designs that complement the surroundings, and protect your finished rug with a clear polyurethane coating.

Materials
- Wheat, gold, rust, and brown pastel sticks (number will vary with rug size)
- Acrylic permanent spray fixative
- Polyurethane coating
- Paper towels

Directions
General instructions: Pastel sticks are essentially powder color with a minimum of non-greasy binder. One advantage to using pastels is that you don't have to wait for drying for the final effect. Another is that you can make clearly defined lines or blend the colors to create a variety of unusual effects.

Be sure the concrete is smooth and clean before you start drawing the rug. Draw the rug design in monochromatic colors, then protect your fingers with paper toweling while you blur and smudge the design to give an overall textured effect. Draw the fringe around the edges last with clear lines so that each tassel is clearly defined.

Spray the rug with acrylic permanent spray fixative. Let dry, and spray another coat of fixative. Let dry. Finally, add two coats of clear polyurethane finish so the rug will withstand normal wear.

Area Rug Made of Gift Wrap

Cover your floor with an area rug of gift-wrap paper, coated with polyurethane varnish for durability. The total cost is minimal, and the design possibilities are endless.

Materials
- 4 8x1½-foot rolls of gift wrap
- 2 rolls of coordinated paper for border
- Wallpaper paste
- ¾ gallon polyurethane clear varnish

Directions
Inside portion of this rug measures 81x104½ inches; tile border is 8 inches (two tiles) deep. Finished size is 8x10 feet.

If your floor is dark, paint area you plan to cover white. (Darker colors may show through after paste is applied to paper.)

Prepare floor with a thin coat of high quality "moisture cure" polyurethane. Follow instructions on container. Let dry. Cut center portion of "rug" to size and apply to floor with wallpaper paste. Patch strips of paper together, overlapping the edges no more than ¼ inch, as polyurethane coating will make the paper slightly translucent and overlapping patterns will show through.

Next, cut and apply borders, aligning edges of tiles. Border measures 89 inches (30 tiles) on short side, and 112½ inches (38 tiles) on longer side. Butt tiles at right angles at corners. Measure width of baseboard and cut border to fit. Prepare baseboard and apply border same as for "rug."

Give floor and baseboard a thin coat of polyurethane. Let dry. Follow with a heavier coat. To ensure long life, recoat once a year with a fresh coat of polyurethane.

266

Decoupage Desk Accessories

This handsome collection of desk accessories add character to any desk. The combination of black with an overlay of liquid pearl in a swirl design provides the perfect background for prints of this type.

The art of decoupage, which originated in Venice in the seventeenth century, quickly spread throughout Europe and later to America. In recent years there has been a widespread revival of interest in decoupage, partly due to the fact that new products have been made available to hobbyists that make the job easier and more enjoyable. Designs can depict the classic styles of seventeenth century art or they can be spirited versions of contemporary art.

Materials
- Blotter
- Boxes
- 10 ornamental metal feet for boxes
- Ashtray
- Paperweight
- Prints for design decals
- Black acrylic paint
- Liquid pearl finish paint
- White acrylic paint
- Sealer
- Decoupage paste
- Decoupage transfer emulsion
- Silver leaf
- Silver braid
- Clear varnish
- Black felt
- Fine silicon carbide sandpaper (No. 240, can be used wet or dry)
- Fine sandpaper (No. 400)
- Polyurethane sponge
- Paste wax
- White glue
- Sharp, pointed scissors
- Glass cleaner
- Waxed paper
- Cardboard

Directions
Blotter: Remove the blotter paper. Put waxed paper under each leather edge for protection.

Paint the leather sides with a coat of black acrylic paint. Let dry; apply a second coat.

Using the liquid pearl finish, pour a small amount into a container. Gather the four corners of a 1½-inch square piece of polyurethane sponge in your fingers and form a ball. Dip the sponge into the pearl mixture, wipe off the excess, and apply to the black, painted leather in a circular motion, forming overlapping circles. Cover all of the leather on the blotter.

Paint the back of each print you use with white acrylic paint, and allow to dry. Apply a coat of sealer to the front of each print, then cut out the designs.

Anchor each print to the leather with decoupage paste on the back. Press down with a damp cloth. Apply a 1-inch wide strip of silver leaf down the outside edge of each leather side. Glue narrow silver braid along the inside edge of the blotter.

Apply ten heavy coats of decoupage transfer emulsion to the leather sides. Allow to dry for two hours between coats. After the final coat, let dry 24 hours. Dampen No. 240 sandpaper, and sand until smooth. Wipe clean with a damp cloth. Apply a coat of paste wax to protect the surface. Remove the waxed paper, and replace the blotter paper.

Boxes: Sand boxes with No. 400 sandpaper inside and out until smooth. Wipe residue with tack cloth. Apply sealer to inside and outside of each box. Allow to dry, then sand lightly. Give each box two coats of black acrylic paint. Allow to dry.

Apply liquid pearl finish, as you did for blotter. Cut and glue white painted prints to boxes, following instructions for blotter. Apply silver leaf to the concave border around lid of large box; glue silver braid around

(continued)

lower edge. On the smaller box, glue braid around lid and bottom edge.

Brush on 20 coats of varnish to each box at 24-hour intervals. Sand, then apply four more coats. When dry, dampen sandpaper and sand as you did on blotter. Coat with paste wax. Silver leaf the feet and attach them in place.

Ashtray: Clean with glass cleaner that does not leave a film. Paint back of print with white acrylic. Let dry, then cut out print.

Glue the design on the bottom. Holding ashtray right side up, press down tightly with a camp cloth to work the air bubbles from under the cutouts.

Apply liquid pearl with sponge to back side. Paint over with two coats of black acrylic, then four coats of varnish. Let each coat dry before applying the next. Glue black felt to bottom when varnish dries.

Paperweight: Cut cardboard slightly larger than the paperweight. Coat cardboard with sealer; when it is dry, apply two coats of black acrylic paint.

Cover cardboard with liquid finish pearl, as before. Use two identical prints to make contoured design. Cut the bird, perch, and tendrils from first print; cut head and wings from second print. Press and contour first print from back side slightly to give it shape. Next, contour head and wings from second print. Adhere in place over the corresponding place in the first print. Keep total contoured height of design so it fits ⅛-inch concave cavity in bottom of paperweight.

Put design on black cardboard, so when paperweight is over cardboard, you have a margin of cardboard around paperweight. Glue design in place. Next, place paperweight in position over design; mark around it.

Remove paperweight, cut cardboard to fit bottom. Apply white glue to lip on back of paperweight; glue cardboard in place. Glue black felt to fit back side of paperweight.

Shadow Box Clock

The clock above features dimensional decoupage, an offshoot of traditional decoupage. Encase clockworks and the delicate cutout designs in an ordinary rectangular wooden box with a hinged lid. Decorate the box with brass hardware and rows of narrow gold braid.

Materials
- 5⅜x11⅝-inch box with removable lid
- Clockworks

- Three feet of ½x⅛-inch molding
- Three feet of ³⁄₁₆x⅛-inch molding
- Sandpaper (No. 400 wet-and-dry)
- Pink paint
- White paint
- Two ¾x⅝-inch hinges
- Narrow gold paper braid
- Three black and white prints
- Oil pencils
- Non-tarnishing wax gilt
- ¼-inch sequin pins
- 1-inch brass ring
- Four 1¼x⅜-inch brass feet
- Pair of catches
- Glass to fit
- White glue
- Sealer
- Silicone adhesive

Directions

Cut out the area from the box where the clock and hinges fit. Sand box until smooth. The lid of the box will be inverted for the shadow box, so place the lid on the box upside down and sand around joint to assure smooth fit. Glue a strip of ½x⅛-inch molding around the inside edge of the cover to support the glass you will insert later.

Wipe the box clean inside and out with a lint-free cloth, and apply a coat of sealer inside and out. Allow the sealer to dry, then sand lightly. Wipe the box again.

Apply two coats of pink paint to the inside and the outside of the box, and to the outside of the cover. Apply two coats of white paint to the inside of the cover. Sand lightly, then apply a third coat of both pink and white paint.

Mount the lid to the box with pair of hinges. Keep the lid in a closed position; glue gold braid border around the edges of each side, front, back, and top. After the glue dries, cut through the braid at the joint between the lid and box.

Color eighteenth century black and white prints with oil pencils before cutting. When coloring, follow engraving lines on print as a color guide for that area. Color with long even strokes, keeping the pencil in contact with paper. Make many strokes close together with a constant pressure applied to pencil. This keeps individual lines from showing. When the coloring is completed, apply a coat of sealer to the front side of the prints; allow to dry. Cut out the colored parts of the prints.

Glue all the parts of the first print inside the box lid. Contour and elevate the cutouts from the other prints. Attach the prints with silicone adhesive at different levels (see photo) to give a three dimensional effect.

Assemble clockworks in the lid. If the hands are too long, trim them to fit the clock face. Put glass in place. Cut ³⁄₁₆x⅛-inch molding to fit the inside edge of the shadow box over the glass. Apply a coat of wax gilt to the molding. Attach the molding with ¼-inch sequin pins. Glue a row of narrow gold paper braid to the face of the molding. Attach the rest of the hardware: Fasten the brass ring at the center top of the clock, the four brass feet to the bottom, and the pair of catches to the lid.

Decoupage Tips

- Modern sealers, used in decoupage, have many advantages such as drying rapidly. However, you must not use them in a humid atmosphere.
- Cuticle scissors are ideal for cutting intricate designs. Embroidery scissors are also good if they are small and have a sharp point.
- Keep a pair of tweezers handy to lift prints from the pasted surface, if you decide to reposition the design in a more becoming arrangement.
- Be sure to have adequate light in your work area; and use a magnifying glass, rather than eyeglasses, when working on fine details.
- When you decoupage on wood, be sure to fill all of the holes, dents, and cracks with wood filler, and sand well before starting.

Box Topped With Transfer Decoupage

Try this method of decoupage that eliminates many of the tedious steps that are necessary with traditional decoupage. This technique is especially good for beginners. You don't even have to cut out each of the designs; simply transfer the print to the intended surface with a special medium that picks up the printed design but not the paper backing underneath it.

The transfer decoupage process allows you to apply almost any kind of printed picture to a great variety of smooth surfaces — wood, glass, china, plastic, and metal. Use this easy-to-master technique to decorate anything from a minuscule pill box to a ceiling-high room divider.

Materials
- Wooden box
- Wood stain
- Transfer medium
- Paper design
- Decoupage finish
- Fine sandpaper
- Paste wax

A

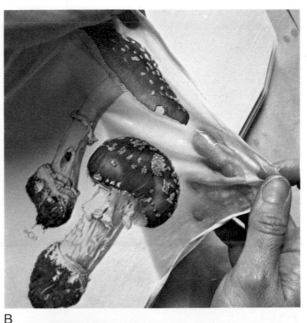

B

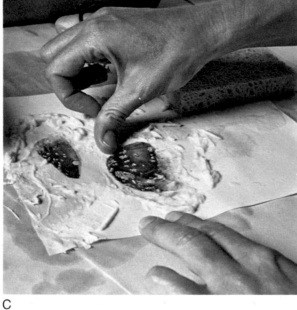

C

D

Directions

Remove the hinges and clasp, and sand the box. Apply a coat of wood stain. With a soft cloth, wipe off the excess stain until you achieve the desired wood tone. Next, use a coat of sealer to protect the stained finish.

Place the print for the top of the box on a flat surface, and brush the transfer medium on the print (see drawing A).

Then, lay the picture on the top of the box (see drawing B). Rub the print with your fingers, and remove the paper surrounding the picture as you go (see drawing C). Be sure no air bubbles remain and that the print is attached securely to the box top.

Apply the decoupage finish with as few brush strokes as possible (see drawing D). Apply two coats to the entire project, then as many coats to the top as is necessary to produce a deep, transparent finish. If any air bubbles appear on the surface, sand well before applying the next coat. Finally, add a coat of paste wax. Buff with a soft cloth, and replace the hardware.

Macralap — Macrame and Burlap Combined

Achieve stunning results with this fast and easy needlecraft technique. All it requires is some burlap and simple handwork such as thread pulling, yarn overcast stitching, bead and ribbon threading, and a basic running embroidery stitch.

As you practice these simple stitchery skills on burlap, the results will look like costly custom-woven yardage that is always so popular for accessories for the home.

With macralap, use a backing to give it a sturdy, substantial appearance such as the fringed place mats and table runner shown on these two pages. Or, achieve a sheer gossamer look such as the window treatment pic-

tured on page 274; leave the macralap unlined, and let the sunlight filter through the open-work designs.

Try this fascinating craft that involves none of the tedious knot tying that is associated with macrame. You'll find that it is an enjoyable hobby, and that you will be proud to display your projects you create.

Materials

Place mats and table runner:
- 1½ yards hot pink 72-inch wide rayon/wool felt
- 4 yards orange burlap
- 1 skein pink washable rug yarn
- 1 skein red washable rug yarn
- 4 skeins orange washable rug yarn
- Tapestry needle

Window covering:
- 2 yards off-white burlap

- 7 yards 2¼-inch lace
- 12 yards off-white scroll type trim
- 120 white wood beads
- 132 glass beads
- Thread and yarn scraps to match burlap
- Spring-tension curtain rod
- 39½-inch piece of ½-inch dowel

Directions

General macralap instructions: Use the following procedure to cut the burlap you use in these macralap projects. With a pencil and a ruler, find the correct dimensions, placing pencil marks lightly on the burlap threads. Grasp the thread at one side of the fabric and pull it out. After you pull the thread out, there will be an open channel in the fabric. Carefully cut the piece of burlap in the middle of the channel. Repeat this same procedure for all four sides of the piece. In order to get evenly sized fabric pieces, pull the threads before cutting pieces. Be sure to ask for cleaning instructions when you buy your fabric (both rayon-wool felt and regular burlap are dry-cleanable).

Place mats: Cut out four 22½x14-inch place mats from the orange burlap. Stay stitch across the 14-inch width, 3 inches in from each end. Pull out two horizontal burlap threads beside the stay stitching. Weave a double row of red yarn using the same pattern.

Measure 3¾ inches from the red yarn. Stay stitch; pull two threads; weave a row of doubled pink yarn.

In the area between the woven rows, draw three diamonds. Pull out all horizontal threads in each. Tie the threads in each diamond into three bundles.

Fill the area around the diamonds with running stitches and overcast with orange yarn.

Turn under edges ½ inch and blindstitch to the 18¼x13-inch piece of felt backing (felt will reach only to the end of the worked

(continued)

pattern). Pull all of the horizontal threads from the burlap at the end of the place mat to make the fringe.

Make three other place mats the same, following the same pattern.

Table runner: Cut a 19x115-inch piece of orange burlap. Stay stitch ½ inch around all four sides of the table runner. The center section of the runner is made just like the place mats except that the design is larger. Allow 8½ inches between the rows of doubled pink and red yarn, make the diamond motif to measure 7x19 inches.

Measure in 32 inches from each end of the runner to make the lattice designs on either side of the center section. Pull the threads to weave two rows of doubled pink yarn; one row of doubled red yarn; two rows of orange overcast; two rows of doubled red yarn; then finish with two rows of doubled pink yarn. Measure nine inches and repeat the same weaving procedure.

Pull all of the horizontal threads within a nine-inch section. Divide the threads into 15 bundles. Tie each bundle two inches from the yarn border. Repeat the tying at the other end, placing the knots two inches from the border and keeping them on the back side of the runner so they won't show. In the center of the threads divide the bundles in half and tie again, creating a lattice effect.

Measure in 32 inches from the other end and repeat the same procedure, pulling the threads, dividing them into bundles, and tying them.

Measure in 20 inches from each end; pull threads, and weave one row each of doubled pink and red yarn. Stay stitch along the outside row of yarn. Pull all of the horizontal threads between the stay stitching and the end of the runner. Lay the runner flat and trim the fringe evenly to a length of about 12 inches. Divide the fringe into 32 sections of 16 strands each and tie each of the 16-strand sections with overhand knots to make tassels.

Cut an 18x72-inch piece of felt. Add an 18x4½-inch piece to make the strip 76 inches long. Turn the edges of the table runner under ½ inch and blindstitch it to the felt backing underneath.

Window covering: Cut the off-white burlap piece 40¼ inches wide and 63½ inches long. Stay stitch ¼ inch around all four sides so it won't ravel. Turn one 40¼-inch end under ½ inch and stitch it down to form the top of the window covering.

Measure down from the top three inches and pull one horizontal thread. Using this open channel as a guide, sew a piece of lace across the entire piece. Measure down 2¼ inches, pull thread and sew a double row of scroll trim. Measure down 2¼ inches; pull thread; sew a second row of lace. Pull out all of the horizontal threads between the lace and trim, on both sides of the trim.

Measure down 10 inches from the bottom of the second row of lace, pull one thread, and sew another row of lace along the thread line. Pull all of the horizontal threads in this 10-inch section. Repeat the above instructions until you have six rows of lace and two 10-inch pulled sections.

Below the last row of lace measure 2¼ inches. Pull a thread, and sew a double row of scroll trim. Measure down 2¼ inches and pull a thread but leave a section 3½ inches deep to serve as the bottom casing to hold the dowel.

Divide the 10-inch pulled thread areas into 17 equal sections. Tie each section in the middle with yarn (tie the yarn in back of the burlap so the knot is not visible). Using heavy-duty thread, secure a double length of thread at the bottom of the top section of the lace, between the eighth and ninth section of the gathered threads.

String five glass beads, five wood beads, one glass bead, five wood beads, and five glass beads on the thread and fasten them between the eighth and ninth sections at the top of the lace below.

Fasten the beads, strung in the same manner, between the fourth and fifth sections; between the 13th and 14th sections; as well as at either end of the gathered sections. Repeat this same procedure for the other areas of the gathered sections.

Fold under ½ inch around all four sides of the completed window hanging and machine stitch. Sew 1½-inch casings at both the top and the bottom of the panel. Adjust a spring-tension curtain rod to fit inside of the window casing, and insert the curtain rod in the top casing. Then, insert a dowel in the bottom casing to make sure the window covering hangs straight and smoothly.

Spectacular Planters from Unlikely Sources

Examine this bevy of ingenious hanging planters, and you'll probably discover that you have some of the construction materials right at home. Enjoy making these planters for your home, or for gifts for indoor gardeners.

Materials
- Paper punch
- White glue

Blue Planter
- Square detergent bottle
- Light blue and rust jumbo rickrack
- Blue and rust 2-inch wide braid

White Planter (upper right)
- White plastic frozen food bowl
- 2 yards decorative band trim
- Matching tassel trim

Gold Basket (center)
- Woven wastepaper basket
- 3 drapery tiebacks with tassels
- Matching cord
- Gold paint
- Masking tape

Hanging Planter (far left)
- Lettuce crisper
- 1½ yards daisy trim
- Wright's stick-to trim
- Single-fold bias tape

Clay Pot Planter (lower left)
- Clay flowerpot
- Fruit applique motifs
- 3½ yards rayon macrame cord

Mini Gold Planter (lower center)
- Egg-shaped pantyhose container
- 5½ yards gold cord (Wright's No. 9963)

Crystal Planter (lower right)
- Clear plastic wastebasket
- Colored paper or foil to line basket
- 5 drapery tiebacks
- Matching cord
- Wire for hanger

Directions

Blue planter: Cut off top of square detergent bottle just below the handle. Makes holes for hangers with a paper punch. Glue one row around top of bottle and another row around bottom. Glue decorative braid around center. Divide the remaining blue rickrack in half and cut to make hangers. Slip the ends through punched holes from outside and knot on inside.

White planter (upper right): Measure around plastic frozen food container and divide circumference into thirds; punch holes with paper punch. Cut three 24-inch lengths of decorator band trim, thread through punched holes, and knot on inside of bowl. Knot ends together at top. Glue companion tassel trim around top edge. Poke a hole at center bottom of container and tie or glue one tassel.

Gold basket (center): Apply gold paint to woven wastebasket. If your basket does not have openwork around top such as the one pictured, cut four holes (two on each side). Pull cord through slide on two tiebacks. Stretch cord out completely and cut at top (remove slide before cutting and use masking tape either side of cut to prevent raveling). Divide basket into fourths. From outside, thread long cord through holes to inside at each quarter (see drawing A).

Take the other tieback and center tassel at center of basket bottom. Bring loops up on either side to quarter marks. Put a slide on each double cord of tieback. Open loop and push through hole next to hanging cord. Pull hanging cord through loop. Adjust cords evenly. Tie knots in top of four hanging cords. Tuck taped ends into center of knot.

(continued)

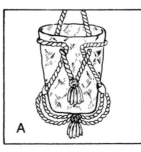
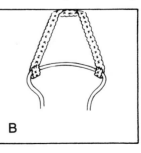

A   B

Hanging planter (far left on page 276): Cut daisy trim into three 18-inch lengths. Weave through the wires of lettuce crisper down sides, across bottom, and up other side. Hand stitch ends of trim at top of frame. Apply stick-to trim onto wrong side of single fold bias tape; cut in two. Staple ends around handles (see drawing B). Spread open curved wires around top of lettuce crisper planter.

Clay pot planter (lower left on page 276): Glue fruit or flower appliques to flowerpot. Cut two 1½ yard lengths of rayon macrame cord. Fold in half and knot all cut ends together. Insert cord through bottom of pot from inside to outside. Pull cord around pot at quarter marks (see drawing C). Tie ½ yard of macrame cord under lip of flowerpot to hold strings in place securely.

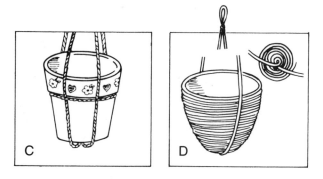

Mini gold planter (lower center on page 276): Use large half of egg-shaped pantyhose container. Remove one-inch of filler at each end of cord. Glue cord around top of container, placing the one-inch unfilled end at an angle to conceal it as you wind and glue cord around egg until you get to center bottom.

Mark vertical lines at each side (see drawing D). Glue cord up one vertical line. Leave the remainder of the cord free with enough to glue down other side and tuck at bottom. When the glue dries, loop a knot at the top of the trim to hang.

Crystal planter (lower right): Line a clear plastic wastebasket with colored paper or foil to conceal the clay pot. Separate the loops of the first tieback (see drawing E). Tassel will be at the bottom of basket when it is completed. Loop the second and third tiebacks through the first, doubling cord over and then under the single cord of the first tiebacks (see drawing F) in next column.

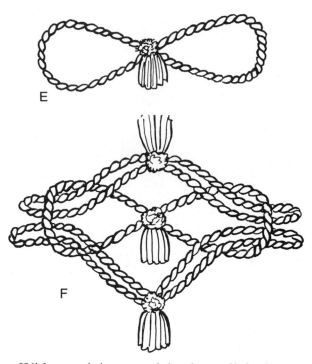

With remaining two tiebacks, pull the loops through the slide to make one long loop. Pull double cord of the long tie through loops of second and third tieback (see drawing G). Take loop end of long tie and weave over and under cords by the tassel. Pull tight. Wire slides together at the top of loop to provide hanger. Insert the lined wastebasket.

Tortoiseshell Pendant

Add glamour to your favorite outfits with an expensive looking tortoiseshell pendant like the one pictured above. No one will guess you baked the disks in the oven.

Materials
- Orange plastic baking crystals
- Brown plastic baking crystals
- Green plastic baking crystals
- Tin lids for molds (different sizes)
- Gold rings, wire, and clasp (from the craft supply store)
- Tapestry needle
- Pliers
- Wire cutter

Directions
Combine equal parts of orange, brown, and green baking crystals to get tortoiseshell effect. Fill tin lids half full of crystals, place on cookie sheet, and bake in a 400-degree oven until they are smooth and glossy (about ½ hour). Let cool, and slip them out of tins. To punch holes in plastic pieces, hold a hot tapestry needle with pliers and insert into disks.

To assemble the dramatic necklace above, use gold rings, wire, and clasp to attratively join the tortoiseshell pieces.

Plastic Mobile

The fragile-appearing plastic mobile above is one that everyone from pre-teen crafters to adults will enjoy making. Hanging in a window, the sunlight filters through and increases the beauty of the rich, jewel tones featured in the plastic designs.

If you're a bargain hunter, look for pieces of scrap plastic rather than buying large expensive sheets. Pieces of almost any size will do.

Use this same technique on other items. Make dog tags, bookmarks, or by punching holes, create designer buttons.

Materials
- Scraps of sheet plastic no more than ¼-inch thick
- Waterproof felt-tip marking pens in a variety of colors
- Black heavy-duty thread
- 12-inch length of ¼-inch dowel

Directions
Do not remove the protective masking paper before cutting sheet plastic. When cutting squares or rectangles, use a straightedge as a guide. Apply firm pressure to the cutting tool, and draw the cutting point the full width of the plastic five or six times. Position the scribed line faceup over a ¾-inch dowel running the length of the intended break. Hold the sheet with one hand and apply downward pressure on the short side of the break. This should result in a clean break. If you are cutting curved shapes, use a saber, band, or jigsaw.

Drill a hole at the center of the top of each piece of the mobile. Use a hand or power drill at very slow speed, with a minimum of pressure.

Adapt designs from books and greeting cards, and paint them on pieces of the mobile with waterproof felt-tip marking pens (see the photo at the upper right of the page). Choose jewel-toned colors that give a stained-glass effect, and outline each one with black paint.

Place the pieces on foil-lined cookie sheets, and put them into a 300-degree oven for a minute or two—just long enough for the plastic to shrink and thicken.

Paint the dowel black. Attach different lengths of heavy-duty black thread—evenly spaced—to the dowel, and tie the other ends of the thread to the holes drilled in the plastic jewel-tone designs.

Dress Form Sculpture

If you've always relegated papier mâché projects to a list of children's rainy day activities, you'll reconsider when you use this technique to create a sophisticated piece of sculpture. Look for the wire expandable dress form in thrift shops, secondhand stores, at auctions, and at garage sales.

Display the life-size sculpture on a pedestal next to a large green foliage plant for contrast. Your friends and family will admire your ingenuity.

Materials
- Wire dress form
- White glue
- Clean newspapers
- White acrylic paint
- Acrylic matte or gloss varnish
- Masking tape

Directions
Place the dress form on a working surface where you can examine it from any angle while decorating. Protect the work area with thick layers of newspapers.

Tear clean newspapers into long strips (do not cut with scissors). You will need a large amount for a project of this size.

Prepare the glue by mixing equal amounts of white glue and warm water in a shallow container. Stir the glue and water mixture until it has a creamy consistency.

Saturate the strips of newspaper in the glue mixture and wrap them over and around the dress frame, leaving some irregular spaced areas of the wire frame exposed. Before the papier mâché hardens, mold it by hand to produce just the form you wish. Use a pointed tool to make sharp indentations in the life-size sculpture.

Use masking tape to protect the metal base while you are working on your project.

After the papier mâché is thoroughly dry, paint the entire sculpture with white acrylic paint. Let dry. Finally, apply a coat of acrylic matte or gloss varnish to act as a sealer.

Art Deco Sculptured Wall Decoration

This three-dimensional wall hanging above a starkly simple fireplace mantel is a refreshing change of pace for those who wish to impart a new look to their surroundings.

The design was inspired by an over-the-mantelpiece featured in a 1930's movie when Art Deco was in vogue. The '30s was the hey-day of Art Deco, and nowhere was it more evident than it was in Hollywood where hotel lobbies, homes, and movie sets were show-cases for the class, sophistication, and svelte of Art Deco. As the years went by, it faded into obscurity. Now, there's renewed interest in this sumptuous style of decorating.

Now, you can recapture the spirit of the '30s in this do-it-yourself project because, although this sculptured wall hanging looks as if it was carved out of marble, actually it is made of foam insulation material that builders use, and is very lightweight. Use a compass and triangle to figure out dimensions of this geometric design.

Materials
- One 4x8-foot sheet of 2-inch-thick foam insulation material
- One 4x8-foot sheet of ¾-inch-thick foam insulation material
- One quart latex paint
- Rubber cement
- Large sheets of paper for making patterns
- Compass
- 30/60-degree triangle
- Band saw
- Drum sander
- Orbital sander
- Sandpaper
- Double-faced pressure-sensitive tape

Directions
From the 4x8-foot sheet of ¾-inch foam insulation material, cut a 30x53-inch piece for the background panel.

Note: The lowest level relief pieces are cut of the ¾-inch foam insulation material; the top relief pieces are cut of the 2-inch foam insulation material.

Enlarge and make paper patterns for all of the pieces, following the dimensions marked on the diagram on page 284. To do this, you will need to use a compass and a 30/60-degree triangle.

To measure the ¾-inch triangular pieces, draw a straight horizontal base line; then draw a line A, B perpendicular to it (see drawing on page 284). On the vertical line, measure 5 inches and 8½ inches from point A. Move the triangle sideways—with the short side of the triangle on the base line—until the long side meets the 5-inch mark. Draw a line from that mark to the base line (point C). Repeat for the 8½-inch mark.

To measure for the center triangle, use both sides of the 30/60-degree triangle. For the side triangles, use the angles formed by line A, B.

Following the same basic procedure, measure the 2-inch-thick triangular pieces, but measure 8½ inches and 12¾ inches on line A, B.

To achieve the rounded edge for the upper two rows of the pattern, draw a vertical line down from point C. Using a point 8 inches from point C as a center, draw an arc with an 8-inch radius.

To make the ¾-inch-thick rounded pieces, again draw a base line and draw line C, D perpendicular to it. For the bottom edge of the rounded piece: Draw an arc with a 5½-inch radius, centered 4 inches up from point C. For the top edge: Draw an arc with a 6-inch radius, centered 7¼ inches up from point C.

To make the bottom edge of the 2-inch rounded pieces: Draw an arc with a 6-inch radius, centered 7¼ inches up from point C. For the top edge: Draw an arc with an 8-inch radius, centered 9½ inches above point C.

(continued)

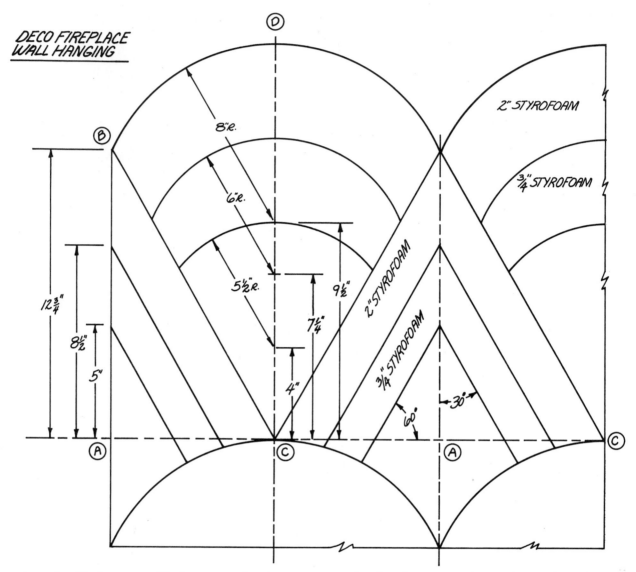

At point C, draw two 60-degree angles (start from the base line) to form the two 30-degree angles centered on line C, D.

Transfer the paper patterns to the foam insulation material (each segment should measure approximately 14¾x17½ inches); use a band saw to cut six each of the ¾-inch-thick pieces and the 2-inch-thick pieces. Next, arrange all of the cutout relief motifs on the background material; trim the pieces slightly where necessary, so they are all uniform in size. Sand all of the cut edges smooth. Use the end of a drum sander to lightly smooth the inside edges of the arc; use an orbital

sander for the outer edges. If you don't have a power sander, you can sand the pieces by hand or rent a sander.

Glue all of the pieces in place on the background panel with rubber cement. If the background panel extends beyond the edges of the relief pieces, trim the background board to fit and sand the edges smooth. Finish your three-dimensional art deco wall decoration by painting it with white latex paint as shown in the photo on page 282 (or whatever color suits your decor).

To hang the panel, position it over your fireplace mantel and make light pencil marks along the edges. Remove it from the wall, attach strips of double-faced pressure-sensitive tape to the back of the panel. Reposition it on the wall, using the light pencil marks as a guide and press in place.

INDEX

Acknowledgments

We are happy to acknowledge
our indebtedness and to express
our sincere thanks to the
following who have been helpful
to us in producing this book:
  Nils Anderson Studios,
    Inc.
  Emile Bernat & Sons Co.
  Burwood Products Company
  Coats & Clark
  Columbia-Minerva
  Janet DeBard
  The Jack Denst Designs,
    Inc.
  Fieldcrest
  Wally Findlay Galleries
  Rug Corporation of America
  Jeri Sutton, The Bee
  Talon
  William Unger & Co., Inc.
  Vonda Jessup and Claudé
    Merritt, Vonda's Trunks
    and Treasures
  Western Wood Molding &
    Millwork Producers
  Window Shade Manufacturers
    Association
  Ray Woods
  Wm. E. Wright Co.
  X-ACTO

Art Nouveau Wall Hanging
on page 34 designed by
Joan Scobey and Marjorie
Sablow. Reused from the
Creative Home Library book,
Decorating With Needlepoint.

Aztecan Motif on page 59
designed by Charlotte Patera.
Reused from the Creative
Home Library book, *Applique*
(pattern No. 58).